# WORLD'S BEST
# CIDER

## PETE BROWN & BILL BRADSHAW

jacqui small

641.229
BRO

First published in 2013 by
**Jacqui Small LLP**

an imprint of
Aurum Press Ltd
74–77 White Lion Street
London N1 9PF

**Publisher** Jacqui Small

**Associate Publisher** Joanna Copestick

**Managing Editor** Lydia Halliday

**Project Editors** Louise Tucker and Hilary Lumsden

**Designer** Robin Rout

**Picture Research** Alex Labbe Thompson

**Production** Peter Colley

British Library Cataloguing-in-Publication Data
A catalogue record for this book
is available from the British Library.

ISBN 978-1-906417-99-4

Printed and bound in China.

This book is dedicated
to friends, family and
cider drinkers everywhere.

Comments welcome to the authors:
Pete Brown: Petebrown@stormlantern.co.uk
Bill Bradshaw: Info@billbradshaw.co.uk

# CONTENTS

# INTRO-
# DUCTION

Cider is the world's most misunderstood drink. Once revered on British dinner tables as 'English wine', it went through a period of being given to lowly farm labourers as a portion of their pay, acquired a reputation for being 'rough', and became something associated mainly with vagrants and under-age tipplers. In the last five years, however, it has enjoyed an extraordinary renaissance.

In some countries it's seen as 'cider beer'. In others it's referred to as apple wine. In the United States, for the last century, 'cider' has referred to sweet, unfermented apple juice, with the resurgent fermented beverage grudgingly having to take on the ugly designation of 'hard cider'.

And yet despite this variety and fluctuation, cider has a soul to it, a consistency. The ice-cider drinker at a fine Montreal restaurant knows nothing of the eccentric cider maker in a dilapidated farm above the Somerset levels, and the Bulmers drinker in an Irish pub may think she has nothing in common with the man 'throwing' *sidra* in an Asturian *chigre*. But they are all touched by cider's unique spirit. Wherever cider is made or consumed, there is a benign, joyful anarchy in the air.

Left on the ground to grow soft and eventually rot, apples would ferment with no human intervention. The 'cider' they produced would most likely be offensive to your palate – not to mention your constitution – but at one step removed, the apple orchard represents the domestication of nature, wildness and civilization coming together to improve their collective lot.

Today, cider takes us back to an earlier, simpler time. It reconnects us with the land and the cycle of the seasons. And maybe, in an increasingly virtual, synthetic and pre-packaged age, that's why cider's popularity is booming around the globe.

Cider has various enclaves of tradition, usually rural areas in both the Old World and the New, populated by a wealth of wonderful stories and a cast of great characters. But despite the shelves of world guides to wine or beer, and similar books on everything from cocktails, rum and whisky to tea and coffee, there's no equivalent for cider.

As soon as we realized this, we set out to remedy it. As we got underway with our gruelling, arduous research (drinking ciders from across the globe), we recognized that our existing knowledge of cider covered only a very narrow band. Then we realized this surely went for just about everyone else – with the exception of a few gurus we celebrate in the following pages. In an age where so many products and cuisines are succumbing to the trend of globally standardized brands and varieties, cider remains unique in its breadth and eccentricity.

For the first time, we hope to give both lifelong cider lovers and novices the full, fascinating picture. This book covers the history of cider from a global perspective, what it is and how it's made, and undertakes a weaving journey through the main cider traditions around the world.

Wherever you look, cider is in the midst of an exciting boom. It's recapturing the imagination of drinkers who grew up with it and grew bored of it in countries where it has centuries of history, as well as those in other parts of the world who are encountering it for the first time.

This explosion began around 2006. In Britain, people credited the 'Magners' Effect', after the very successful marketing campaign that relaunched cider in an appetizing new light. In the United States it seemed like a natural progression from craft beer. But everywhere we've been, a renewed interest in cider began, apparently for different reasons, at around the same time. It's as if a cidery shock wave went around the world, a psychic pulse hitting the minds of discerning drinkers everywhere, and making them think, 'Hmm... I fancy a cider.'

From the Winter Banana and Newtown Pippin apple varieties of the United States to the lost but not forgotten Bodenham Beauties and Spring Grove Codlins of the Welsh Marches, from the sake cider of Japan to the apple wine of Frankfurt and the working man's apple 'Champagne' of Argentina, from the global corporation to the deep countryside collective, discovering the world of cider is a raucous, fascinating, meandering, chaotic, thirst-quenching journey of a lifetime.

## A Note on the Ciders

We see this book as the start – not the end – of a process of bringing together the diverse world of cider. There are undoubtedly gaps in our knowledge, and we look forward to filling those as quickly and as satisfyingly as possible. We do not claim that the 244 ciders in this book are definitively *the* best 244 in the world – but 244 *of* the best. Every cider in this book is one we enjoyed and one we think worth trying. But everyone's palate is different. And call us lightweights if you must, but we were unable to visit every single cidery in the world in the time we had to write this book. So we have made this selection not as the last word in great cider, but as a comprehensive and democratic representation of the astonishing array of flavours and styles that exist, offering something for everyone, from the novice to the connoisseur.

If you're a cider maker who feels wronged at your exclusion, or a cider drinker who cannot believe we've omitted your favourite, let us know (see page 4 for contact details). Because, as the global cider revolution grows, we'd love to bring you an expanded, improved second edition.

Cheers!

'I MUST NOT PRESCRIBE TO OTHER PALATES, BY ASSERTING HOW GOOD CIDER MAY
BE MADE, OR TO COMPARE IT WITH WINES: BUT WHEN THE LATE KING (OF BLESSED
MEMORY) CAME TO HEREFORD IN HIS DISTRESS, AND SUCH OF THE GENTRY OF
WORCESTERSHIRE AS WERE BROUGHT THITHER AS PRISONERS; BOTH KING, NOBILITY
AND GENTRY, DID PREFER IT BEFORE THE BEST WINES THOSE PARTS AFFORDED.'

From 'Aphorisms Concerning Cider' by John Beale, in John Evelyn's *Pomona*, 1664.

# CĪDER BASĪCS

# HISTORY OF CIDER

Go back far enough in the history of alcoholic beverages and there's one shapeless, formless mother drink from which all others emerged. Archaeological evidence now shows us Stone Age people figured out that anything with natural sugar will ferment into alcohol, given the right conditions. The earliest drinks contained grapes, barley, honey... whatever would bubble away to provide a buzz.

Whenever cider emerged as a separate drink is lost in time; its history is frustratingly vague compared to that of wine or beer. And there are two problems that will probably always keep it this way: the cider-making process itself and the language surrounding it.

We know that modern apples trace their roots back to the *Malus silvestris*, an ancient apple grown in what is now Kazakhstan, and its pilgrimage west in the spoor of animals and humans, until it was hybridized with European crab-apple varieties as long as 10,000 years ago. Archaeologists have found carbonized pips in early settlements from 6500 BC, and the Greeks and Romans had perfected the grafting of apple trees before the birth of Christ.

Given that you make cider simply by getting juice out of apples, many historians argue that it is older than civilization, at least as old as beer or wine. Squeeze out the juice, and cider makes itself. But not everyone agrees – because, while you can squeeze oranges or lemons by hand, apples are very firm. The first stage of cider-making is to break up the apples into a consistency where you can actually squeeze them. And that process takes equipment.

We know that the Romans made cider, both at home and across Europe. They had heavy wooden presses to make olive oil, and outside olive-pressing season it made sense to use this equipment for something else. One reason press owners were keen to do this was that they were expensive pieces of equipment, so it made sense to utilize them as much as possible. In fact they were so expensive that good presses only belonged to wealthy households. Cider may be seen as a simple, rustic drink today, but Roman cider mills belonged to large estates.

This, plus the lack of any written evidence to the contrary, leads drinks writer Ted Bruning to conclude that early cider-making was not as widespread as we might think. In his book *Golden Fire: the Story of Cider*, Bruning presents cider's and perry's very earliest mentions. Pliny included it within a tract entitled '66 Varieties of Artificial Wine', saying 'Wine is made, too, of the pods of the Syrian carob, of pears, and of all kinds of apples', and in '41 Varieties of Pear' he includes the Falernian, 'so called from the drink which it affords, so abundant in its juice'.

Early cider-making was part of the practice of good estate management. Before refrigeration, harvest time was followed by a succession of clever ways of preserving nature's bounty in such a manner that it wouldn't spoil or rot quickly. Apple juice could be kept even longer in barrels than apples stored in a cool cellar.

One might reasonably ask whether, having squeezed the juice, it was drunk fresh or fermented into cider. How do we know the Romans weren't big fans of cool, sweet apple juice? The answer to that is simple: if it wasn't drunk within a day or two, it became cider whether you liked it or not, thanks to the wild yeasts on the skin and in the flesh of the apple.

Having presented as much of the written record of early cider as we can find, Bruning looks at the hassle involved in early presses and concludes that cider-making was not a widespread activity. Those who made it did so to preserve apples as some kind of faux wine, always second best and unloved. But if there's one thing cider people agree on, it's that they never agree on anything. And there is a counter-theory.

First, as apples age they soften, and eventually rot. While most cider makers (and drinkers) might not like the idea of using fruit that's on the turn, there are still those even today who think soft apples get the best results, and this attitude used to be much more widespread than it is now.

Second, apples can be crushed using a simple mortar and pestle principle. There's evidence of small-batch cider makers in Wales, for example, using a large bucket and pounding apples with heavy sticks to crush them. Such a method was labour-intensive but could reduce three to four bucketfuls of apples to pulp within 10 minutes. It was still being used on smaller Welsh farms in the early 20th century. So there's no reason to doubt it could possibly have been used for as long as we've had bowls or buckets strong enough to withstand a bit of beating. From a pulp, the juice could have been extracted relatively easily with only the most rudimentary tools.

OPPOSITE, TOP LEFT: The Royal Warrant awarded to Bulmers for its cider.
OPPOSITE, TOP RIGHT & BOTTOM: Accounts from Sheppy's farm, Somerset, 1853, including sales of cider.

---

7 Yearlings 1 Bool 2 Breeding Sows 3 fat Pigs
About 20 Geese 3 Horses 5½ Acres of Wheat
3½ Acres of Oates 2 Acres of Barley 3 Acres of Beanes
5 Acres of Cleaver Seed 40 50 Sacks of Potates
1 Ton of Skim cheese 50 fleeses of Wool 30 Bushels
of Wheat in Sack 35 Hogsheads of Cider 64 Tons
of Hay One mot of Cleaver at 4 about 4 ton

Receit For the Burn for the Cows
2 oz of Allum
2 ob of blue stone
1½ oz of bôle armenia
½ oz of Cor'osive Sulliment
Mix them in quart of boiling Soft Water
when cold put into a bottle and keep
for use NB shake the bottle before
using it

James Sheppy

---

Brought Over

1845 Advance to Thomas Sheppy Oct 15th 15 0 0
14 Gallons of Cider for Hay Making 10 6
Paid for Rent for Briggs ground to Mr Dimmins
July 31 Do for 4 Sugar at 6½
1846 July 18 22 lb of cheese at ___ per lb
1847 April 2 10 lb of cheese at 6 per lb 3 4
June 5 10 lb of Do at 6 2 6
1848 January allowance in part cash 7 3 6
1844 Oct 4 Paid Mr Sheppy half Years Rent 105 4 8
1843 May 12th Settled for Money Remited in cash 105 7 4
Nov 12th halling 50 Bushels for James Sheppy Do 10 6
18 Do 50 Do Do 10 6
20 Do 50 Do Do 10 6
22 Do 50 Do Do 10 6
30 one Sack of Wheat 4 0
Dec 17 halling 50 of Wheat 10 6
19 Do 50 Do Do 10 6
50 Part of Days Work for man
Jany 1 Do Do
2 Do Do
Do 50 Wring for
3 Do
21 halling 50 of Wheat 10 6
23 Do 60 of Do 12 6
Paid for 10 Bushels of Wheat 3 0
30 halling 75 Do 15 7
Feby 3 Do 55 Do 11 6
25 Flax Delivered to Inwod Mill for James Sheppy 89
89 Bushels of Wheat at 6 per Bushel
March 12 83 Do & 15 lb of Wheat

---

1863 Brought for Solsbin Butter Form Inwod
Farm John Sheppy
April 3 82 lb of Butter at 11 per lb
3 82 lb of Butter at 11 per lb 3 15 2
10 90 4 2 6
Sept 23 Recid for Butter 10 12 8

1866 March 25th Account of Live Stock
John Sheppy at Inwod Farm Congresbury
25 Cows & heifers in Calf at 14 each 350 0 0
7 Yearlings at 5 10 each 38 10 0
4 Weaning Cattes 8 0 0
2 Grasing Heifers 24 0 0
1 Meety Stag 16 0 0
1 Bool 8 0 0
1 Sow & pigs 10 0 0
2 Fat pigs 12 0 0
1 Nag Colt 14 One cart Colt 10 24 0 0
2 Working Mares 490 10 0
50 Fat Sheep at 50 each 75 0 0
565 10 0

1866 March 25 account of dead Stock John Sheppy
10 Acres of Wheat in Mow 50 0 0
16 Sacks of Barley at 16 per Sack 12 0 0
25 Do of Potatos 8 0 0
20 Hogshead of Cider at 50 per Hog 50 0 0
5½ Wheat on the Ground 16 0 0
7 Acres of clover on the Ground 7 0 0
Money in cash & depts 195 10 0 143

Bruning himself tells us how the 4th-century writer Palladius describes a method of crushing the fruit, soaking the pulp and then wringing it through a bag.

Such methods were undoubtedly inefficient and labour-intensive. And Bruning is surely correct when he says that cider-making didn't take off on a large scale until much later. But it could quite easily have happened on a small domestic scale, as many household activities did.

This brings us to our second problem: that of language. If cider was ever made on a small scale, the people doing so didn't leave any record of it. That doesn't make it less likely; most people were illiterate and there's not much of anything written down beyond affairs of law and state for most of human history. The trouble is, even when people did write things down, they didn't actually have a word for cider.

We've already seen that Pliny referred to cider as wine. Northern Spain bases its claim to having invented cider on a reference by Strabo in 60 BC, but the Greek scholar actually refers to *zythos*, a word for beer. Some have said that 'cider' itself is the descendant of the Hebrew word *shekar*, which was translated into Latin as *sicera*. But a basic analysis of *sicera* in its ancient usage clearly shows that it was an umbrella term for all kinds of strong drink except wine. Before the 9th and 10th centuries, wherever cider was made, it will be forever linguistically hidden behind other drinks.

Cider really starts to appear properly during the reign of Charlemagne (r. 768–814), whose Frankish empire stretched from northern Spain to Normandy and modern-day Germany, with a capital city in Frankfurt, thus spanning three of today's most important cider-making areas. Charlemagne himself was possibly the first to give cider and perry their own names – *pomatum* and *pyratium*. While those names never stuck, they show that cider was a recognized drink, and they were included in the plan of *Capitulare de Villis*, a detailed set of regulations for how royal estates should be managed, which said that *siceratores* should be present on each estate to make beer, cider and perry. Around this time, there are hundreds of references to vineyards and orchards in legal documents such as wills. The fact that they are always referred to together suggests that both were cultivated for drink.

The weight of such references is overwhelmingly centred in northern Spain. Asturias was a separate kingdom recognized by Charlemagne and the Pope, and was the first major centre of apple cultivation.

It's not clear who was responsible for the spread of cider-making throughout Europe, though the extent of the Frankish empire certainly helped. There's evidence to suggest the Asturians spread apple cultivation across Europe, although it was already practised in Brittany by the 4th century, and wild apple trees were sacred to the Celts as the hosts for mistletoe.

ABOVE: Bulmers of Hereford in the early 20th century.
Apples were gathered in piles, or 'tumps', to allow them
to mature before pressing.

We can only speculate as to how many of these apples were made into cider. But the old word *sicera* was appropriated by the Asturians in the 9th century to refer specifically to the fermented apple drink, and gave us Spanish *sidra*, French *cidre* and ultimately English *cider*.

Following Charlemagne there's gradually more evidence of cider-making along the rainy, temperate Atlantic coast, from Asturias through Normandy and Brittany, up to Ireland and the west of England. By the 13th century, pressing technology had much improved, and we start to see more specific references to cider in estate management and wills.

From around the 14th century Europe suffered a period of climate change often dubbed a 'mini-ice age'. Vines withered in areas of northern Europe where they had once thrived, and England, Germany, France, Normandy and Brittany turned to cider instead. Production techniques improved and cider became an important drink in rural areas, to the extent that most farms had an orchard.

In the 16th century, pioneering cider makers in Normandy's Cotentin Peninsula made a science of cider, studying and publishing works on apple varieties, soil types and pressing techniques. In the early 17th century, the gentlemen cider makers of Herefordshire followed suit. Cider crossed the Atlantic to North America with early colonists, each spreading their traditions. The English took cider to the United States, where it became the staple drink of the frontier. The French took it to Quebec, and the Spanish to South America. In each region today, the links with the parent tradition are clearly recognizable.

Cider was also an important drink in Australia by the 19th century, and during the 20th it spread across the world to countries that never had a cider-making tradition. It is one of the fastest-growing drinks in the world, sweeter than beer, less potent than wine, simple and yet capable of complex greatness.

Welcome to the cider revolution.

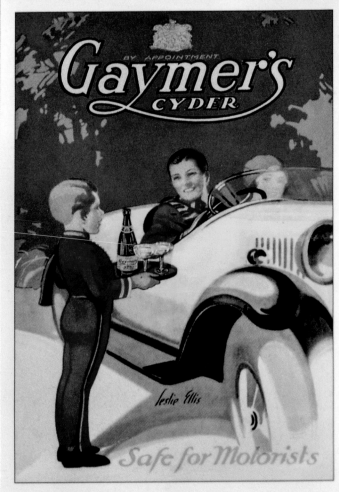

RIGHT: Early to mid-20th-century cider advertising. Obviously certain claims would not be allowed today.

# APPLES, ORCHARDS AND THE CĪDER YEAR

MAYBE THE REASON WE'VE
MADE THE FORBIDDEN
FRUIT INTO AN APPLE IS
THAT ORCHARDS EVOKE THE
IMAGE OF EDEN IN OUR
COLLECTIVE MIND'S EYE.

ABOVE: Blossom time, which is around May in apple-growing countries of the northern hemisphere, is the most beautiful time to visit a cider orchard.

In the entire canon of human history, myth and storytelling,
no other fruit possesses the sheer potency of meaning as the apple.

Most people in Christian countries, believers or not, are familiar with the image of Eve presenting Adam with an apple, the fruit of knowledge, which saw them expelled from Eden. But the Bible never names the 'fruit of the tree which is in the midst of the garden'. It was probably a pomegranate, as the region where Eden was supposedly located was too hot for apple cultivation.

In our own times, in the Big Apple, the apple of your eye may well believe that an apple a day keeps the doctor away. But you have to hope that one bad apple hasn't spoiled the bunch.

The apple's gate-crashing of Eden shows how adept it is at slipping into big, meaningful narratives. Yet maybe the apple is truly miraculous.

Cut horizontally, an apple reveals five seed chambers, shaped like flower petals. And in each apple, every one of those seeds carries a genetic imprint that is entirely different from its siblings and its parents. If those seeds were planted and developed into new trees, any resemblance to other apple trees living or dead would be purely coincidental. Every apple tree can potentially give birth to thousands of new varieties.

While it hasn't been proven beyond doubt, the best available evidence suggests that the ancestor of *Malus domestica*, the culinary apple we know today, comes from a wild tree on the mountain slopes of Kazakhstan. Here, trees with huge canopies grow to heights of 18 metres and yield a frankly surreal variety of fruit. Mammals such as bears ate the tastiest fruit and excreted the seeds in gradually wider circles, and humans (and their horses) on great trade routes such as the Silk Road are thought to have done something similar since the Bronze Age.

In this way, the apple spread across Asia and Europe. Within certain climatic bands, each time it encountered new growing conditions – varying seasons, pollinators, soil types, pests and weather – there were at least some among that infinite variety of seeds that found the new conditions to their liking, and apple varieties spread – and multiplied as they spread.

Cuneiform tablets reveal that in ancient Mesopotamia, the art of grafting was discovered almost 4000 years ago. If a cutting from a tree or vine taken from a desirable parent is notched onto a groove in another tree and the graft takes, the resultant fruit will resemble the parent rather than the rootstock – so grafting is a form of cloning rather than sexual reproduction.

The Chinese also practised grafting in the 2nd millennium BC and the ancient Greeks and Romans mastered the art. So when at random a seedling tree, or 'pippin', produced fruit that was appealing, it could be replicated – at least in similar conditions to where its parent grew. According to Pliny, the Romans cultivated 23 different apple varieties, some of which they took to England.

And so we can deduce that orchards have been planted in Europe for at least 2000 years. Domesticated Roman trees encountered the much older *Malus silvestris* (humans were eating apples in France and Britain from at least 3800BC) and our modern cider varieties descended from that meeting.

Maybe the reason we've made the forbidden fruit into an apple is that orchards evoke an image of Eden in our imagination. Before civilization there was only wilderness, and Eden's bounty and apparent safety suggest it wasn't that. An orchard, both symbolically and practically, is the taming of the wilderness – partial domestication, in which nature is guided by man.

There is something utterly fantastical about an orchard that inspires both serenity and giddiness. An orchard full of cider varieties, such as that belonging to the Hecks family business in Somerset, is a useful reminder of the delicate balance between randomness and order, between wildness and domestication. Some apples are no bigger than plums, while others are the size of small grapefruit. Some hang in bunches like grapes, while others – no more than two inches across – line spindly, delicate branches that somehow fizz out from the heart of the tree, like hair full of static electricity. Some are as dark and rich as Bordeaux wine. Others are green-streaked with dark-purple stripes like gang scars. The vivid brightness of the laden trees, studded with jewels, makes the heart leap.

Apple cultivation measures the passing of the seasons. An orchardist must graft before the growth starts and hopes that when this growth occurs it is not affected by late frosts. In spring beehives are placed to help pollinate the trees, and if all goes well we marvel at the beauty of the apple blossom. In autumn apples are picked as and when each variety is ready. Then, as the temperature falls and the sun lowers, the fruit is milled and pressed. The cider is stored to ferment throughout the winter, and as we wait for the fermentation to complete, we also wait for the trees to wake and begin their cycle again.

The cycle takes a full year, and is marked with rituals that recognize the primacy of nature, as well as revealing how inventive we are at creating excuses to drink freely.

Industrial cider makers using concentrated juice can produce cider all year round, but most cider fans would say it's not as good, that 'the craft cider maker works with the seasons, not against them'.

BELOW: The elegant beauty of a cider orchard shows humanity and nature working together at their very best.

## The 'T' Word

Those who don't know cider can have a snide attitude if the word *terroir* is used in conjunction with it. Social conditioning tells us that this is a concept exclusive to the sophistication and subtlety of wine.

But if we accept that climate (or microclimate), temperature and soil can have a profound effect on one particular fruit – which we do, because it's true – then logically it would be bizarre to suggest it has no such effect on other fruits.

Julian Temperley of Burrow Hill uses findings from the research station at Long Ashton to support his claim that the limestone outcrops and slopes of Kingsbury Episcopi, Baltonsborough and Wedmore on the

edges of the Somerset Levels are *terroir* without equal. He says there's a clear difference between Dabinett apples grown here and those from anywhere else, for example.

Across the Channel, French cider maker Eric Bordelet names one of his ciders 'Argelette', after the prehistoric rocky soil on the lower slopes of the granite hills where he grows his trees. He shows geological maps of the region to anyone who visits. There's an overlap between the most passionate believers in the *terroir* of cider and the producers of some of the world's greatest ciders that is too consistent to be coincidence.

## A Cider Lover's Guide to Apple Varieties

It's technically possible to make cider from any apple variety, although we have tried one made entirely from crab apples and it's not something we'd advise anyone to taste. Or make.

Crabs aside, it's common to find ciders made from culinary (eating) apples such as Bramley or McIntosh, and dessert apples such as Cox's Orange Pippin or Cortland, as well as a huge array of cider apples.

In 1903, the Long Ashton Research Station established four different classes of cider apple: sweet, sharp, bittersweet and bittersharp. Any cider apple should ideally have high levels of sugar for fermentation, so the difference between them is in their levels of tannin and acidity. The most common variety of cider apple is the bittersweet, with good tannin and low acidity.

Occasional varieties such as Dabinett and Kingston Black offer such a good balance of different elements that they can make single-variety ciders. But the vast majority of ciders, just like most great wines, require a blending of different varieties to achieve the best result.

RIGHT: Crates of apples at Hecks Orchard, Somerset, waiting to be pressed.
OPPOSITE: The many different colours, textures and patterns of cider apples.

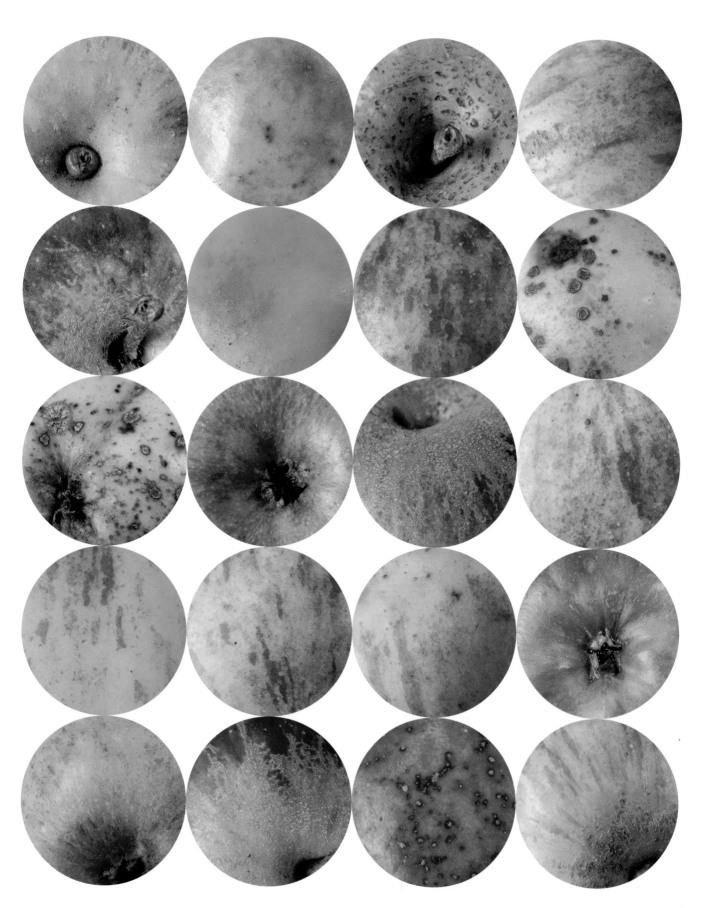

# HOW CIDER IS MADE

Like many of the most rewarding things in life, cider is ridiculously easy to make. But it's much harder to make good cider than bad. Given that views on what constitutes good and bad cider are themselves hotly debated by different cider makers, it would be impossible to arrive at any consensus on how you make the very best. So here we simply offer the basics.

## What is Cider?

Simplistically, cider is fermented apple juice. As wine is to grapes, cider is to apples, although 'cider' is also used to refer to unfermented apple juice in the United States.

What constitutes *good* cider is a complicated question. But generally when you taste a cider that truly impresses you, the chances are that it will have a very high juice content (80 per cent plus), will not have been made from concentrate and will have no added sweeteners, colourings or artificial flavourings.

OPPOSITE: Traditional cider-making display at Apple Day, Burrow Hill Farm, Somerset.

## The Basic Process

Get some ripe apples that have a high concentration of sugary juice in them. Break these apples down into a mush. Squeeze out the juice. Then, allow naturally occurring yeast to ferment this sugar-rich liquid, so that some or all of the sugar turns to alcohol. You could do this in your own home – it really is that simple. And that complicated. So let's break it down step by step.

## Sorting and Washing

Harvesting can be a crude process. The first stage of production involves the apples being rinsed and checked so they can be cleaned and sticks, leaves, twigs and any rotten apples can be taken out.

## Milling

You can't simply squeeze an apple like an orange or lemon – the fruit is too firm. So apples must first be broken up into a soft mush. Historically there have been various methods for doing this, with the most primitive using a simple mortar and pestle principle. From this we graduated to a hollowed-out log with a large, heavy wheel, sometimes lined with spikes or knives, running over the apple-filled groove.

This evolved into the traditional stone mill, one of the most evocative images of cider-making. A large stone wheel is attached to an axle, which allows it to be pushed around a circular trough. Ancient olive presses of this type were driven by slaves, but by the time they were common in 18th-century England, the power came from horses plodding gently in a circle.

In the late 19th century a mechanical hopper with blades inside known as a 'scratter' became increasingly popular. The apples are poured into a hopper at the top, and the pulp, or 'pomace', is collected below. This principle, through wildly varying designs, remains the norm today.

## Pressing

The basic process simply requires the pomace to be wrapped in something permeable and squeezed. But to do this on a large scale requires a greater source of pressure than a pair of human hands. Traditionally the pomace was packed into straw or, later on, horsehair or sackcloth, to make a 'cheese'. These cheeses were piled into the base of the press with a board placed on top. One or two great wooden screws were then turned by levers to press down and slowly flatten the cheeses to extract the juice, which was collected from channels and grooves at the base of the cheeses.

This principle is still widely used today. Hydraulic presses mostly replaced the hand-cranked version after the Industrial Revolution, and today there are various types of hydraulic and mechanical presses. A version of the traditional cheese press is still prevalent among craft producers, but in North America in particular 'accordion presses' are also common, where the pomace is loaded into a long series of narrow slats, which are then squeezed horizontally. Larger-scale presses carry out a similar process inside giant cylindrical tanks.

## Blending

It's difficult to know where to mention this in the process, but it's also essential. The vast majority of ciders are a mix of different apple varieties and there's a fine art to the blending. Many traditional cider makers do it by eye, mixing the fruit together before pressing. Others will press different fruit varieties separately and mix together the precise proportions they want prior to fermentation. Others still will ferment finished ciders separately and blend them by taste and intuition to create a perfect product.

## Fermenting

Fermentation is one of nature's true miracles. Yeast is a naturally occurring micro-organism whose sole aim in life is to consume sugar, which helps it multiply. The by-products of the process are alcohol and $CO_2$.

This is a perfectly natural process that occurs anywhere there is soft fruit or pressed juice, if the temperature is right, and it's the basis of any (decent) alcoholic drink. Throughout human history we've tried to control it, but even now the best we can do is influence it.

Pomace contains wild yeast and, left alone, it will ferment the juice into cider naturally. The advantages of this are that you get a natural product that is likely to have greater complexity because of the astonishingly diverse wild yeast culture. The risk is that fermentation is less controllable, less knowable and the results have a wider margin of error, thanks mainly to an increased risk of bacterial infection. The alternative is to remove the wild yeast and add a single-strain cultured yeast instead to produce a cleaner fermentation. Wine and Champagne yeasts are the most common types used in cider.

Fermentation under scientific conditions can happen in a few days, but artisanal cider makers tend to

## Ageing and Storage

Some artisanal cider makers believe that once a cider had finished its fermentation, it's ready to drink, cannot be improved and is best drunk fresh. Others ferment or age it post-fermentation in wooden barrels such as whisky casks, where it might take on additional characteristics from the wood, the microflora that live in the grain, or the remains of the spirit that was previously stored in there.

Once it is finished, cider may be filtered or pasteurized, or not. It may have added colourings, flavours or preservatives, but obviously such practices are frowned upon by artisanal makers and drinkers.

Cider is packaged in a variety of formats: barrel, keg, bottle and, for mass-market producers, cans. Farmhouse-style cider may also be packaged in a 'bag in box', a cardboard box containing a sealed bag that shrinks as the cider is drawn from it, keeping air from the remaining liquid to improve its shelf life.

ferment their products slowly over several months at low temperatures. Some traditional cider makers – and cider drinkers – believe that once the cider is 'working' in its fermentation vessel, you leave it until its ready. But if the yeast is not healthy, or doesn't have enough nutrients, it can die and the fermentation can go awry, producing musty, eggy, even faecal aromas. Hardcore farmhouse cider fans often say there's 'no such thing as bad cider' and may even declare the 'rougher' it is, the better. We've judged at cider competitions where we've been offered cider that smells of human excrement and have been told, by the 'expert judge', that this is what the cider maker intended.

To prevent such horrors, other cider makers constantly monitor and taste throughout fermentation, and if they can tell that the yeast does not have enough nutrients, they add some. This in itself is an old tradition – folk tales of dead rats being thrown into the vat to add a bit of body do have a basis in scientific fact. But these days it's more likely to be added sugar if there's not enough in the juice, and chemical yeast nutrient.

# CIDER FLAVOURS

When we began writing this book, a leading drinks writer said to us, 'Interesting, but what can you write about cider? It tastes of apples. What else is there to say?' We respectfully dedicate this section to that person. And if all you've ever tasted is fizzy, mainstream commercial cider, then welcome. And prepare to have your mind opened.

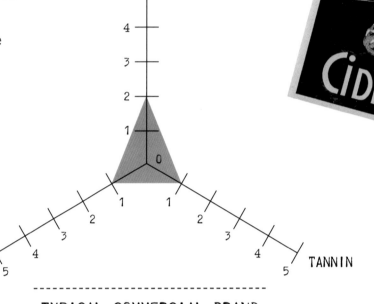

## TYPICAL COMMERCIAL BRAND

• Pretty bland – so all scores are low
• Balanced, bit slightly sweet, so that's higher than the others

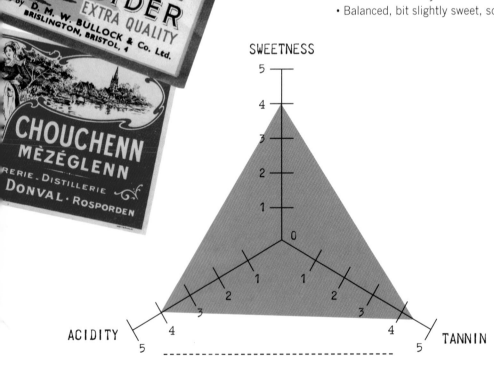

## TRADITIONAL FARMHOUSE

• Big and full-bodied, so all scores are high
• Lots going on, but it's all in balance – so scores are similar

### The Basic Flavour Spectrum

Most ciders are marketed, and classified in competitions, as sweet, medium or dry. This clearly works up to a point, but it doesn't offer us the full picture.

Dryness may mean that all the sugar has been fermented – an absence of sweetness. Or it may refer to the presence of tannin, which is a distinguishing feature of many cider apples. Tannin is an astringent, bitter compound that has a drying effect in the mouth, and makes juice feel thicker and more full-bodied. And apart from sweet and dry, many ciders, like white wine, also vary from low to high acidity.

Finally, we have the intensity of flavour to consider: each aspect may be light or full-on.

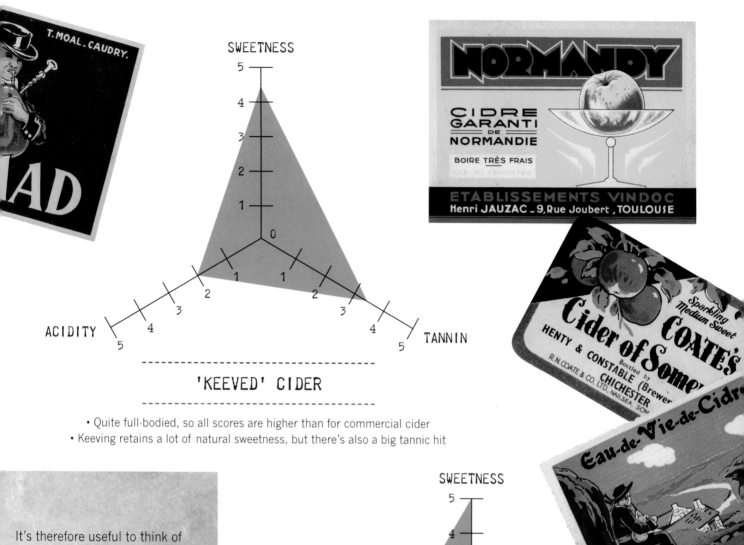

## 'KEEVED' CIDER

- Quite full-bodied, so all scores are higher than for commercial cider
- Keeving retains a lot of natural sweetness, but there's also a big tannic hit

It's therefore useful to think of the basic cider flavour spectrum on three axes: sweet, tannic and acidic, each of which could be high or low.

Different styles of cider quickly produce very different shapes, thanks both to their relative balance and intensity, as you can see in the diagrams shown on this page.

It's worth exploring these key dimensions in a little more detail, as well as some of the secondary flavours that complement them.

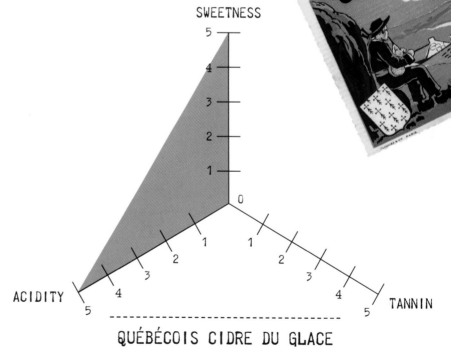

## QUÉBÉCOIS CIDRE DU GLACE

- Massive sweetness and acidity in balance
- No tannin

## Sweetness

If you're familiar with processed food and drink, sweetness can be one-dimensionally saccharine and quickly becomes cloying and sickly. Natural sweetness is both richer and more palatable, and in cider it can take on syrupy, vanilla or honey notes.

## Acidity

Can be an appley sharpness reminiscent of a Granny Smith, a citrusy zing or sourness. If the cider has been exposed to air, ethanol may undergo an anaerobic fermentation to become acetic acid – aka vinegar. In Asturian and some British farmhouse ciders, a degree of acetic acid is considered positive, but at any significant level it is unpleasant to drink (though it does make great vinegar).

## Tannin

This is often about texture more than flavour but tannin can add straightforward bitterness or astringency, or a dryness that can be minerally. It's sometimes reminiscent of eating chalk.

## Secondary Flavours

**Fruit** More complex than simple sweetness or acidity. It's generally considered undesirable for cider to taste like unfermented apple juice, just as wine is considered disappointing if it tastes of grape juice. But the character of the apple should shine through, albeit not in the same way as in the raw fruit. Cider may also evoke many other flavours such as citrus, banana, melon, pear or vanilla.

**Funk** An imprecise term to cover a number of flavours that can be good or bad. Traditional English farmhouse cider can have a cheesy character, or notes that we describe as 'barnyard' – like wet straw, damp animals, musty, earthy or even manure-like. It can also be eggy, resembling cooked vegetables, or phenolic, like sticking plasters. Funkiness in cider is like spiciness in food: some people are going to hate it whenever it's present. Others will really go for it, even to extremes. But most would agree that it works best when complementing other flavours rather than overwhelming them.

**Floral** Cider can have a perfumed character that may even evoke specific flowers such as rose, geranium or orange blossom.

**Caramelized** Some styles have hints of caramel sweetness, butterscotch, toffee or dried fruit such as raisins or figs.

**Butter** In aged or vintage ciders a pleasing buttery smoothness develops, thanks to a secondary, or malolactic, fermentation that breaks acidity down into something mellower.

## Alcoholic Strength

Typical cider fruit ferments to a natural alcohol level of 6 to 8 per cent alcohol by volume (ABV), but may go as high as 10 per cent ABV if the fruit is especially rich in sugar. Alcohol can be boosted higher than this by the addition of extra sugar to keep the yeast fermenting, but if it reaches a high enough level, alcohol will kill the yeast. It's rare to see pure cider above 9 or 10 per cent ABV.

Most cider is lower in alcohol than the standard range of fermentation. This is achieved by watering it down, 'back-sweetening' fermented cider with unfermented juice, or stopping the initial fermentation early.

This range of alcohol content means that in strength as well as character, cider sits somewhere between beer and wine, and draw comparisons with both.

## Carbonation

Cider may be still or sparkling. A natural fizz can be created by bottling cider at the correct gravity before it has finished fermenting (*méthode ancienne*) or dosing with sugar and yeast at bottling (*méthode champenoise*). These methods can be difficult, inconsistent, time-consuming or expensive, so many ciders are 'force carbonated' with the addition of $CO_2$. Purists frown on this method, but it is possible to vary the degree of carbonation from a gentle sparkle to an aggressive fizz.

## Common Styles

Most ciders are served in glass bottles. They may be still or sparkling, and may contain any of the flavour characteristics described above. Cider also has within it several distinct examples of styles or sub-genres. As with flavour, we make no attempt here to classify every single cider into a specific style; this would be a life's work, probably with a padded cell and straitjacket at the end of it. So the following list does not cover every single cider, and probably allows some to feature more than once. It's not exact but, trust us: it's better than the alternative.

**Scrumpy/farmhouse** Still and unfiltered, arguably the most natural and traditional way to make cider. Tends to be opaque, can run from pale gold to deep amber, and is likely to be 6 to 8 per cent ABV with strong, funky and tannic flavours that even vary from barrel to barrel.

**'Keeved' cider** Lower in alcohol, higher in fruit sugar and sparkling, around 3 to 5 per cent ABV. (For a description of keeving see page 84.)

**'Apple wine'** Offers a great balance of sweetness and acidity but with little or no tannin (common with cider made from culinary rather than cider fruit). More frequently found in Germany, Quebec and New England.

**Bottle-fermented** Naturally sparkling, often (but not always) higher in alcohol. Usually served in Champagne-style bottles.

**Commercial 'beer-style'** Lower in alcohol (around 5 per cent ABV); usually (let's be polite here) delicately flavoured. Packaged, promoted and drunk as an alternative to beer. This accounts for the majority of cider volume in the UK, Australia, United States and South Africa (see page 34).

**Single varieties** Some varieties of apples, such as Dabinett and Kingston Black, offer the cider maker the right characteristics to make a balanced, satisfying cider without blending.

## Cider Derivatives

At a risk of upsetting some purists, we're with Burrow Hill's Julian Temperley, who defines cider as all the produce of the orchard. The apples can be pressed and drunk as fresh juice, fermented into cider, which can then be distilled into apple brandy. These drinks can then be combined or concentrated to produce other products.

**Cider brandy/Calvados** Distilled cider – what brandy is to wine. Usually around 40 per cent ABV. The most celebrated style is Calvados from Normandy (see pages 70 and 74).

**Pommeau** Brandy blended with unfermented apple juice, between 15 to 20 per cent ABV and barrel aged, for around three years (see page 80). Perfect aperitif or *digestif*.

**Ice cider/cidre de glace** Apple juice frozen before fermentation to increase the concentration of sweetness and acidity (see page 214). Top alternative to dessert wine.

**Perry** Not a cider derivative at all but a close sibling – basically, 'cider' made with perry pears rather than cider apples for a drink that is often more delicately floral, but can also be fruity and highly tannic (see page 38).

# COMMERCIAL BRANDS

It's customary in the worlds of both beer and cider to criticize large, mainstream manufacturers at least as enthusiastically as artisanal craft producers are celebrated. It's also a little lazy and not always helpful to the general reader.

We're no great fans of the biggest commercial ciders that dominate the market in the UK, Ireland, United States, Australia and South Africa. But neither do we feel we have the right to criticize the millions of people who drink them. Here are the facts about the brands you see advertised, so you can make up your own mind.

Artisanal ciders can only be made in the autumn, (unless their fruit is cold-stored in special facilities). This is when the apples are ready and the cider from them varies in character, depending on the season, quality and size of the harvest. Commercial producers who supply supermarkets and bars year-round simply cannot function in this way. Also, buyers of large commercial brands expect their cider to taste exactly the same time after time. Therefore, if a cider maker wants to operate on a large commercial scale, it's inevitable that compromises must be made.

Rather than using fresh juice from pressed apples, to achieve both volume and consistency, large-scale producers must use juice from concentrate for some, if not all, of their volume. Concentrate can be shipped economically over long distances and stored for long periods before water is added back. When drinking cider ice-cold straight from the neck of the bottle, many people will detect no difference in flavour in cider made from concentrate. But when tasting cider carefully, poured into a glass and served at the correct temperature, concentrated juice tastes different because the process breaks down some flavour compounds and may even add a papery or cardboard note.

The next thing to note is the actual percentage of apple juice in the cider. Juice, even from concentrate, is expensive. Since supermarkets have become more powerful than the producers who supply them, they can dictate the quantities and price points they want. Large-scale cider makers often have to supply at a given price, and the only way to meet that price is to reduce manufacturing costs.

Most commercial brands are therefore watered down, which has to happen anyway to get to the commercial norm of 4 to 5 per cent ABV. Some higher-quality brands add unfermented apple juice, but it's more common to add water, then add sugar or other flavourings to prevent the cider from tasting too thin. Apple juice content in commercial ciders varies widely: the statutory minimum content is 35 per cent in the UK, 50 per cent in the United States.

The popular palate also prefers lighter tastes that are easier to drink quickly. Dilution is often balanced with the addition of sweeteners, artificial aromas and colourings and other adjuncts to create a balance of sweetness and lightness that is constantly tweaked in reaction to market research to have the maximum appeal to modern palates weaned on sugary soft drinks.

There are obviously degrees of compromise, so when judging commercial brands it's important to differentiate between products that are very light in flavour and those that are actively unpleasant to drink. Magners and Stella Cidre may taste watery to fans of artisanal cider, but some cheaper products have harsh chemical notes to them and can only ever be drunk ice-cold, where these flavours are masked. Not everyone appreciates the funk of Somerset farmyard cider. But the mainstream drinker still has a right to expect better than products made so cheaply they are actively offensive to the palate.

ABOVE: Cider filtration on an industrial scale.
RIGHT: Apples at Westons, waiting to be pressed.

If you drink mainstream cider brands, that's fine.
But you might want to know what's really in the bottle.

'I DON'T THINK THERE'S ANY SUCH THING AS THE PERFECT CIDER. I ALWAYS THINK THERE'S ROOM FOR IMPROVEMENT.'

Not everyone agrees with Peter Mitchell or likes what he says. We've met cider makers who become heated at the mention of his name and say the only reason to listen to him is so you can do the opposite.

# THE AUTHORITY PETER MITCHELL

The more even-handed cider maker might suggest that his methods favour commerce over craft, that he teaches how to make cider that is technically perfect but not necessarily interesting.

And then there are those craft cider makers, scores of them around the world, for whom attending a Peter Mitchell course is a life-changer, a mandatory starting gun on a new career.

The opinions may vary, but what's absolutely certain is that his name will come up in conversations about cider almost anywhere in the world. It only seemed fair to find out what the man himself has to say.

Mitchell studied physiology and biochemistry and then completed a masters degree in applied microbiology and biotechnology, with a research thesis on malolactic fermentation. He has been making cider since 1982, and has won numerous awards for his products. He has consulted with just about every large-scale commercial cider maker in Britain, and runs regular cider-making courses in the UK and North America. He has also taught across Europe, Asia, Australasia and South Africa – pretty much everywhere in the cider world, in fact, except France and Spain, where producers, he says, 'like to look after their own stuff'.

Mitchell's technical proficiency is beyond doubt. But in a cider world where few people agree about anything, what sort of philosophy does he preach? 'A good cider is one that people want to buy,' he says. 'It should be free of technical faults. Cider is easy to make, but it's easy to get faults and cider doesn't hide faults well. All I'm arguing is that you need to use skill and care in the production, using the best methods and technology available.'

It's this emphasis on technical proficiency that upsets some, but Mitchell does not see himself as standing against traditional methods. 'Traditional cider makers always wanted to do the best,' he says. 'People have been using yeast nutrients for centuries. We've always known that if it's bubbling away, it's well, and if it's not, it's dying. We know more about the process now, and I'm sure our ancestors would have wanted to know that, too.'

It's hard to find much to disagree with there. But when I ask him his thoughts on the current global boom in cider-making, he replies: 'I think the growth will continue, but it's not without risks. I worry that people are trying to do too much, too soon. If there's too much innovation people get bored of it. And if you're trying to plant an orchard, make cider and sell it at a high price point all at once, you're trying to master a whole set of different processes far too quickly.'

The cider world is full of passionate innovators who may be frustrated by this point of view. Some who have taken his courses suggest he is trying to force everyone to make technically perfect cider without character. 'I don't think there's any such thing as the perfect cider,' counters Mitchell. 'I always think there's room for improvement.'

It takes time and money to make cider, and Mitchell's philosophy seems to be 'learn to walk before you try to run'. It's sound advice, but may be conservative for some.

And so we arrive at another schism in the world of cider. Is it better to have consistency and reliability, with no chance of a nasty surprise, or to play Russian Roulette and chance upon unimaginable delights with the threat of unspeakable (and undrinkable) horrors lurking? It seems that, where cider is concerned, there will always be room for both.

**Peter Mitchell**
Mitchell Food and Drink Ltd
74 Culber Street, Newent,
Gloucestershire GL18 1DA
**www.mitchell-food-drink.co.uk**

OPPOSITE: Peter Mitchell makes his own cider as well as advising others. His Out of the Orchard range also includes a crisp, fine perry.

# PERRY

Just as there are many distinct varieties of cider apple, all entirely different from culinary apples, so perry pears are a world away from culinary pears. Yes, they are part of the same family. But they are the black sheep of that family.

If perry pears were people, they'd be like Matt Damon's character in the film *Good Will Hunting*: a difficult outcast with no friends, troubled and destructive, lashing out and hurting anyone who attempts to nurture them, but with genius hidden inside, waiting to be released.

Let's make no bones about this: perry pears are absolute bastards. The trees take ages to grow and produce fruit, and perry makers talk about planting 'pears for your heirs'. The small, ugly fruit is incredibly temperamental and vulnerable to pests and diseases. It's much more difficult to prise from the tall, high-canopied trees than a cider apple, and yet it must be collected at precisely the right time, and this varies widely for different varieties. Too early and the fruit is hard as stone. A couple of days later and it's soft and mushy. The flesh is viciously tannic; one American super-taster we met with a surprising affection for tannin described biting into one as 'like being punched in the face in a really awesome way'. Even if you're brave enough to take a bite you may get an unwelcome surprise: perry pears rot from the inside out, which means you may only discover the fruit is worthless when it's too late.

Let's say you persevere this far, growing and successfully harvesting perry pears. Perry-making then often requires the fruit to be macerated before pressing, during which time it's vulnerable to infection. It's higher in citric acid than cider apples, which can easily convert to acetic acid (our old friend vinegar) at this time.

Bad perry – which is what you're most likely to get – is one of the nastiest drinks you will ever taste. Imagine stepping in a cowpat covered in nail varnish remover and you're almost there. And whether your perry is good, awful or indifferent, it contains high levels of sorbitol, a sugar alcohol that causes flatulence and diarrhoea if consumed in large quantities.

So why on earth does anyone bother with this wretched, unfriendly drink? Because good perry – if you're lucky enough to find it – is like drinking angel's tears. Some resemble cider. Other sparkling perries have a balance and delicacy rivalled only by the finest Champagnes, with a graceful elderflower note on the nose that even French fizz can't match.

The comparison with Champagne is a crucial one in understanding perry, and a fascinating chapter in the broader history of alcoholic drinks. Read any book on wine and it will probably tell you that the *méthode champenoise* (or *méthode traditionelle* if you're doing it outside the Champagne region) was discovered by accident and then developed by a monk called Dom Pérignon around 1700.

What they neglect to tell you about is the firm documentary proof that English cider and perry makers were doing the same thing years before Dom Pérignon was even born.

Sparkling wine such as Champagne is made by dosing it with sugar after bottling to create a secondary fermentation. Of course, if you bottle before fermentation has finished this won't be necessary, and there are records of bottling cider with corks going back to 1632 at Holme Lacy in Herefordshire, the estate of Lord Scudamore. Twenty-one years later, Ralph Austen told the Royal Society that he had seen what would become known as *dosage* practised widely in the county:

---

'CIDER MAY BE KEPT PERFECT GOOD MANY YEARES IF BEING SETTLED IT BE DRAWN OUT INTO A BOTTLE AND WELL STOPPED WITH CORKS AND HARD WAX MELTED THEREON.. PUT INTO EACH BOTTLE A LUMP OR TWO OF HARD SUGAR OR SUGAR BRUISED.'

---

Then in 1676, John Worlidge described bottled cider and perry undergoing the *remuage et dégorgement* (riddling and disgorging) process, by which bottles are turned and matured, even though those terms had not been invented yet because the French still didn't know about it.

OPPOSITE: A good perry is closer in character to fine wine or even Champagne than it is to commercial 'pear cider'.

To bottle sparkling wine, cider or perry successfully you don't just need the drink, you need the bottle. And not just any bottle: it needs to be strong enough to withstand the pressure from the carbonation building up inside. While the invention of such strengthened glass is lost in time, glassmakers employed by Sir Kenelm Digby (a friend of Scudamore's) claimed in court to have mastered the method by 1632, the same year Scudamore was bottling cider and perry. Almost a century later, when the French finally acquired the bottles to make Champagne, they still referred to this strengthened glass as *verre anglaise*.

Remains of the world's most legendary perry tree still survive in the grounds of Holme Lacy. Only a few rooted branches are left, but records from 1790 show it once covered three-quarters of an acre and yielded up to nine tonnes of fruit a year. Herefordshire and its neighbouring counties of Gloucestershire and Worcestershire have always been, and still are, seen as the world centre of

perry production, with locals insisting that 'perry pears flourish only within sight of May Hill', which stands between Gloucester and Ross-on-Wye.

Even here, though, perry nearly vanished for good. It's hard to imagine why, but in the 19th century many farmers decided perry pear trees were uneconomical and not worth the bother. Despite a campaign to propagate them and the establishment of various collections of trees throughout the 20th century, they remain rare. One well-meaning perry fan by the name of Francis Showering attempted to establish big enough orchards to launch a large-scale commercial perry in the 1950s, but those anti-social perry trees were having none of it.

After several attempts, Showering resorted to importing concentrated pear juice. His product, Babycham, introduced perry to a generation, particularly women, many of whom remained unaware that the sugary concoction served in a Champagne bowl and advertised

LEFT & FAR RIGHT: Perry trees. Alone.
They prefer it that way.

by a cute cartoon deer was perry at all. A generation later, the less childlike 'fun, fabulous and female' Lambrini pulled a similar trick, so tacky it gave even alcopop drinkers someone to whom they could feel superior.

The terminally unfashionable image these brands created, plus the fact that few people knew what perry was, led some commercial brands to launch 'pear cider' variants – like cider, but made with pears instead of apples. Arguably, this confuses things still further. Most commercial pear ciders are made with imported pear juice concentrate rather than perry pears. Some are 'pear-flavoured' apple ciders, while others are 100 per cent fermented from culinary pears. While the Campaign for Real Ale (CAMRA) refuses to recognize 'pear cider', the National Association of Cider Makers insists perry and pear cider are interchangeable terms.

The life of the perry drinker therefore remains uncertain, frustrating and hazardous to the taste buds, punctuated by frequent trips to the toilet. But it is a vocation that can offer unparalleled delight. With its subtlety and delicacy, perry promises eternally to deliver the greatest flavour you've ever experienced, but always keeps it tantalizingly out of reach. If you keep drinking, it promises, just around the next corner it will hit you in the face with a big sloppy kiss. But it never quite does.

I suggest this to Herefordshire cider and perry maker Tom Oliver, regarded widely, along with Gloucestershire's Kevin Minchew, as one of the two best perry makers in the world. He smiles. 'Yes, perry is a journey. The first sip is not the whole story. As you drink more, you're opening up your senses to its hidden depths. If we could go back through every perry I've made in the last 15 years, there are three I could give you where you'd turn that final corner and arrive. But that only happens in a vintage year.'

Better keep going, then.

ABOVE: Perry pears do not look or taste like culinary pears. Vicious little critters.

# TASTING CIDER

If it's a hot day and you want to glug down a frosty bottle from the neck, it takes a brave or arrogant person to tell you that you're drinking your cider wrong.

Some of us have far higher concentrations of taste buds than others, which creates dramatically different perceptions of flavour. There's also an emerging body of research that seems to prove that taste cannot be separated from other stimuli and that context, environment, mood and memory all make something 'taste' different.

So there's no right or wrong way to taste something. But if you're reading this book, you're probably interested in experiencing the full flavour that cider has to offer – hence this guide to tasting. However, we're not saying this is the right way to drink, merely that it's the best way to appreciate the full character of your cider, if that's what you want.

The principles of tasting any food or drink are the same. We think of taste as something that happens on the tongue and we use the words 'taste' and 'flavour' interchangeably, but all five senses contribute.

First, select a glass that allows you to pour in a decent glug of cider but still has enough room for you to get your nose in for a good sniff. A wine glass, half-full, is perfect. Here we go...

# 1
## Have a Look
It's often said that 'the first bite is with the eye'. Appearance certainly gives us a clue as to what to expect. Does it look light and clean? Or heavy and rich?

# 2
## Swirl and Sniff
'Flavour' is actually a composite of taste and aroma, and most of it is aroma. Drink straight from the bottle and you're cutting your nose – and about 80 per cent of the flavour compounds – out of the equation. Swirl the glass to release the volatile aromas, and get your nose in for several good inhalations. It might seem pretentious but, go on: no one's looking.

# 3
## Have a Sip
By 'sip', we mean a good mouthful. You have flavour receptors not just on your tongue, but all over your mouth. The more receptors it hits, the more you're going to get out of your cider. So swirl it around, coating the whole of your mouth. And be mindful: focus on what's happening in there. Allow your brain to make associations and respond to the stimuli it's receiving.

# 4
## Remember to Swallow
Yeah, you can spit if you want. When you're tasting cider or wine professionally you may be getting through as many as a 100 at a time and the whole spittoon thing is about simple survival. But if you're not judging competitions, it's worth remembering that the finish of a drink is an important part. The way cider leaves your palate tingling after the swallow is the final part of the experience. Well, almost...

## Temperature

Cider should best be served chilled – not warm, and not ice-cold. If it's too cold the flavour is masked (which is precisely why some commercial brands suggest it). You want it to be refreshing on a hot day, but if you do want to get the full flavour, a temperature of around 8–10°C is perfect.

# 5
**Repeat!**
If it's good, you want to drink more of it. We're here to enjoy ourselves! But drinks do change as you consume more. Sweet or strong flavours may become cloying in greater volumes, while some subtler flavours may develop quite beautifully as more of it hits your palate. Around two-thirds of the way down the glass, you'll have got a pretty rounded view.

# TASTING SYMBOLS

Following our broad classification of flavours on pages 30-33, we've devised the following to help distinguish the ciders in this book. Any particular cider may possess one, two or more of the following:

 **STILL**

 **SPARKLING** Either Champagne-style traditional-method or forced carbonation.

 **BIG** Full-bodied, powerful and juicy.

 **ESPECIALLY TANNIC AND DRY**

 **BARNYARD FUNKINESS** May have cheesy, spicy or earthy notes.

 **ADDED FRUIT** Or other flavour adjuncts.

 **KEEVED** For lower alcohol and higher residual sweetness.

 **CALVADOS OR OTHER CIDER BRANDY**

 **POMMEAU** Or similar mix of distilled spirit and cider or apple juice.

 **ICE CIDER/CIDRE DE GLACE**

 **PERRY**

 **WINE-LIKE** Comparable to wine: delicate and refined, balance of sweetness and acidity with little or no tannin.

 **REFRESHING** A delicately flavoured, quenching refresher, probably consumed in a way comparable to beer.

**NOTE** Cider brandy, ice cider and Pommeau are still unless otherwise stated.

# PLANET
# CIDER

# A WORLD OF CIDER

Cider is produced across the entire world. Names may vary, but the unique characteristics of each region ensures an even greater range of tastes to enjoy.

MAIN: These hands tell the story of a life spent in the cider industry.

OPE

# SPAIN

# SPAIN

Say 'Spain' in a game of boozy word association and the answer that will come back immediately is 'wine'. Famous for Sherry, Rioja and Tempranillo, Spain has the largest vine acreage of any country and is the world's third-largest producer of wine, behind France and Italy.

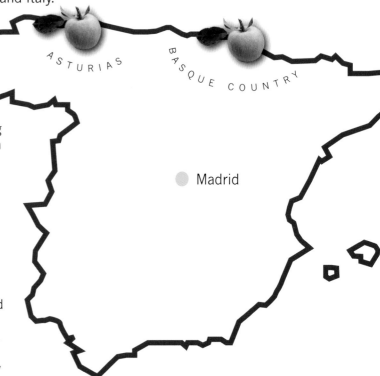

But the world of drink is never as simple as that – and neither is Spain. This fiercely regional country still resists notions of a centralized state, and with regional identity comes dramatic variation in food and drink traditions.

The northern coast is where Spaniards come on holiday. While much of Europe flocks to the searing temperatures of southern Spain, the native population chill out in *España Verde*, enjoying the cool, maritime climate along the Bay of Biscay in Galicia, Asturias, Cantabria and the Basque Country. The geographical barrier of the Cantabrian and Basque Mountains help make this region feel separate from the rest of the country and it has always been resistant to invasion. There's more rainfall than in the rest of Spain and the northern slopes of the mountains are lush and green, making this perfect apple-growing country. The fierce local pride here is reflected in the claim that this could have been the very birthplace of cider-making.

Any Spanish cider maker will tell you that the Greek philosopher Estrabón (Strabo) recorded cider being produced in the region in 60BC because there was very little wine. There's just one problem: in the original text, Estrabón referred to *zytho* – the Greek word for beer. He uses the same word elsewhere in the text to refer to a barley-based drink that is obviously beer. There is no reason why he would use the word to mean a completely different drink without specifying that he was doing so.

The Asturians call Pliny in their defence, who wrote that there was little barley in the region at the time, but lots of apples. Given that there was no specific word for cider for centuries after the first records of its manufacture, it is plausible that Estrabón used *zytho* in the same way the Romans often referred to cider as wine.

If we accept that, it's also plausible that the Asturians spread cider-making to other regions. 'There are records of legions from Asturias – the *Hispanum Asturium* – serving among the Roman armies that conquered Britain,' says Eduardo Coto, a passionate advocate of Asturian *sidra,* 'and it's generally accepted that the Romans introduced cider to Britain. Could it actually have been the Asturians? Then, in AD794, a council took place within Charlemagne's empire at which members of the Asturian court were present. It led to the foundation of the city of Frankfurt – now one of Europe's main cider-making regions. Coincidence?'

There are hundreds of references to cider and orchards in wills from around the 8th and 9th centuries, which often refer to 'vineyards and orchards' together, implying that the fruit was being grown to press into drink. We know Charlemagne referred to cider specifically, and while he never mentions the location of the *siceratores*, sheer weight of evidence suggests apple-growing and cider-making were more established in Asturias than anywhere else during his reign. Certainly by the 12th century, apple cultivation was the central part of the Asturian economy.

What is also beyond doubt is the passion for cider in the region today. 'Cider isn't just a drink; it's a lifestyle for the Asturians,' says Tess Jewell-Larsen, a cider writer living in the region. Asturians drink an average of 54 litres of cider per head, per year: more than anyone else in the world (if you calculate the figures at a regional rather than national level). Asturian *sidra* has received a Protected Designation of Origin, or PDO, from the EU, and a regulatory board keeps a close eye on apple growers, cider makers and *sidrerías*.

Cider is made and drunk across *España Verde*, but its focus is Asturias. As soon as you leave the airport in the capital city of Oviedo, the roadsides are dotted with *sidrerías*, and the 'Apple Town' of Villaviciosa (literally, 'fertile valley') has a higher concentration of cider-focused bars than we've seen anywhere else. Villaviciosa is home to El Gaitero, Spain's largest cider brand. It is named 'The Piper' after one of the four statues of musicians in the central town square. The export version is an excellent sparkling cider, slightly musty, and a little smoky. But in supermarkets across Spain it's more common to find Champagne-style bottles of light, spritzy varients of around 4 per cent ABV. These are stocked alongside sparkling wines rather than the canned brands imported for tourists, and sell for as little as two euros a bottle. Crisp, fruity and refreshing, they prove that cheap, commercial cider doesn't have to be rubbish. But this is not the stuff that cider drinkers get excited about.

Traditional Asturian *sidra natural* reminds some people of West Country British cider and others of Frankfurt's *Apfelwein*: comparisons that may add weight to Eduardo's theories of cider propagation. However, it has a defining characteristic that separates it from both – and from anything else. French and English ciders rely on bittersweet apples, using sharp apples for balance and aroma. In Asturias, the sharps are the stars of the show. Typically, the blend will be 40 per cent sharp, 25 to 30 per cent medium-sharp, 10 to 15 per cent sweet and just 20 to 25 per cent bitter or bittersweet. These apples are fermented naturally with wild yeast, and develop high levels of volatile acidity – the presence of acetic acid. Most cider makers around the world think of this as a technical fault, dismissing it as 'microbiological spoilage', but it's the defining characteristic of Spanish *sidra natural*, and part of the definition in its European PDO. In most ciders, acetic acid is kept below 0.5 grams per litre. Above two grams, and it's vinegar – undrinkable to most palates. *Sidra natural* hovers around 1.5 grams per litre. But it can't be judged properly unless it's served correctly – as we'll see in the following pages.

Basque *sagardoa* tends to have even higher volatile acidity than Asturian *sidra*. These ciders are often made by small, family businesses that produce just one type, which is stored in giant chestnut vats in cellars that are usually open to the public. From January to April it's *txox* time in the Basque region – home to over 70 cider makers. *Txox* is the local phonetic spelling of the sound that the small peg in the front of each giant barrel makes when it's pulled out. Stalls line the streets, and the cider is sold cheaply until it runs out. As the weather gets warmer, the bulk of the cider is then bottled. Wherever you go in the Basque Country or Asturias, the welcome is almost as heady as the cider. It's served with generosity and warmth – although you might be asked to sing a song in return. Cider production here has had its ups and downs, but is now being supported by the government and thriving again. Not everyone likes sharp *sidra*, but the new wave of Nueva Expresión ciders are different in style, more balanced and wine-like.

Spain in general will probably always be better known for its wine than anything else. But drinking wine was never this much fun.

LEFT: El Gaitero, 'The drink that speaks the truth', according to its classic ads.
BELOW: El Gaitero headquarters in Villaviciosa, Asturias – showing off because it's one of the few cider regions in the world with palm trees.

MAIN: The vast, chestnut-wood maturation tanks at El Gaitero. Big doesn't always have to be bad.

# CIDER THROWING

When a cider tradition stretches back as far as 2000 years and defines a culture, one might expect a bit of ritual and theatre. The way cider is served in northern Spain does not disappoint.

In a *sidrería*, when you order a bottle of *sidra* the waiter will pour it for you – sometimes at a special pouring station, because this is no ordinary pour. A wide glass, chunky-looking but impossibly delicate to the touch, is held in the left hand, which is extended down to the ground as far as the server can reach. The bottle is held in the right hand, which is extended as far as possible skywards. Ideally, this creates a distance of about a metre between glass and bottle.

Staring straight ahead, the talented server, or *escanciador*, then tilts the bottle and 'throws' the cider through the air. Done perfectly, it hits the side of the glass, which is so thin it vibrates with the impact, until there's between a half-inch and an inch in the bottom which you drink quickly, then gesture to the *escanciador* for a repeat performance.

There is far more to this technique, known as *escanciar un culín* ('pouring a shot' or 'gulp') than mere mixologist-style showing off. This dramatic passage from bottle to glass temporarily aerates the cider, so by the time it is handed to you it has a sparkling, mousse-like consistency reminiscent of Champagne. As well as having a delightful mouthfeel, it takes the edge off the characteristic acetic character of the *sidra*, making it much more mellow than if poured in a normal way, turning sharp, flat cider into liquid sherbert. We've tried it ourselves (over the sink) and it's remarkable the difference it makes to the same

FAR LEFT & LEFT: It can take a lifetime to perfect the skill of being an *escanciador*, but it does make you lots of friends. BELOW: The soft, sherberty, mousse-like cider is best drunk quickly. Darn.

cider poured from the same bottle. The problem is, the effect only lasts for a minute or so, which is why, to be enjoyed at its best, you have to down small quantities quickly. When bottles of *sidra* are sent to competitions and festivals around the world without anyone who knows how to pour them properly, this particular style is often misunderstood and unfairly maligned.

Back in the *sidrerías*, the aim is to pour one good mouthful, and if there are any dregs after the first gulp then it's quite common to tip them on the floor rather than go back to a glass that's lost its fizz. Some *sidrerías* have special drains for this, but a night spent in most will end with your shoes glued to the sticky floor.

The origin of this tradition comes from the way cider is served straight from the huge chestnut barrels in traditional cider houses. The pressure of the cider trying to get out of the hole, which is unplugged by the removal of a tiny peg, sends it shooting in an arc across the room. If pouring from the bottle is a special skill, the guys who manage to pull the peg from the barrel with one hand and hold a glass stretched away from them in the other should be seen, catching the arc as it shoots through the air onto the right part of the glass. There's one danger with these exquisite small glasses: you very quickly lose track of how much you've drunk. Considering Asturians drink an average of 54 litres of cider a year each, those *escanciadors* in the *sidrerías* must be constantly busy.

# THE *SIDRERÍA* AND SPANISH CUISINE

Whatever your tipple, Spain has one of the best drinking cultures in the world. Everywhere in the country, bars are relaxed and numerous, and it's common to drink a small glass of something at any time of the day. When you do, it will often be accompanied by a small snack.

Tapas restaurants in other countries often seem to miss the whole point of what tapas is. A *tapa* is not a meal – neither a main course nor a starter – but a few bites to accompany a drink. Order a range in one restaurant to share, or have one with each drink and move on somewhere else.

In most places, food and drink traditions have evolved together, playing off each other, and the cider country of northern Spain is no exception. Here, tapas are more commonly referred to as *pintxos* in the Basque Country or *pinchos* in the rest of northern Spain, after the cocktail sticks they're often served with. People still drink cider in

*sidrerías* rather than at home. A traditional *sidrería* may only serve cider, but it's increasingly common to find a *chigre*, or bar, that serves a variety of drinks. The oldest Basque cider bars served no food and people would bring their own, but this has now changed dramatically.

The acidity of *sidra natural* makes it a perfect foil for fatty food, as it cuts through the grease and enlivens the palate. Chorizo cooked in cider is simple perfection, and a regular feature of any Spanish restaurant or bar. Salt cod and thick rib-eye steaks are also common and delicious accompaniments.

And then there's the cheese. Cider and cheese is as good a match as cider and pork, and *España Verde* is very proud of its cheese. The Basques make wonderful ewes-milk cheeses, including the firm, smoky *Idiazábal*, which is a natural partner to sharp *sargado*. Not to be outdone, Asturias is often referred to as *el país de los quesos*: 'Land of Cheese'. *Cabrales*, a strong blue cheese which, like the cider, has its own protected *denominación de origen*, is famous throughout Spain and beyond, and has an acidity of its own that works well with *sidra*.

The most famous regional dish is *fabada Asturiana*, a rich stew made with chorizo, white beans, pork shoulder and *morcilla* (black pudding). Cider pairs wonderfully with all these ingredients, and one is never far away from the others. But Asturias is also famous for its fish and seafood. Fresh squid, crab, sea urchin and sea bass go with crisp cider in a zingier way than the creamy dishes.

Although the whole approach of the *sidrería* is informal and rustic, some grow to titanic proportions. Petritegi in San Sebastián is often fully booked, despite having 700 seats. This may have something to do with the 15,000-litre-capacity barrels, from which guests can serve themselves year-round.

In fact, San Sebastián has more Michelin-starred restaurants than anywhere else in the world. While the local Riojas might feature more commonly on the menus in the best places, cider is undeniably at the heart of one of the world's most admired cuisines.

ABOVE & OPPOSITE:
*Sidrerías* are frequented by young and old alike.
RIGHT: The Tierra Astura chain of *sidrerías* sets cider drinking in a modern setting.

# SPAIN CIDER SUGGESTIONS

## BUZNEGO
Gijón, Villaviciosa, Asturias
www.sidrabuznego.com

### Zapica Sidra de Asturias
(6% ABV)

Golden and bright with a faint green hue. Clean aromas of ripe apple, followed by a very fruity flavour with notes of honey and fresh grass. Moderate acidity with a long finish. Beautifully balanced.

## CASERÍA SAN JUAN DEL OBISPO
Tiñana, Siero, Asturias
www.caseriasanjuandelobispo.com

### L'Alquitara del Obispo
(40% ABV)

Very fragrant apple and spirit aroma. Intense flavours of crisp, dry apples and skins, delicate yet warming. The local legend is that it was created by a bishop who was killed by three Norman knights when they attempted to get the recipe from him.

## CASTAÑÓN
Quintes, Villaviciosa, Asturias
www.sidracastanon.com

### Sidra Natural Castañón
(5.5% ABV)

Rarely has the term 'natural' been more appropriate. With a musty aroma, hints of chalk, wild yeast, leaf and apple core in among the fruit, this is like drinking the entire orchard rather than just the fruit.

## CORTINA
Amandi, Villaviciosa, Asturias
www.sidracortina.com

### Sidra Natural
(6% ABV)

Hazy yellow, with an aroma of sweet apple, vanilla and a characteristic slight acetic edge. Flavour is light, tart, with good acidity and a sourness that is not overpowering.

### Villacubera DO Sidra Nueva Expresión
(6% ABV)

Pale golden colour with greenish hue and gentle carbonation. Subtle, ripe fruit notes. Floral and light with very gentle acidity and the slightest touch of woody tannin.

### EL GOBERNADOR
Villaviciosa, Asturias
**www.sidraelgobernador.com**

**Sidra brut nature Emilio Martínez**
(8% ABV)

Vivid green apple and citrus aromas, followed by a fresh-fruit palate that's rounded yet sharp, and finishes dry and zingy.

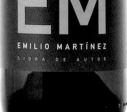

### HERMINIO
Colloto, Oviedo, Asturias
**www.llagarherminio.com**

**Zythos Nueva Expresión DO**
(6% ABV)

Pours a deep, hazy gold. A tart, green-apple aroma followed by a dry, phenolic flavour with fresh fruit and a dry, astringent finish.

### ISASTEGI
Tolosa, Guipúzcoa
**www.isastegi.com**

**Sidra Natural** (6% ABV)

Hazy yellow, with big farmyard and acetic aromas. On the palate there's a lot of tart apples, moderately sweet and boldly acidic, with a mouth-puckering finish.

### JR CABUEÑES
Gijón, Asturias
**www.sidrajr.es**

**Sidra Natural** (6% ABV)

Light golden colour; fresh, clean aroma with a hint of woodiness. Light, rounded flavour with slight acidity and a soft, pleasant, drying aftertaste.

### LOS SERRANOS
Ribadesella, Asturias
**www.licoreslosserranos.es**

**Aguardiente de Manzana** (40% ABV)

A family business since 1895, creating liqueurs and spirits from a variety of fruits. This one is produced slowly and is carefully aged for a perfect balance of apple character, big oak and spirituous warmth.

### MENÉNDEZ
Gijón, Asturias
www.sidramenendez.es

#### Val d´Ornón DO (Sidra Natural) (6% ABV)

Straw-yellow, with a clean and fruity scent that takes you right back to the orchard. Well-balanced on the palate, with light acidity and a pleasant finish.

### PANIZALES
Mieres, Asturias
www.llagarpanizales.com

#### Sidra de Hielo Panizares (9.5% ABV)

This rare ice cider pours a coppery amber colour, with aromas of apple skin, peach and banana. It has slightly lower residual sugar than its Canadian counterparts, and is faintly sparkling, so it's fresh and fruity rather than massively overpowering.

### PETRITEGI
Astigarraga, Guipúzcoa
www.petritegisagardoa.com

#### Sidra Natural (6% ABV)

Pours pale yellow with a sour-apple and lemon aroma. On the palate it's citrusy, medium-bodied with a sharp, tart-apple bite. It's essential that this is poured in the correct manner to be enjoyed properly.

### TRABANCO
Gijón, Asturias
www.sidratrabanco.com

#### Sidra Natural (6% ABV)

One of Asturias' largest cider makers shows that big doesn't have to mean bland. On the nose you get the whole apple, not just the juice. The flavour is a complex mixture of ripe and cooked apples, subtle herbs, good tannins, funky wild yeast and strong acidity.

#### Poma Áurea Sidra de Asturias (6.5% ABV)

Made from a selection of hand-picked apples from the best orchards in the region, pressed on old wooden presses before being fermented in old wooden barrels, this is bottled with fresh apple must to prompt a secondary bottle fermentation. The result is a very dry cider with a powerful apple-and-barnyard aroma and layers of orchard fruit, flowers and dried fruit that keep revealing themselves.

## VALLE, BALLINA Y FERNÁNDEZ
Villaviciosa. Asturias

www.gaitero.com

### El Gaitero Extra
(5.5% ABV)

A superior sparkling cider, it's astonishing how cheaply this is positioned and sold in Spanish supermarkets. Fruity aromas and a light, fresh, slightly acidic palate make it a perfect drink for the climate.

## VALVERÁN
Sariego, Asturias

www.llagaresvalveran.com

### Sidra 20 Manzanas
(10% ABV)

Valverán has been making cider since 2010 and combines Asturian tradition with a modern approach influenced by wine-making. This rare ice cider is matured in oak barrels for 12 months. Thick, sweet apples laced with honey, oak and vanilla hints with an odd (for an ice cider) touch of funk.

## VIUDA DE ANGELÓN
Nava, Asturias

www.viudaangelon.com

### Prau Monga DO (6% ABV)

Golden yellow and lightly carbonated. Intense aromas of ripe fruit, followed by a balanced flavour with an acidic edge – a perfect example of the Asturian cider style.

## ZAPIAIN
Astigarraga, Guipúzcoa

www.zapiainsagardoa.com

### Sidra Natural
(6% ABV)

The house cider in one of the Basque region's greatest cider houses, and a favourite for the *txotx*. A light, easy-drinking start to a meal or tasting session, best drunk chilled.

## ZELAIA
Hernani, Guipúzcoa

www.zelaia.es

### Sidra Natural
(6% ABV)

Another *txotx* favourite. Hazy yellow with tart apple and citrusy, lemony aromas. A lightly acidic profile with a long, medium-dry finish.

# FRANCE

# FRANCE

In an echo of their historically fractious relationship, France and Britain are great rivals for the title of world's best cider producer. Knowledgeable advocates in each country could make a strong case: Herefordshire or Normandy perry? Breton *cidre brut* or Somerset farmhouse cider? It's a close call wherever you look.

But consider what each country shows of itself to the rest of the world and the picture changes dramatically. Britain – the biggest cider maker on the planet – exports brands such as Strongbow and Bulmers to an ever-increasing number of countries. What these sweet, industrial ciders full of juice concentrate, water and sugar lack in true cider character, they make up for in slick marketing and design.

By contrast, French cider is harder to find outside the regions that make it. But when you do so it's likely to be a bottle-conditioned beauty in a Champagne-style bottle with a cork-and-wire stopper and an elegant label that looks unchanged since the 1930s. It hides in expensive restaurants priced appropriately, and people swoon over its quality. And yet France is one of the few countries where cider is still considered boring and old-fashioned, with sales stagnating as dedicated drinkers become a passing generation.

And yet, just a century ago, France drank more cider than wine. Were it not for deeply held institutional prejudice and a few chance twists of fate, haute cuisine around the world – dominated as it is by France – could well have developed with cider rather than wine as the natural accompaniment to food.

Cider certainly goes back a long way here. Fossilized pips and paintings on France's incredible prehistoric cave walls reveal that people have always eaten apples here. Caesar's cider-loving Romans passed through en route to conquering Britain, and Strabo mentioned the abundance of apple and pear trees in Gaul. When Charlemagne instructed that *siceratores* be on hand on his estates to prepare *pomatum* and *pyratium*, his Frankish empire centred on what is now France, and eventually gave the country its name.

By the 11th century there were known orchards in Cotentin and the Pays d'Auge in Normandy. But France really dates the birth of cider to the 13th century, and the dramatic improvement (the French say 'invention') of the apple press.

However, apples remained second best. As in the rest of the vine-growing areas of Western Europe, wine was considered the superior drink, and cider was mainly a cheap substitute for farmers. But the mini-ice age hit Europe, vines gradually disappeared from the cool north-western climes of Normandy and Brittany, and apples came to the fore. By the beginning of the 14th century orchards were being planted by nobles as well as farmers,

and 300 different apple varieties were grown. The cider was still generally considered to be poor quality, though, until the arrival of some gentlemen from northern Spain.

There had been a long relationship between Spain and northeast France, thanks to the fishing routes across the Bay of Biscay that led to the arrival and adoption of bittersweet Spanish cider apple varieties such as Bisquet, still in widespread use today. In the late 15th century, the Spaniard Guillaume D'Ursus impressed the French king in battle and was granted estates in Normandy. Here, he grafted new apple varieties and introduced more sophisticated cultivation and propagation techniques. When King François visited him in 1532, he bought several barrels of D'Ursus's *pomme d'épices* ('spiced apples') and made cider very fashionable.

Others followed D'Ursus's example, bringing in apples and techniques over the Bay of Biscay, improving trees and production techniques. In 1588, Charles IX's

OPPOSITE: Traditional cider maturing in Brittany.

Caen

Paris

NORMANDY

Quimper    Rennes

BRITTANY

PAYS BASQUE

BY THE END OF THE 19TH CENTURY,
THE GOVERNMENT ESTIMATED THAT
A MILLION PEOPLE WERE EMPLOYED
IN CIDER-MAKING. FRANCE HAD
THE LARGEST ACREAGE OF APPLE
CULTIVATION OF ANY COUNTRY IN
THE OLD WORLD. SO WHAT HAPPENED?

personal physician, Julien Le Paulmier, wrote *De Vino et Pomaco*, a 'Treaty of Wine and Cider', which praised cider for its health benefits and popularized it across France.

Cider's popularity grew steadily – and then dramatically. In the late 19th century phylloxera, a relative of the aphid with an insatiable appetite for the roots of vines, all but destroyed French wine production. Orchards grew to fill the gap, and in 1889, Fabienne Cosset declared that cider had replaced wine in Paris. By the end of the 19th century, the government estimated that a million people were employed in cider-making and France had the largest acreage of apple cultivation of any country in the Old World. So what happened?

Wine production eventually recovered, of course – and was then aggressively promoted by the French state. The fact that Calvados production was legally restricted, and Pommeau, the apple juice and brandy aperitif, was banned outright for many years, purely because each one rivalled brandy or wine, tells us all we need to know about how jealously the French guard their wine industry.

And maybe French cider simply isn't French enough for the French. The two main cider-producing regions – Normandy and Brittany – feel separate from the rest of France. Normandy was colonized by invaders, while Brittany never fully signed up to be part of the French nation, retaining its separate Celtic identity. The Pays Basque – another significant cider-producing region – is also famous for its separate sense of identity.

Then there were the two world wars. The first saw cider production grind to a halt as the government requisitioned alcohol and its means of production to make explosives. In the second, cider was devastated by German occupation, and Normandy in particular – the heart of French cider production – was destroyed by fierce fighting following the Allied invasion.

After the war cider slipped further down the table, losing out to beer as France's second favorite drink, after wine. It increasingly became seen as staid and old-fashioned, something that Grandpa drank, only to be dabbled with in the summer. But it remained popular in its northwest heartland, and the producers there began to fight back. New *basses-tiges* (low-stem) orchards were planted to replace the traditional tall, gnarled *hautes-tiges* trees, greatly improving yields and efficiency. In Normandy and Brittany, where the climate and soil create perfect conditions for cider apples, both regions created *appellations d'origines contrôlées* (AOC) for their cider, Pommeau and apple brandy.

In this broad range of products from the apple, as in its cuisine more generally, France demonstrated its ingenuity in getting the most out of nature's harvest and preserving it for as long as possible before we had the benefit of refrigeration. Fresh apples have finite value for the person who grew them, and they soon go off. Turn them into cider and it increases their value and keeps for up to a year. Distil that cider into Calvados and it's potentially so valuable that it can be used as currency, and it keeps indefinitely. Finally, Calvados can be blended with fresh apple juice to create Pommeau, to give a second strand to the value chain, not to mention a rich array of flavours for the table.

Because artisanal ciders are never pasteurized, cleanliness is vital. No water, carbon dioxide or cultivated yeast is added, and the proportions of apples are carefully specified for any cider wishing to meet its AOC. Typically 60 to 70 per cent of the apples will be bittersweets, with no more than 10 to 15 per cent sharp, acidic apples. While French cider shares hints of barnyard funk with English farmhouse cider, it's far more likely to be sparkling than still, with the *méthode ancestrale* – where the cider is bottled before it has finished fermenting – still in widespread use. The preservation and refinement of the old method of keeving, where full fermentation is prevented, means naturally sweet, sparkling ciders are one of the defining characteristics of Normandy and Brittany. Sweet *cidre doux* is typically up to 3 per cent ABV. *Demi-sec* is between 3 and 5 per cent, and then fully fermented *cidre brut* is 5 per cent or above.

As with any country, the bulk of the total volume is made up by industrial brands that disregard the care and attention of the AOC. Typically they are 50 per cent fresh juice and 50 per cent concentrate, pasteurized and artificially carbonated. In line with pleasing as many people as possible they are have an artificial sweetness to them. But while brands such as Ecusson and Loïc Raison hardly compare to artisanal ciders, they embarrass industrial brands from other countries, retaining far more of cider's true character in both style and substance.

Cider will always be second best to wine in France. But in a country that takes food and drink so seriously, where tradition and craftsmanship have always been revered, even second best means that France leads the world in the artistry of cider-making.

ABOVE: Cider for sale.
OPPOSITE, CLOCKWISE FROM TOP LEFT: Simple pleasures. The refreshing, natural fizz of French cider. Cider can be aged successfully for years – if it's good enough. It's the apples that matter.

# CALVADOS

Wonderful though French ciders are, for many who make them they are not finished products – merely a necessary stage on the way to creating something they consider far more special.

Brandy, whisky and gin were well known across Europe before the self-styled 'Lord' Gouberville, a royal forester in Normandy, learned about wine distillation and applied it to cider in the mid-16th century.

The results obviously went down well. So many cider makers followed his example that in 1606 they formed a guild of *distillateurs d'eau-de-vie de cidre de Normandie*. But, not for the last time, the French authorities decided that the produce of the apple was so good, the precious wine industry needed to be protected from it. Production of cider brandy was banned outside the provinces of Brittany, Normandy and Maine.

Nevertheless, inside these districts the art of creating cider brandy improved. After the French Revolution, Normandy was divided into *départements*, one of which was named 'Calvados', and the name gradually became associated with the apple brandy of the northwest.

While production may have been restricted to a few regions, consumption gradually spread. In cafés and bistros near the factories that grew with the 19th-century industrialization of France, *café Calva* – coffee with a shot of Calvados – became so popular that if you wanted a straight coffee you had to be very clear about it. 'Bad coffee, bad Calva, bad work' became a popular saying, until the practice was eventually discouraged. But the good stuff spread, too.

Calvados production ground to a halt during World War I, when the government requisitioned alcohol for the arms industry. It was threatened with a similar fate after the German invasion of 1940. Armagnac and Cognac were exempted because of their *appellations d'origines contrôlées*, so the cider makers moved swiftly to gain similar recognition. Calvados was granted its appellation in 1942, which saved it from disappearing and ensured its high standards.

When cider is first distilled it creates a clear *eau de vie* with fresh, fruity overtones. It becomes Calvados after a minimum of three years' ageing in wooden barrels.

'The ageing does three things,' says Christian Drouin, one of Normandy's most celebrated cider makers. 'It gives the spirit character from the wood – flavour, structure and tannin. Over time, notes of vanilla,

cinnamon, coffee and smoke develop. Secondly, the Calvados oxidizes as the wood breathes and exposes it to the air, turning that fresh-apple flavour into marmalade, baked apple and dried fruits. And finally, we lose the "angel's share". Three or four per cent of the volume in the cask evaporates every year it ages, which leads to both concentration and mellowing of the flavours.'

There are three different appellations for Calvados: the main Calvados AOC; Calvados Domfrontais, which recognizes a spirit made from both apples and pears, common in southern Normandy; and Calvados Pays d'Auge, the finest variety, which must be made with ingredients from this most celebrated of French cider-making regions and which must undergo double distillation in a traditional alembic pot still rather than the more recent innovation of single continuous distillation.

Outside the appellations there are many farmers who make their own Calvados, and there are even travelling stills to help them do it. There's a long tradition of distilling poor cider, so it doesn't go to waste. But Drouin – who holds the appellation Pays d'Auge – insists you have to put the finest stuff in to get the best result out. 'The most common fault in cider is that it turns to vinegar,' he says. 'If you distil it, it makes disgusting Calvados! So people age it in a barrel and hope that will make it nice. It doesn't. You could age it for a hundred years and you'll just get a century-old disgusting vinegary drink!'

Calvados is aged in a variety of different barrels, and then different ages are carefully blended. The age listed on the bottle refers to the youngest constituent of the blend, and high-quality Calvados is usually made up of blends of vintages that are much older than the one specified. Drouin uses some that are 60 years old.

Calvados is a beguiling drink that manages to combine the sophistication of years of oak-ageing and the warm glow of alcohol spirit, and yet still retains the imprint of the original fruit character. It's difficult to find anyone who makes it – either French Calvados or equivalents such as Somerset cider brandy – who does not consider it to be both the finest expression of the apple, and the ultimate example of the cider maker's art.

OPPOSITE: The shrine to Calvados that is Pierre Huet's cellar.

# THE MODERNIZERS DOMAINE DUPONT

In 1887, Jules Dupont arrived at an estate known as La Vigannerie, a country manor with farmland and orchards, and began work as a tenant farmer. While raising cattle, he also made cider and Calvados, which sold so well that he was able to buy La Vigannerie in 1916.

His son, Louis, succeeded him in 1934, focusing on the cattle and selling Calvados in bulk to local merchants. When he died in 1974, his wife, Colette, assumed control of the business at the renamed Louis Dupont Family Estate, and passed it to her son, Etienne, in 1980.

Etienne was far more fascinated by the drinks side of the business than his father, particularly the Calvados. He spent time in the Cognac region learning as much as he could about double distillation, and then planted new orchards. He was instrumental in the creation of the *appellation contrôlée* (AOC) Pays d'Auge in 1996, establishing beyond doubt that his business sat at the heart of France's finest cider-producing region. He was

joined by his son, Jérôme, in 2002. Between them, they have made Dupont arguably the world's most recognized name in French cider and Calvados.

The family's manor house is flanked by two elegant rows of sheds: brick buildings with arched fronts. On one side sit the cider shop and offices. A new pressing area was under construction when we visited. On the other side, the locked sheds contain rows of barrels, in which the Calvados sits ageing. A steady stream of tourists from the United States, Japan and Russia wander around the grounds. This is hardly surprising; in America, Dupont cider is a regular feature on decent wine lists, retailing for up to $35 a bottle.

'Yes, we are among the people who export quality cider the most,' says Jérôme Dupont. 'There are other ciders, industrially produced, that are not as interesting in their expression, but we export across Europe, to North America, Australia and Asia.'

Combining tradition and innovation to dazzling effect is a family affair for one of the world's most celebrated cider makers.

There's a clear love of cider here that seeks to express itself not only in the Calvados, for which Dupont is most famous, but also in fresh, sparkling apple juice, Pommeau and a full range of ciders that even incorporates ice cider, all of which are produced to a superlative standard and regularly win bags of awards.

'Historically, cider and Calvados producers in Normandy were farmers,' says Jérôme. 'They followed traditional methods but were not really aware of the science of it. We think tradition is important but we also make a great study of the whole oenological dimension, the principles of wine-making. For example, double distillation of our Calvados Pays d'Auge gives us a very clean and delicate spirit, while Canadian ice-wine-style cryo-concentration allows us to make our dessert wine, the *Givre*. The combination of tradition, oenology and the right Normandy apple varieties gives us all we need to make rich and expressive wines on our *terroir*.'

Combining elegance and authenticity, even the labels suggest tradition and modernity at the same time. Is this the winning formula to revitalize French cider? Jérôme smiles. 'Well, Calvados drinkers tend to be from the spirits crowd, while cider drinkers split in two: on the one hand we have the historical drinkers, and on the other a new generation coming in from the craft-beer scene. We're trying to appeal to several different audiences. But I think we try to focus on the ciders and spirits that best express the character of our apples and *terroir*, and do this in the most interesting way we can gastronomically.' It seems like a winning formula to us.

FROM FAR LEFT: Some of Dupont's Calvados blends contain spirit that's decades old. The father-and-son team: Jérôme Dupont loves them apples, while his father, Etienne, admires them at their very best – as the basis of Calvados Pays d'Auge.

**Domaine Dupont**
14430 Victot-Pontfol
Pays d'Auge, Normandy
**www.calvados-dupont.com**

# NORMANDY

In the 10th century, the northern coast of France was there for the taking. Viking raiders plundered freely, and eventually invaded as far as the gates of Paris. The French king negotiated with the Norsemen, granting them the coastal region northwest of Paris in return for tributes and the promise to protect the land from all other invaders. The Norsemen became the Normans, quickly adopting the language and many of the customs of their new home, and Normandy was named after them.

In Norse tradition the apple is the fruit of immortality. The goddess Iðunn was the Keeper of Apples, which she fed to the other gods and goddesses to preserve their eternal youth. More generally, apples represented long life, wisdom and love. Here in Normandy, those who revered the apple had the perfect soil and climate to grow a bounty of them. For a culture that also regarded the enthusiastic consumption of alcohol as a way of life, a dedication to cider-making was a foregone conclusion.

Which is just as well, because they made terrible wine.

One wine writer in the early 19th century noted, 'I know very few people who have tasted the wines, and even the most renowned ones, of lower Normandy. These few people declare unanimously that such Normandy wines were undrinkable.'

To be fair, the local climate didn't really suit vines, especially after it cooled in the 13th century. The vines were replaced by grain, and in times of war and famine (of which France experienced more than its fair share), that grain was used for bread rather than beer, leaving cider to emerge as Normandy's favorite tipple.

Traditional orchards had high trees under which livestock could be grazed, fertilizing the roots and doubling up the use of the land. It made perfect sense for every farm to have an orchard, and cider-making

became a default activity for any Norman farmer. In the region of the Pays d'Auge, the poor, flinty soil meant the trees had to work hard, producing smaller fruit that was more intense in flavour and which therefore made superior cider. By contrast, the clay and limestone soil of the Domfrontais region in southern Calvados was ideally suited to the strong, deep roots of perry pear trees. By the 19th century the quality of Normandy's *cidre*, *poiré* (perry) and Calvados was recognized throughout the nation.

Normandy was, of course, the site of the Allied invasion that led to the liberation of Europe from the Nazis in World War II. Key towns were devastated by the bombing on D-Day, and the months that followed saw some of the most vicious fighting of the war as the Allies clawed their way through the region's narrow lanes and high hedgerows. Relief was at hand thanks to the locals who dug up barrels of Calvados they had hidden from the Germans to share with their liberators. This spread the fame of Calvados around the world, and it remains the official drink of regiments such as the Royal Canadian Hussars.

Apart from the tourist sites on the landing beaches, you'd never guess at the war's devastation today. Normandy is almost a fairy-tale landscape, seemingly perfectly preserved from the Middle Ages. Its green slopes and winding roads are punctuated by half-timbered black-and-white buildings, many of them serving as *gîtes* for tourists from abroad, or second homes for affluent Parisians. Claude Monet grew up here, and the imagery of the coastline and Norman countryside is central to his work, a key inspiration for Impressionism.

ABOVE: Age stamps used for wax Calvados seals.
OPPOSITE: A former travelling cider press has taken up permanent residency at Christian Drouin's farm, Domaine Cœur de Lion.

'WE SHOULDN'T EVEN
TRY TO COMPETE ON
COST. IT'S MUCH
BETTER TO FOCUS
ON QUALITY.'

The sense of Normandy as a kind of grown-up playground for the French is reinforced by some of the drinking customs. The *trou Normand* – 'Norman hole' – is famous as the gap between courses in a meal that must be filled with a cheeky shot of Calvados. And the *café Calva* survives here, too: everywhere we went, people finished their meals with a coffee, and finished the coffee in turn with another shot of Calvados swirled into the dregs of the still-warm cup.

Normandy also produces much of France's milk, butter and cheese – another benefit of those dual-purpose pastures-cum-orchards. It's thrilling for any cheese lover to look at the map and spot places called Camembert, Livarot and Pont-L'Évêque, just a few miles from each other in the heart of cider country. It's no coincidence that French cider and these soft, creamy cheeses are a heavenly combination.

The cider tradition in Normandy is still very much one of farmhouse production, and the 40-km *Route du Cidre* takes you past many places where you can roll up to an ancient barn, see the cider being pressed and buy some to take away. But while this is a wonderful journey of exploration for the happy, cheese-filled tourist, the variable quality of farmhouse production has contributed to cider's image as something quaint and old-fashioned rather than a drink to be taken seriously.

Cider orchards began to disappear in the 1970s, grubbed up to make way for more lucrative grain, with many surviving traditional trees devastated by storms. In the 1980s, EU milk quotas precipitated a dramatic fall in farmers' incomes. The government therefore began subsidizing the planting of more modern, higher-yielding orchards on dwarf rootstock, the *basse-tige* varieties that can yield fruit in only four years. Industrial cider producers were happy to buy the harvest, creating a guaranteed income stream for farmers. But when apple prices fell in the economic slump of the 1990s, many growers decided to invest in presses of their own to top up their income.

Adam Bland is an English cider maker who relocated to Normandy in 1991, when he became disillusioned with the constant price squeeze and quality among British commercial brands. The fruit he sells to the cider factory guarantees an income that allows him the freedom to experiment with some very fine ciders and perries of his own.

Bland (he admits it's not the best name for someone making flavourful products) is in the heart of the

ABOVE LEFT: Normandy's traditional architecture is a great excuse to visit...

ABOVE CENTRE: ...but it's the produce of the orchards that's the real draw.

*appellation d'origine contrôlée* region for Normandy and grows the varieties that conform to the AOC's exacting standards. 'But we don't bother with the AOC,' he says. 'It's a pain because the government runs it all very closely. It's a huge amount of hassle. But you have to admit the apple varieties make very good cider.'

At the heart of Normandy is the Pays d'Auge, in the northern part of the Calvados district. Since 1996, the *Cidre Pays d'Auge* AOC has represented the highest standard in French cider-making. The selection of the apples and each step of the process they go through is carefully codified. This ensures quality and the maintenance of tradition, but is perhaps restrictive when it comes to giving cider the innovation it needs to gain greater contemporary appeal.

But while there are frustrations, most cider makers agree that quality is paramount. 'Here in France we have some of the highest production costs in the world,' says cider and Calvados maker Christian Drouin. 'We shouldn't try to compete on cost. It's much better to focus on quality. For example, we don't press as much juice as we could – we get 580 litres of juice from one tonne of apples, whereas a new press could get 850 litres. But when you leave the press running, you extract the flavours from the seeds and the skin, and it becomes a little rougher. It's like Champagne: the best juice is from the first pressing.'

Cider makers such as Bland, Drouin and Domaine Dupont stand a class apart from the traditional cider of Normandy's farmhouses. They bring a wine sensibility to cider, not pretending that cider is wine, but applying the same degree of care and craft to it. If they continue with what they're doing, it's hard to imagine cider retaining its staid, downmarket image for long.

ABOVE: The enticing shop at Christian Drouin's Domaine Coeur de Lion.

# THE *TERROĪRĪSTE* ERĪC BORDELET

The first time we meet France's most revered cider maker, he's unfolding geological maps of his local area within a minute of shaking hands.

'Here you see we have three kinds of rock. We have the granite from the higher ground, the same as Brittany. Over here we have the schist – dry and minerally – and in the middle we have the granite cooking up the schist. It's complex geology: a *grand cru* ("great growth"). Each soil type gives a different character to the fruit.'

It would take a brave or extremely foolish person to say within earshot of Eric Bordelet that the concept of *terroir* cannot apply to apples as much as it does to wine.

Bordelet's orchard is a geological oddity, unlike any other we've visited. Centred around the Château de Hauteville – a ruin he is in the process of restoring, with his ciders ageing in the pitch-black cellars – the effect of the collision of rocks is plainly visible. On one side of the château the soil is dry and minerally, grass studded with bright wild flowers and buzzing insects. You could be fooled into thinking you were in Provence. But turn around and look at the other side of the château, and the green, mellow pasture could be in Somerset.

Bordelet jokes that the Pays d'Auge ends at one edge of his property. The boundaries of the soil types are echoed by the fact that he is just outside both Normandy and Brittany, somewhere at the top of the Pays de la Loire, and therefore outside the appellations that apply to each of the two famed cider-making regions. This is one reason why he calls his products *sidre* rather than using the conventional French spelling. 'But the granite and flint soils, pear trees and cider culture all reinforce the fact that we are closer to Normandy in character,' he insists.

This outsider status seems to suit Bordelet perfectly. He grew up on this farm, but left and travelled, spending 12 years working in Parisian restaurants, most of that as a sommelier. There he learned a great deal about wine, and cites the late Didier Dagueneau of Pouilly-Fumé as his mentor and inspiration.

When he returned to the family business, he brought an entirely different approach from the one he'd grown up with. He ignored the apple varieties recommended by cider's governing bodies in favour of others he had personally researched, planting new orchards on dwarf rootstock at the same time as launching what is clearly a lifelong quest to save obscure local perry pear varieties. 'There are many old trees we don't even know the names of,' he says, 'I don't care about that now – the emergency is to save the varieties by grafting them. Maybe one day when I retire, I'll research what they are.' Bordelet also made the farm biodynamic – a principle about which he is as passionate as everything else in his operation.

With his pugnacious, single-minded drive and determination, close-cropped hair, grizzled expression and magnificent, tusk-like moustaches, Eric Bordelet resembles the *sanglier*, the wild boar that are still hunted across this part of France. But the elegance in his work sends you searching for far less earthy comparisons.

His ciders (80 per cent exported) are testament to a delicate and vividly creative approach. Widely celebrated by sommeliers, wine writers and his cider-making peers, they are some of the finest in the world. Bordelet doesn't need appellations and tourist routes. All he needs is his fruit, and the precious *grand cru* of soil that creates it.

---

'THERE ARE MANY OLD TREES WE DON'T EVEN KNOW THE NAMES OF.'

---

OPPOSITE: Eric Bordelet (below right) makes his excellent ciders (above far right) in the grounds of a ruined château (above right) and ages them in its dark cellars (below far right).

**Eric Bordelet**
Château de Hauteville
53250 Charchigné, Normandy
**www.ericbordelet.com**

# POMMEAU

Behind every great but quirky drink in the world there's a creation myth. And like all creation myths, it's always the same story told in a slightly different way. The story behind freeze distillation, smoked beer and Pommeau is that they were each created by accident, and almost thrown away until someone just happened to taste them and realize what a wonderful concoction had resulted from the fortunate mishap.

Pommeau is a blend of unfermented apple juice and Calvados. It has been suggested that it was originally created when some apple juice fell into a barrel of Calvados. No one seems to be able to explain the physics of how this might have happened – what with barrels being tightly sealed and only having a narrow aperture even when open, and the improbability of a large quantity of apple juice just sitting above this aperture. So we're more inclined to go with the less interesting but much more likely theory that it was created as a way of helping unfermented apple juice store for longer without spoiling, making the most of the harvest, or even the simple fact that mellowing fiery, intense spirit with sweet, sharp, fresh juice seems like an obvious idea for a cocktail (which is even today often made from scratch in Brittany).

Typically, Pommeau is two-thirds apple juice to one-third apple brandy *eau de vie* (Calvados with only one year's maturation in the barrel, which is therefore not yet quite Calvados). This gives it an average of 17 to 18 per cent ABV, making it a perfect aperitif or *digestif*, or even an alternative to dessert wine. Like ice cider, which it resembles in passing, it pairs phenomenally well with cheese or foie gras.

The drink has a curious recent history. From 1935 to 1972, its production was illegal under French law. This seems a little harsh, given that similar products made with brandy and grape juice – Pineau des Charentes and Floc de Gascogne, made with Armagnac – had no such restrictions. But this is because the law was designed to protect French wine production. (Incidentally, the legend is that Pineau was also created by accident in 1586.)

Once it was legalized, thanks to intense lobbying by Calvados producers, it didn't take long to define the best apples, blending and ageing processes needed to create perfect Pommeau. Pommeau de Normandie received its AOC in 1991, and Pommeau de Bretagne followed six years later.

Once blended, Pommeau is aged in the barrel for around three years (the minimum ageing by law is 14 months). A young Pommeau combines the character of the Calvados with a juicy freshness that makes it perfect when chilled. As it ages, it gains an earthy complexity from the wood and the oxidation in the barrel, developing an appetizing mahogany colour and ripe-apple, dried-fruit, caramel, vanilla and butterscotch notes that make it comparable to Madeira.

Pommeau is less well known than Pineau, but French brands are now sold in around 20 countries, and cider makers such as Julian Temperley in Somerset and Finnriver in Washington State have developed their own takes on the drink. Temperley also suggests mixing it with lemonade to create the Pimms-like 'Orchard Mist', or even with a bone-dry sparkling cider for the *kir*-like, heady 'Orchard Mischief'.

Accident or not, Pommeau's intriguing character and lithe flexibility make it a wonderful addition to the bounty of the orchard, a drink that completes a comprehensive range of precious drinks from the humble, all-conquering apple.

ABOVE: Pommeau is a stunning aperitif or *digestif*.
OPPOSITE: There's magic happening behind this bung!

ONCE BLENDED,
POMMEAU IS AGED
IN THE BARREL
FOR AROUND
THREE YEARS
(THE MINIMUM
AGEING BY LAW
IS 14 MONTHS).

# BRITTANY

The history of Brittany is a story of resistance, of stubborn refusal to give in. As fans of *Asterix the Gaul* will know, this is a region that fought hard against Roman occupation. It was never part of Charlemagne's Frankish empire, and didn't want anything to do with the rival claims of French and English kings. Like their Celtic counterparts in Wales and Cornwall, and the Asturians in northern Spain, there's still a very real sense among Bretons that this is a separate state.

Even today, Brittany feels cut off from the rest of France. The rugged, sea-battered peninsula sticks out to divide the stormy Bay of Biscay from the English Channel. The landscape is littered with standing stones and dolmens as ancient as Stonehenge. Finistère – the department furthest west – means 'end of the earth' in French, and the ancients believed the world ended over the horizon.

The Bretons fiercely protect the customs and traditions from their Celtic past, and the language spoken in the rural areas of lower Brittany is a clear relative of Welsh. Like the other Celtic races, apples feature strongly in Breton mythology. The apple is the fruit of science, magic and revelation, and the locals believe this was the true location of Avalon: the legendary 'Island of Apples', and the true home of the Arthurian legend.

The climate is certainly suited to apple-growing. Brittany is not revered internationally in the same way as Normandy, but it has remarkably strong cider traditions that are famous across France, and produces about 40 per cent of the nation's cider. Much of the juice is sold to industrial producers, but there is a thriving artisanal scene that replicates anything Normandy can do, each time giving it a specific Breton name. As well as cider, traditionally known as *chistre*, there's Pommeau de Bretagne and *Lambig*, an apple brandy, each one having earned its own appellation.

So is there a qualitative difference between Breton and Norman cider? Hervé Seznec of Manoir du Kinkiz believes so. He makes *cidre Cournouaille* (Cornwall cider) in the district of the same name, and it is this style that has earned Breton cider its own AOC. 'Breton cider tends to be stronger and drier than Norman,' he says. 'We have more sun, which means higher sugar and more alcohol. It also introduces greater aroma to the fruit, particularly apricot notes. But the main difference is the minerality in flavour that comes from the granite soil. It is a natural expression of our soil – more concentrated.'

Cider is seen as a softer, mellower alternative to wine here, and while it is increasingly regarded as old-fashioned, it's still widely drunk in Brittany's traditional *crêperies*. The natural sweetness of a traditionally 'keeved' cider is the perfect partner to the creamy richness of the crêpe. In an illustration of the area's strident individuality, the cider is usually served in a *bolée*, a ceramic bowl that resembles an English teacup.

For all its oddness, Brittany is a welcoming and bewitching destination for tourists. Little of its cider, Pommeau or *Lambig* is exported. Which gives you all the more reason to go and sample it where it is made.

ABOVE: Bretons drink their cider from a traditional *bolée*.

OPPOSITE, ABOVE: Gwen *eau de vie* – a young distilled apple spirit without barrel-ageing.
OPPOSITE, BELOW: Hervé Seznec does important quality checks on his Manoir du Kinkiz Calvados.

# KEEVĪNG

Here's a dilemma: a lot of people like sweet cider, but if you ferment cider completely naturally, all the sugar ferments to dryness. So without adding artificial flavourings like industrial cider factories do, how can an artisanal cider maker create an all-natural product that's still full of sweetness?

The answer is keeving.

The amazing thing about this strange process, once you finally get your head around it, is that something like the result of modern microbiology has in fact been practised for centuries. It was common in England by the mid-1600s but, as it's a great deal more fiddly than simply adding sugar or artificial flavourings to cider, it eventually disappeared, though some craft cider makers are now reviving it. In France, where production standards have been better maintained, it is a widespread practice.

Keeving really does show an extraordinary understanding of the apple's biology. For a keeved cider, bittersweet apples are collected and milled as usual. They have to be predominantly bittersweets – if there's too much acidity, this prevents the enzymatic activity that comes later from working as well as it should. The apple pulp is then left to macerate overnight. This can only be done in cool temperatures, when the natural yeast present is sluggish and doesn't feel like getting to work on fermentation. Over this maceration period, oxygen gets to the pulp and starts to break down the cell walls. This releases pectin into the juice.

When the rich brown juice is pressed, the cider maker adds enzymes that trigger the keeving process. The traditional addition is a mixture of salt and chalk, or even wood ash – which leads you to speculate how on earth anyone figured out how to do this – but the modern practice is to add calcium chloride.

As the juice stands, the pectin converts into pectic acid, which then reacts with the enzymes to form an unsightly and insoluble jelly-like substance that floats to the top of the liquid, buoyed by the gas bubbles from the beginning of the slow fermentation. The French neatly negotiate the fact that it doesn't look very appetizing by giving it a pretty name: *le chapeau brun* (brown hat). English cider makers, in a rare feat of poetic description, used to call it the 'flying lees'.

The gel binds much of the protein and takes it out of the clear juice below the 'hat', or falls to the bottom to create a sediment. (Here the descriptive powers of the French momentarily fail them: they refer to this part as '*défécation*'.)

If the yeast starts to multiply and ferment too soon, the brown hat turns white and you get a full, vigorous fermentation that produces a straightforward cider. However, if the keeve works, the clear juice from the middle of the vessel is extracted into a fresh container, leaving the hat and the protein behind. The yeast still present in the juice is starved of nutrients, and is too weak to perform a full fermentation. By the time it has finished, there is still a significant amount of natural sugar left in the juice which, if managed correctly, will not fully ferment.

So keeving creates a cider that has a wonderful deep colour, thanks to the oxidization, brilliant clarity due to the removal of the protein, and a full, sweet flavour because there is so much natural sugar left in the juice. And, if that's not good enough, the residual yeast will produce a natural sparkle after around four weeks in the bottle.

That cider makers believe the finished product is well worth all this effort tells you everything you need to know about its quality.

OPPOSITE: *Le chapeau brun*, the ugly-looking by-product that tells a cider maker that the beautiful process of keeving is working.

KEEVING REALLY DOES
SHOW AN EXTRAORDINARY
UNDERSTANDING OF THE
APPLE'S BIOLOGY.

# FRANCE CIDER SUGGESTIONS

## CIDRE LE BRUN/ CIDRE BIGOUD
Plovan, Brittany
www.cidrelebrun.com

### Cidre Artisanal Brut Le Brun (5.5% ABV)

Fermented naturally and bottle-conditioned. There's a slight funk and woodiness on the nose, and rich but dry apple flavour on the palate, with citrus and farmyard hints.

### Cidre Artisanal Biologique Le Brun (4% ABV)

Just about as natural as you can get: the apples are left to age and dehydrate slightly to increase the flavour, and then once pressed, the juice is left to mellow before fermentation. Sweet and slightly funky, with wonderful complexity and balance.

## BLAND & FILS
Dives-sur-Mer, Normandy
**No website**

### Brut (5.5% ABV)

A slight 'horsey' aroma, then on the palate there is sweetness balanced by healthy barnyard funk with a lovely dry and astringent finish.

### Poiré Demi-Sec (4.5% ABV)

Buttery yellow, lots of sweetness in the mouth balanced by nice acidity, with a clean, crisp finish.

## DOMAINE BORDATTO
Jaxu, Pays Basque
www.domainebordatto.com

### Txalaparta (8.5% ABV)

Fermented on the lees in oak barrels for five months and then bottle-conditioned, this is complex, structured, with good tannic length.

## ERIC BORDELET
Charchigné, Normandy
www.ericbordelet.com

### Poiré Granit (3.5% ABV)

Named for the granite through which the perry pear trees' roots struggle. Sublime, with great acidity and a huge wallop of fruit. Incredibly sophisticated for something with such a low alcohol level.

### Sydre Argelette (4% ABV)

Named after the *grand cru* of rock on which the trees grow, this has a wonderful bone-dry spine decorated by sweetness running down it, and an incredible structure, with distinct minerality enhancing the tannins and acidity.

## CIDRERIE DU CHÂTEAU DE LÉZERGUÉ

Ergué-Gabéric, Brittany

www.chateau-lezergue.com

### Cidre Fermier Demi-Sec
(4.5% ABV)

Peachy, golden colour and floral aroma, with rich fruit balanced by mineral acidity and pleasant soft tannins. A great example of Breton *cidre* and a multiple award-winner.

## ADRIEN CAMUT

Pays d'Auge, Normandy

No website

### Calvados 18-year-old
(41% ABV)

Considered by some to be the best Calvados there is. Notes of plum, prune and spice complement the huge baked-apple and rich, oak-barrel character.

## LES CELLIERS ASSOCIÉS

Pleudihen sur Rance, Brittany

www.valderance.com

### Blanc de Pommes
(3% ABV)

Ciders with such low alcohol should theoretically have excessive sweetness, but made with a careful blend of acidic apples, this one manages to be bright, vivacious and refreshing, never cloying – a perfect aperitif.

## LA CIDRERIE DE COLPO

Colpo, Brittany

http://cidrerie.colpo.pagesperso-orange.fr

### Cidre de Colpo Brut
(4.5% ABV)

Slightly sweet with low bitterness and refreshing acidity – the perfect accompaniment to the local crêpes.

## DOMAINE DUCLOS FOUGERAY

Saint-Michel-d'Halescourt, Normandy

www.domaine-duclos-fougeray.com

### Cidre Extra Brut (6% ABV)

Balanced, with a good tannic structure, this cider gives off aromas of almond and liquorice, displaying a nice acidity on the finish. Wonderfully refreshing, rustic, tannic and acidic.

## DOMAINE DUPONT
Pays d'Auge, Normandy
www.calvados-dupont.com

### Calvados du Pays d'Auge (40% ABV)

Pale gold, like fino Sherry. Floral, apple and citrus aromas, then a full-on hit in the mouth, supple and rounded with a hint of vanilla adding to the comfort and warmth.

### Cidre Dupont Reserve
(7.5% ABV)

Six months' ageing in Calvados casks helps create an aroma that has all sorts going on: there's a hit of barnyard funk with apples and hints of pineapple. On the palate it's much more delicate than the huge aroma leads you to expect. A little funky, more pineapple with lemon, and the influence of the Calvados finally coming through.

## CHRISTIAN DROUIN
Normandy
www.calvados-drouin.com

### Cidre du Pays d'Auge
(3·4% ABV%)

Vivaciously sparkling, with a riot of aromas, including fresh asparagus, floral hints, pineapple, rubber, and fresh hazelnut. The flavour is full-bodied and tangy, with sweet apple and juicy fruit.

## FERME DES LANDES
Côtes d'Armor, Brittany
www.fermedeslandes.com

### Cidre Fermier Brut
(5% ABV)

Made with 17 varieties of organic apples. Golden amber and slightly cloudy, with a bready nose, fresh flavour and slight bitterness and astringency.

## DOMAINE DE LA GALOTIÈRE
Vimoutiers, Normandy
www.lagalotiere.fr

### Cidre Cuvée Prestige
(5% ABV)

The producer credits the excellence of this cider to the south-facing chalk and clay slopes on which the apples are grown, creating a cider that is bright-yellow with a powerful fruit aroma, full body and pronounced tannins.

## MANOIR DE GRANDOUET

Pays d'Auge, Normandy
**www.manoir-de-grandouet.fr**

### Cidre Fermier Brut
(5% ABV)

Cloudy orange with big fruit flavours and a distinct smoky hint. Full-bodied but dry – a great introduction to Normandy farmhouse cider.

### Pommeau de Normandie AOC (17% ABV)

From this perfectly preserved family farm, the Pommeau is aged in oak for three years to create a beautiful amber colour with soft apple and oak flavours and dried-fruit aromas.

## CALVADOS PIERRE HUET

Cambremer, Pays dAuge, Normandy
**No website**

### Cidre Pays d'Auge
(3.5% ABV)

One of the most respected makers of Calvados shows excellence across his entire range. The sour-apple nose has hints of wood and barnyard. The palate is moderately sweet, a little funky, with long, fresh acidity.

## CIDRERIE 'MANOIR DU KINKIZ'

Quimper, Brittany
**www.cidre-kinkiz.fr**

### Pommeau de Bretagne AOC (17% ABV)

By the terms of its AOC, Breton Pommeau must be aged in oak barrels for at least 14 months. This one goes much further, ageing for two to three years. This gives it a rich, sweet complexity with wood, spice and caramel lingering alongside the deep rich fruit, and a long, satisfying finish.

### Le Cornouaille AOP
(5.5% ABV)

Full-bodied, earthy, rustic and barn-like but balanced, with super-ripe apple flavours and powdery mineral tannins wrapped in a superb mousse. Its butteriness is offset by pleasant acidity.

### Sélection Cordon Or Fine Bretagne (40% ABV)

A very special blend of the manoir's oldest brandies. Big apple aromas still survive, giving way to a palate of phenomenal roundness, smoothness and complexity.

## LEMASSON
La Manche, Normandy
**www.cidre-lemasson.fr**

### Cidre Bouché Bio Brut
(5% ABV)

Organic and bottle-conditioned, this is a great all-rounder, balancing sweetness, acidity, tannic bitterness and dry astringency.

## LOÏC RAISON
Britanny
**www.loicraison.fr**

### Traditionnel Bouché
(5.5% ABV)

Hazy yellow with tart apple aroma and a little burnt sugar. Sweet and slightly syrupy on the palate, with a creamy mouthfeel and short, dry finish. The market leader in France isn't up there with the best farmhouse ciders, but compare it to commercial, mass-market brands anywhere else and it's outstanding.

## DUCHÉ DE LONGUEVILLE
Anneville-sur-Scie, Normandy
**No website**

### Antoinette Brut (4.5% ABV)

Another 'industrial' French cider that puts its peers in other countries to shame. Light, sweet apple aroma and a simple, sweet palate with long, fresh acidity and a tannic hint. A great refresher.

## CIDRERIE DE MENEZ BRUG
Fouesnant, Brittany
**No website**

### Cidre de Fouesnant
(5% ABV)

Typical of the Cornouaille AOC-style: hazy blonde with good fruit character, light dusty notes and a long finish.

### CIDRERIE NICOL
Surzur, Brittany
www.cidres-nicol.fr

**Cidre Bouché Breton**
(5.5% ABV)

Ripe, sweet apple aroma with a hint of vanilla, followed on the palate with dry, crisp fruit flavours, a hint of spice, and a slight tartness.

### ALAIN SAUVAGE
Grandouet, Normandy
**No website**

**Cidre de Tradition AOC Pays d'Auge Demi-Sec**
(3-3.5% ABV)

Fruity apple, not as sweet as you might expect. Local chefs love this, as it complements earthy offal dishes perfectly.

### CYRIL ZANGS
Glos, Normandy
**No website**

**Cidre 2010** (6% ABV)

Sparkling, rich-coloured cider that combines juicy, mouth-watering apple fruitiness with a wild-yeast sourness and yet still manages to be drier than you'd expect from French *cidre*, finishing with a smoky tannic bite. Rustic, and yet sophisticated at the same time.

**This Side ® Up** (6% ABV)

This bottle-conditioned cider is a hymn to *terroir*: made from apples grown on a coastal clifftop, there's a seaweed and mineral tang laced through the fresh-apple flavour, with chalky dryness, a slight funk and a beautiful mousse. Fantastic – a real cider drinker's cider.

Im gemalte Haus gibts Äppelwoi
Rippcher un aach Worscht des aane is
zum Futtern des annern für de Dorscht

# GERMANY

# GERMANY

The passion for cider in some parts of Germany can be neatly summed up by one brief conversation at the Frankfurt *Apfelwein* (apple wine) festival.

**Me:** 'It's very interesting for me to learn about German cider-making culture, because growing up in the UK, I believed we were the only country in the world that drank it.'

**German Cider Maker:** 'Really? You drink cider in the UK?'

**Me:** 'Yes, cider is huge there! In fact, Britain drinks more cider than the rest of the world put together.'

**GCM:** 'No, I think you are mistaken.'

**Me:** 'Honestly, I'm not. I've seen the figures.'

**GCM:** 'Figures? Ah, but these figures: do they include the cider bars in the Sachsenhausen district on the south side of the River Main in Frankfurt?'

**Me:** 'Um, well, I'm not sure. Perhaps not.'

**GCM:** 'Well, there you are, then.'

Even if he, my conversational partner, had realized he was comparing the consumption in 50,000 pubs and thousands of shops and supermarkets to around 30 bars, I think he would have remained defiant.

Whereas we have cider, *cidre* and *sidra* in other European countries, there's no direct word for cider in Germany – instead, they refer to it as *Apfelwein* (sometimes corrupted to *Ebbelwoi*), *Most* (from the Latin for squeezed fruit) or *Viez* (thought to derive from the Latin for 'wine'). And in the German version of the cider renaissance, wine is definitely the most pertinent comparison.

*Apfelwein* can be traced back to the Emperor Charlemagne, known locally as *Karl der Grosse*, the enthusiastic proponent of cider-making, whose Frankish empire stretched from Normandy to central Germany. Overall, Germany remains far better known for its beers and wines, but historically vine and apple cultivation have enjoyed a yin-and-yang relationship. Wine was always popular, but changing weather patterns, blights, taxation and regulation caused growers to switch between the apple and the grape at various points. One theory on the derivation of the name *Viez* is that it comes from the Latin for 'substitute' – or 'vice'. Whenever grape harvests didn't work, people would switch to cider instead. For the most part, apple wine is described historically as a simple drink, between 3.5 and 5 per cent ABV, consumed for its refreshing qualities by farm workers and travellers through the country.

This culture is kept alive today in the *Viezstrasse*, a 150-km-long tourist route from Saarburg in the western Rhineland-Palatinate state to the border with

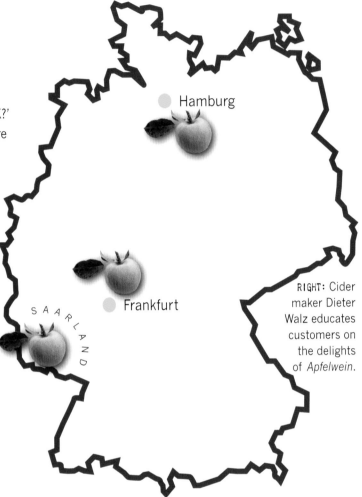

RIGHT: Cider maker Dieter Walz educates customers on the delights of *Apfelwein*.

Luxembourg. Apple trees line the route, which is also dotted with old presses, small *Kelterei* (literally 'wine presses', but now a widely used term for any wine or cider maker) and simple bars selling locally made, light, fruity *Viez*.

At a national level, though, these old traditions have been overshadowed by commercial imports offering drinkers a sweeter alternative to beer. The biggest cider brand in Germany is in fact Stowford Press from Westons, followed by Magners. Recent launches such as Cape Cide – a South African-styled brand – and BCidr, a 'fruity and fresh composure of apple wine and fruit juice', are introducing new people to cider, but it remains a niche market compared to beer. Within it, the old *Apfelwein* tradition has been described by marketeers as 'irrelevant'.

They'd be taking their lives into their hands if they dared say that in Hessen. *Apfelwein* is the Hessian national drink, more popular than anything else.

The passion for it here can best be summed up by the reaction to a statement from the EU in 2006, when it was mooted that the term 'wine' should legally apply only to fermented grape juice, effectively banning the term *Apfelwein*. This prompted widespread public outrage in defence of something which was obviously central to Hessen's culture and sense of identity. After just a couple of days the plan was dropped.

The Hessen *Apfelwein* industry is centred on Frankfurt. In 1903, an American visitor recorded details of massive *Apfelwein* factories here, with mazes of conditioning cellars that seemed to go on forever. Over 60 cellars remain in Frankfurt today. The market leader, Kelterei Possmann, produces almost 20 million litres of *Apfelwein* annually. Big players such as Possmann sell chunky, old-fashioned-looking one-litre bottles of fresh, crisp, slightly acidic *Apfelwein*, but are now also moving into *Äppler* – more stylishly packaged products to compete against the imports.

Most of the traditional products from the big players are very similar – uncomplicated, refreshing, with a homespun, rural feel to them. And since the 1980s, they face an increasing challenge from a new generation of producers seeking to change the meaning of *Apfelwein*.

Heavily influenced by wine makers, producers like Jörg Stier just outside Frankfurt and Peter Merkel out on the low mountains of the Odenwald began experimenting with new techniques. The old *Apfelwein* had always had more premium variants, including bottle-conditioned Champagne-style varieties that were exported as far as the United States until the outbreak of World War II. Now, sparkling *Apfelwein* as well as carefully selected single-apple varietal wines became the object of close attention from a growing number of producers. To compensate for the relative lack in tannins in German apples, use of the *Speierling*, or 'service fruit' was revived. This is a rare tree that produces a crab-apple-style fruit which has intense bitterness before it's fully ripe. Charlemagne himself identified it as useful in cider-making, and now small quantities of its juice are regularly added to cider, as are other fruits such as quince and sloe.

Producers such as Norman Groh are introducing distilling to their operations, and Sherry-style wines are also increasingly common. Rather than the old-fashioned *Ebbelwoi*-style *Apfelwein* packaging, these products are presented in smart, modern wine-style bottles and are being promoted to local restaurants as the perfect accompaniment to food.

'The old apple-wine culture was declining, to the point where it was very rustic and you could only find it in old, traditional bars,' says Konstantin Kalveram, who as well as selling his own Apfelweinkontor brand has written books about and acts as a tireless international ambassador for *Apfelwein*. 'We're creating a new apple-wine tradition. But simply put, if you want a crisp, full-bodied drink with the right balance of fruit, acidity and tannins, produced by a variety of fruits grown on local fields that really reflect our regional produce and culture, apple wine is a real treat.'

Hessian apple wine makers are not only reviving their own traditions, but voraciously learning all they can about everyone else's, and mixing them up. With the annual *Apfelwein im Römer* event in March, Frankfurt also plays host to an increasing number of cider makers from around the world who meet and exchange notes – and drinks – and then hold an exhibition to display the world of cider alongside *Apfelwein* both old and new.

And so we get this curious contrast: outside Hessen, especially outside Germany, few are aware that a cider tradition even exists in the country. Inside, you can be forgiven for thinking that Frankfurt is the centre of the cider universe. Slowly, the world of cider is converging here.

**ABOVE:** *Apfelwein* is part of the very identity, the very brickwork of Sachsenhausen.
**OPPOSITE, ABOVE:** You've got to think cleverly to keep up with serving demand in bars like Wagner.
**OPPOSITE, BELOW:** One of Sachsenhausen's many squares, usually full of people drinking *Apfelwein*.

# SACHSENHAUSEN

In the 17th century, a Frankfurt farmer received permission from the city magistrates to sell his apple wine in a simple tavern on the south bank of the River Main, just across from downtown Frankfurt. Soon he was joined by others, and a cluster of taverns became known as the city's 'apple wine district'. Sachsenhausen was born. It quickly became traditional for Frankfurt's citizens to walk across the bridge and spend their leisure time drinking *Apfelwein* just as enthusiastically as their counterparts in Bavaria quaffed beer.

The district survived the bombing that destroyed much of Frankfurt, and remains a pleasing contrast to the glass-and-steel modernity of the city centre. But on a chilly Saturday morning, it seems German youth have perhaps been trying to achieve what Allied bombers did not. The place looks exhausted; the very buildings seem hung-over. The old cobbles seem to be grouted with broken glass and cigarette butts. The burger joints and bars (there's even a Hooters here) show that the party energy has moved up quite a few notches over the last few decades.

But the heart of Sachsenhausen is still *Apfelwein*. Many of the bars make their own, and this is signified by wreaths of evergreen branches hanging outside. *Apfelwein* is traditionally served in a *Bembel*: a fat, grey stoneware jug decorated with blue detailing. These sit in windows and above doorways and arches everywhere you look, signifying that seemingly every other building is an *Apfelwein* house.

At this time of day most places around the main square are closed – both opening and closing hours are very late here compared to normal bars. But as Bill and I wander deeper into Sachsenhausen, we find Wagner, possibly the most famous of all Sachsenhausen's *Apfelwein* bars. Today it sits amid a row of delis, supermarkets, restaurants and bars in what is clearly a foodie hot spot.

Inside, it's refreshingly simple, a throwback to a previous era. The wooden floor is stained black and filled with large, communal tables and simple benches. Packed coat hooks line the walls, reinforcing a sense of communality and trust. Rows and rows of glasses of *Apfelwein* are poured ready on the bar.

*Bembels* of *Apfelwein* come according to the number of 330-ml glasses they contain, the most popular sizes being 4er and 6er. The glasses themselves feature etched diamond patterns that catch the light and make the cider sparkle. This design supposedly goes back to when people ate food with their hands, which got greasy, and the glass – which used to be expensive – could easily slip from your grasp.

The thing to eat with *Apfelwein* is the notorious *Handkäse mit Musik* (hand cheese with music). *Handkäse* is a sour-milk cheese shaped by hand that looks shiny and translucent, like a peeled pear. It's often topped with caraway seeds and raw onions, served swimming in a mix of oil, vinegar and water and is sometimes eaten with bread and butter. It goes wonderfully with the *Apfelwein* if you like tart, acidic, vinegary flavours with sour, sweaty cheese. Ask about the music, and you'll be told 'that comes later', as the raw onions have their way with your digestive system.

Wagner has a very family-friendly atmosphere, a long way from Hooters just up the road. It may have its own range of branded souvenirs, but it's faithful to the old *Apfelwein* tradition and offers a perfect sociable Saturday afternoon if you're killing time until the more bacchanalian element of Sachsenhausen kicks in.

ABOVE: *Bembels*, the traditional blue-painted ceramic jugs used to contain and serve *Apfelwein*.

OPPOSITE: The contents of a *Bembel* are quickly consumed in a large social gathering like this one.

## THE ORCHARD-DWELLER
# ANDREAS SCHNEIDER

Andreas Schneider must have apple juice running in his veins.

'My parents settled in Nieder-Erlenbach and planted orchards in 1965, four years before I was born,' he says. 'I am a child of this orchard and I grew up under the trees, helping my father gather sticks after pruning, and then later climbing the trees to cut them myself. Being out there gave me a respect for nature and made me who I am.'

A passion for apple wine had been with Schneider all his life. But he came to feel that the traditional apple wine culture had 'lost its face, lost its personality'. He began specializing in single-varietal apple wines, beautifully packaged. 'People want to spend their money on quality,' he says, 'and that money allows me to experiment, learn more, and improve the quality further.' He now makes a wide range of drinks, including fresh *Apfelwein* served straight from the barrel, bottled wines distinguished by vintage, single variety and even the orchard, and bottled sparkling wines: some from carbonation, others from bottle fermentation.

'His *Apfelweins* with residual sugar are loved by people who don't even like *Apfelwein*,' says Konstantin Kalveram of Apfelweinkontor. 'But his dry *Apfelweins*, from the old varieties in his own orchards with their tannins and dominant malic acid, are fantastic, too.'

So what's Andreas' secret? 'We wait!' he laughs. 'That's how we make *Apfelwein*: by waiting. We wait and hope the frost doesn't kill our lovely spring blossom. We wait for the summer weather to give our fruit its natural content, and we wait for just the right moment to pick it in the autumn. Then we press the juice, allow it to settle for a couple of days, take it to the fermentation room and let the wild yeasts do their work, and wait again! I taste them all – some years more than 50 varieties – to find just the right moment to bottle them and put them in cold storage.'

Andreas sees Frankfurt as the world capital of cider. Together with colleague Michael Stöckl, he devised the annual *Apfelwein im Römer* event, which ran for the first time in 2009, bringing together cider makers and their products from around the world. Frankfurt might be a convenient place for Andreas to hold the event, but he argues there's more to it than that.

'Germany has the greatest diversity of cider-making in the world,' he explains. 'We are the only country that produces all known styles of apple wine, from Spanish *sidra* to Canadian-style ice cider, to Port- and Sherry-style ciders.'

The world of cider is unexpectedly diverse in our increasingly interconnected age. In some ways this is part of its charm. But cider needs people like Andreas Schneider to help it discover its common identity – or as he would say, its personality and face.

'I believe the time is ripe for apple wine; it's just a question of time,' he concludes. 'We have to be aware that wine has had 2000 years to grow its culture, so we have to be patient and wait! But the lighter, fruity style of apple wine could be the key to its future success.'

OPPOSITE: Andreas Schneider is immediately recognizable, thanks to his awesome ponytail.

'WE WAIT!
THAT'S HOW WE
MAKE *APFELWEIN*:
BY WAITING.'

**Andreas Schneider**
Am Steinberg 24
60437 Frankfurt, Nieder-Erlenbach
**www.obsthof-am-steinberg.de**

# GERMANY CIDER SUGGESTIONS

### APFELWEINKONTOR
Frankfurt
www.apfelweinkontor.de

**Wein aus Äpfeln 2012 Trocken** (6% ABV)

Pale and delicate, crisp and refreshing, very clean with light structure. If not for the deep, apple aroma, this could fool you into thinking you were drinking a decent Riesling.

### BEMBEL WITH CARE
Heppenheim
www.bembel-with-care.de

**Apfelwein Pur** (5% ABV)

Distinctively packaged, this screams 'new generation' in terms of its attitude. The cider is clean, sharp and much drier than more traditional *Apfelwein*.

### DIETER WALZ
Odenwald
www.apfelwalzer.de

**Apfelwalzer Trocken** (8% ABV)

Bottle-conditioned and lightly sparkling, with a pleasant apple aroma, well-balanced fruit, sweetness and acidity.

### FREYEISEN APFELWEIN
Frankfurt
www.freyeisen.de

**Freyeisen Apfelwein** (5.5% ABV)

An aroma of sweet crushed apples with a trace of violet, followed by initially sweet apple with a hint of caramel that finishes drier as the gentle tannins take over. Faint cheesiness and a slight tangy aftertaste.

## JÖRG GEIGER
Schlat, Baden-Württemberg
www.manufaktur-joerg-geiger.de

### Birnenschaumwein aus der Champagner-Bratbirne Trocken
(8.5% ABV)

This bottle-conditioned, Champagne-style perry has great tannic structure, vivid pear aromas and good acidity while remaining clean and crisp. So full of flavour, and so drinkable.

## KELTEREI JOACHIM DÖHNE
Kassel, Hessen
**No website**

### Schauenburger Apfelschaumwein Trocken (10% ABV)

Fermented using the *méthode traditionelle*, deep gold with fresh apple aroma, this *trocken* style is dry (which is what the word *trocken* means), but with a little residual sugar for a perfect balance of freshness, acidity, yeast and dryness.

## KELTEREI NÖLL
Frankfurt
www.noell-apfelwein.de

### Apfel-Secco (5.5% ABV)

Brightly sparkling with a fresh aroma, vivacious mouthfeel, balanced fruit and acidity with a great dry, slightly bitter finish.

## KELTEREI POSSMANN
Frankfurt
www.possmann.com

### Frankfurter Apfelwein
(5.5% ABV)

The biggest of Frankfurt's *Apfelwein* brands has a light aroma of sour apples followed by a dry, acidic flavour with light citrus notes and a long, clean finish.

## KELTEREI STIER
Maintal-Bischofsheim
www.kelterei-stier.de

### Bischemer Speierling
(6% ABV)

Made with the *Speierling* or 'service fruit', with a fruity, crisp aroma reminiscent of light green plums. Unripe apricot and green-apple notes on the palate, and the *Speierling* adds a long, dry, astringent finish.

## MOST OF APPLES
Dahlem, Lower Saxony
www.mostofapples.de

### Barrique Cider of Apples No.1 (11% ABV)

Possibly the oddest cider in this book: changes every year, but this expression sees apples aged with vanilla, red pepper, chillies, quince, red- and blackcurrants and lavender, aged for 15 months in French oak. The result is a riot of flavours and sensations, probably closer to dessert wine than anything else, with Sherry spirituousness and vanilla sweetness among the highlights.

## OBSTHOF AM BERG
Kriftel
www.obsthof-am-berg.de

### Krifteler Apfel-Quittentischwein
(10.5% ABV)

A wine-like cider made with a blend of apple and quince, with added fructose to achieve a fresh, stimulating cider in which the quince notes combine well with the apples.

## OBSTHOF AM STEINBERG
Frankfurt
www.obsthof-am-steinberg.de

### Goldparmäne Deluxe
(4% ABV)

Full-bodied, nutty, ripe apple aroma. Fresh acidity and delicate tannin support a full fruit flavour that balances wonderfully with fructose, malic acid and tannin.

## Wildlinge auf Löss 2011 (4% ABV)

Varies from one vintage to the next, thanks to the wild-apple varieties being aged on lees. The fermentation was stopped early on the 2011, giving huge apple aromas with hints of caramel and vanilla, and a full taste of ripe apple fruit.

## RAPP'S KELTEREI
Karben, Hessen
www.rapps.de

### Meisterschoppen
(5.5% ABV)

Mainstream, traditional *Apfelwein* with a deep orange colour, full apple flavour, soft acidity and a hint of cheesy must.

## TREUSCHS
Reichelsheim (Odenwald)
www.treuschs-schwanen.com

### Treuschs Apfelwein
(7-8% ABV)

Image icons

A *cuvée* (blend) of apples and pears, with a crisp, fruity character – refreshing and delicate.

## WEIDMANN & GROH
Friedberg/Ockstadt
www.brennerei-ockstadt.de

### Trierer Weinapfel
(6% ABV)

A single-varietal made from the Roter Trier Weinapfel apple. A British-style cider where the apples are stored before fermentation for a full, ripe flavour with hints of spice, plenty of acidity and long tannin.

# AUSTRĪA

# AUSTRIA

While there are many parts of the world that are partial to cider and perry, and some where the drink goes beyond that to influence the local culture, there are very few places indeed that can claim cider and perry have influenced the identity of the region, even down to its physical landscape. In Austria's *Mostviertel* ('cider quarter') in the northeastern state of Lower Austria, the cider is so good they named the place after it.

Vienna

MOSTVIERTEL

Cider and perry are drunk throughout Austria. The word *Most* (pronounced *mosht*, deriving from the Latin for 'pressed juice') applies to both cider and perry, and also to apple and pear blends, or *cuvées*. Some parts of the country share an *Apfelwein* tradition similar to that of Germany. But south of the Danube, in the mild climate of the gently rolling Alpine foothills, it's all about the pears: the passion for perry in the *Mostviertel* is beyond anything in the rest of the world, leaving even Herefordshire and Normandy standing.

The area is named after its main feature: the largest unbroken area of pear trees in Europe. Some are up to 200 years old, and it's estimated they include up to 300 different varieties of pears.

Minstrels were singing about the virtues of *Most* as long ago as 1240. Five hundred years later, it received a dramatic boost when Empress Maria Theresa, Archduchess of Austria, came to the throne and implemented a programme of reforms to improve Austria's international standing, which included agricultural incentives to plant fruit trees. In the *Mostviertel* the focus was on pear trees, which were planted in spaced rows along the roads. Maria Theresa's son, Joseph II, continued the programme, awarding medals to anyone who planted more than 100 trees, and ordering that more trees should be planted to celebrate weddings.

The *Mostviertel* quickly became famous for its trees and the drink made from them. In 1938 it was calculated that there were a million fruit trees in the region, and perry was the favourite drink among farm workers.

Traditional production methods were simple: pears were left to fall to the ground and ripen before being collected and pressed. The juice was then cellared in wooden barrels to ferment naturally for six to 12 weeks. Some perry makers left it there, allowing the dead yeast to alter the flavour, while others racked it off to fresh barrels.

Most *Most* (sorry if this gets confusing) was bottled, but some was left in the barrel so customers could call at farmhouses and fill their own containers. This allowed what remained in the barrel to oxidize, so quality could be variable. Perhaps because of this, the popularity of *Most* declined after World War II. As incomes

rose, this farmhouse drink was seen as inferior to beer and wine. The famous trees began disappearing as farmers planted corn instead.

The renaissance began in the 1990s, when a group of *Most* producers came together to improve the quality

ABOVE: Such is the enthusiasm for perry in Austria that the architecture sometimes celebrates it.

of the drink. They worked with restaurants and bars to promote it and, crucially and cleverly, they realized the landscape was the key. Ancient perry trees lining the roads are a defining characteristic of the area, and when they blossom in late April and early May, the green hills are carpeted in brilliant white. The *Most* producers used this wonderful spectacle to encourage tourism, and established the custom of *Tag des Mostes*, or *Most* Day. On the last Sunday of April, up to 100,000 people descend on the region to drink perry – and drink in the view.

The best way to appreciate it now is to take the *Moststrasse*, a 200-km circuit of the region, clearly signposted, that's perfect for cars or bikes, with various hiking trails leading from it. The trees are a constant, as are the distinctive four-sided farmhouses built around central courtyards. These are impressive, imposing

structures, and it's a common saying in these parts that '*Most* built all these houses'. Some brands of *Most* are sold in bottles with a square base to symbolize the connection.

Of course, a 200-km cider trail is thirsty work, which is why many of these farmsteads supplement the hotels and restaurants along the way with their own bars known as *Heurige*. These offer fine perry with simple food such as meat and ewes-milk cheese, in appealing rooms full of wooden beams and basic furniture.

In nodding recognition to the wealth created by *Most*, the keenest revivalists of the tradition came together to form a cooperative called the *Mostbarons*. To join, you have to demonstrate a passion for promoting *Most*, a love and knowledge of its tradition, and a desire to innovate and move that tradition on. There are currently 19 *Mostbarons*. They're recognizable by their floppy black hats with red bands and white plumes, and the

ceremonial suits (men) and dirndls (women) they wear for formal occasions.

Thanks largely to their efforts, 60,000 new pear trees have been planted since 1995, and some of the traditions are changing. While some producers believe the notoriously antisocial pear tree needs to be given its own room and left well alone so it isn't competing for nutrients with its siblings, much of the new planting is in orchards. Michael Oberaigner, chairman of the Austrian *Mostsommelier*'s Guild, tells us why: 'I learned about *Most* production from my grandfather, so I'm familiar with the old ways,' he says. 'The disadvantage with the old, scattered trees is that some of them are up to 30 feet high, and when the fruit falls, it gets damaged. We're planting orchards of bush trees now and farming more intensively to see if it improves the quality of the fruit.'

The production process has changed, too. It's now far more scientific, with cultured strains replacing wild yeasts, and stainless steel replacing wooden barrels in the search for cleaner, fresher flavours. The annual 'Golden Pear' competition not only celebrates the best, but also gives feedback and guidance to those who need to improve. The *Mostbarons* are just one of various cooperatives, some of whom are pooling their expertise to create collaborative products that showcase the region's bounty at its very best.

Today's *Most* is between 4 and 7 per cent alcohol and is sold and drunk like wine. It can be sweet or dry, with the sweetness being achieved by reducing the temperature to stop fermentation and then removing the yeast. It is always 100 per cent juice, with no water or concentrate added. Great on its own, it's spectacular with the local cuisine, which has also evolved with *Most* at its heart.

*Most* is only made in four of Austria's nine districts, but it's popular across the country. Demand is growing steadily, and what's particularly telling is that as cider grows ever more popular globally, the big international commercial brands hold less than a 5 per cent share of the market here – and that's falling. People want to drink *Most* because they are increasingly interested in regional produce. And here's a product that has defined and shaped not just the drinking habits, but the cuisine, the people, and the very landscape that surrounds it.

ABOVE: The *Mossviertel*, best seen by taking the 200-km *Moststrasse* route through its rolling pasture.

# AUSTRIA CIDER SUGGESTIONS

## STEINERNE BIRNE
Haag
www.steinernebirne.at

### Speckbirne Birnenmost Trocken
(6.5% ABV)

Bright, pale yellow, with fresh citrus and pear on the nose. On the palate it's full-bodied yet low in tannin, with firm acidity providing a long finish.

## HANSBAUER
Haag
www.hansbauer.at

### Florina Apfelmost
(6.9% ABV)

Pale, almost wine-like, with a very fruity, flowery aroma and a grated-apple-peel character with fresh, elegant acidity on the palate.

## SEPPELBAUER
Amstetten
www.seppelbauer.at

### Apfelmost Barrique
(7.2% ABV)

Golden yellow in colour with aromas of ripe apple and vanilla. Aged for a year in oak barrels, the wood character really comes through.

## DIE SCHNAPSIDEE
Reichhub, Austria
www.die-schnapsidee.at

### Apfel Elstar (45% ABV)

Single-variety brandy made from the Elstar apple, which is popular among Alpine distillers because it has a full-bodied, lasting character. Here it's light and fruity, with fresh apple flavours all the way through.

## PANKRAZHOFER
Tragwein, Austria
www.pankrazhofer.at

### Birnenmost Winawitzbirne (6.2% ABV)

The soft, fruity aroma has a very faint, musty hint. Very sharp and refreshing in the mouth with crisp fruit-skin and fruit flavours.

UNİTED
KİNGDOM

# UNĪTED KĪNGDOM

Just like France, Spain and sometimes Germany, cider drinkers in the United Kingdom (UK) believe their country is cider's spiritual home. Many believe it is cider's *literal* home: that cider was invented here, and is only drunk here. British cider books invariably have a short chapter on cider's history that mentions the Romans and the French in passing, before helping build a purely UK-centric version of events.

One of the pleasant quirks in writing this book has been the surprised reaction we get from friends and colleagues when we tell them there are both ancient and developing cider cultures in other parts of the world. To be fair there are some extenuating circumstances, and as authors we can't just write off our fellow Brits as ignorant. Britain does produce and consume around half of all the world's cider. At least one brand is available in every single pub, supermarket and convenience store. And Britain is home to by far the largest commercial cider brands in the world.

It's a different matter if we measure quality rather than quantity, though even then, Britain puts in a good bid for world's best cider – *if* you look in the right places. In our cider suggestions, there are more British entries than there are for any other countries, and we swear on the contents of our drinks cellars that this is not just favouritism. We're perfectly happy to admit that the UK is also home to some of the very worst liquids ever to have the audacity to call themselves cider. In food and drink, the British excel at being simultaneously great and awful.

Cider possibly came to Britain with the Romans, but any record of it being made vanished with them. We know apples were grown here, but if they were being pressed for juice this could only have been on a small scale. It's hazy, because there were no early words for cider – it was either classed as a form of wine, discussed

in terms of various different fruit beverages or covered by the Biblical word *shekar* – thought by some to be the forerunner of 'cider', but actually meaning any strong drink. The absence of records, at a time when nothing much was written down, does not mean cider wasn't made. But it does mean any production was not worthy of special note. The Normans are credited with reintroducing cider to Britain on the basis that they had a strong cider culture across the channel. But there is no firm evidence of cider production (whereas there is plenty for beer) until 1205, when Robert de Evermue, Lord of Redham and Stokesley, paid part of his tax bill with 400 pearmains (a French-originated apple variety) and four hogsheads of 'wine of pearmains'.

Britain had in fact been very fond of wine until the Middle Ages. Wine went wherever Christianity did as part of the sacrament, and the monasteries of England usually had vineyards. But, as with France and Germany, beginning around in the 13th century average temperatures fell and the vines withered. England began

OPPOSITE, ABOVE: Samples at the Royal Bath & West Show: a rural event that includes the world's largest cider competition.
OPPOSITE, BELOW: The Burrow Hill cider bus, a perennial feature of the Glastonbury Festival.

to depend on France for its wine. And when England and France were at war – which was most of the time – non-French alternatives were sought and championed.

The 15th and 16th centuries saw a great many orchards planted. By the 17th century it was common for farmhouses to be built with cellars to keep cider cool, the width of the doors being testament to the size of the vats. Cider-making became common across various regions in the south of England. On the east side, populations were dense and communications better, and apples were grown for eating in London – for a long period, the largest city in Christendom. To the west populations were sparser, but the *terroir* and climate suited apple trees better.

In the 17th century, various scientifically minded gentlemen began evangelizing cider as English wine, focused on cultivating special apple varieties, and pioneered methods such as keeving and bottle-

conditioning to create expensive products that were every bit as good as the finest French wines. Huge tomes were published, encouraging the planting of orchards and giving information on how to make superlative cider. Many of these contradicted each other, as cider makers still do.

But cider never did become Britain's answer to fine wine. The Herefordshire gentlemen were too far away from the main cities. Upper-class London preferred Port, while the working class drank pints of porter. Over in East Anglia, where apples also grew particularly well, Aspall and Gaymers made fine ciders, but the majority of the flat farmland was given over to crops rather than orchards. Where apples did grow, they were usually eaten rather than turned into cider. The same applied in Kent, where one of England's greatest orchard counties became more famous for its hop garden (the opposite of Herefordshire, where hops are also grown in abundance).

Over in the rural west, particularly in the Three Counties (Herefordshire, Gloucestershire and Worcestershire) and in the southwest (mainly Somerset and Devon) cider carried on as a simple farmhouse drink, with none of the refinement of the stately homes. It was typically made with whatever apples were handy, whatever couldn't be used for anything else, and was given to farm workers as part of their wages. Key times on the farm such as harvest were labour-intensive, and fit, strong workers would travel to the farms that offered the best

wages – and the best cider. Such part-payment in kind was made illegal by the Truck Acts of the 19th century, but still continued unofficially.

The decline in demand for farmhouse cider came from two directions. After World War II farming became mechanized, and the thirsty itinerant farm worker eventually moved to the city and began drinking beer, that urban mirror to rural cider. Secondly, industrialization and improved communications allowed bigger, commercial cider makers to flourish, and it became easier for farmers to sell apples to the big guys on long-term contracts then buy the cider back from them rather than make it themselves. As cider declined in favour of beer, the bigger players swallowed up their competitors until there was just a handful of producers left.

By the mid-1980s, cider's cheapest variants were getting cheaper, and dominated its image overall. As cider became sweeter, it became the choice of underage drinkers experimenting with alcohol for the first time. And as it became cheaper, it became the drink of choice for homeless alcoholic street drinkers. Both groups converged on park benches and in bus shelters, highly visible to the general public. Both drank from garishly coloured, eye-catching but cheap, tacky-looking two-litre plastic bottles. Far more effective than any ad campaign, cider's most visible drinkers made it look undesirable in an age that was increasingly image-focused.

Cider sales plummeted. In the key regions, orchards were grubbed up and replaced with other crops. With no one else really interested, Bulmers and Gaymers soaked up much of the remaining market and came to dominate it – at one point Bulmers' flagship brand, Strongbow, had a 90 per cent market share of cider in pubs.

Catering to the budget end of the market and exploiting lower levels of duty, some producers created super-strength 'white ciders'. With little (if any) juice content, these foul chemical concoctions (yes, we have tasted them out of professional necessity) were sold purely on having the highest alcoholic bang-per-buck you could buy if your income was based on scrounging spare change.

To most other people, cider became an irrelevance.

There was still some demand. Strongbow retained nationwide distribution and continued to advertise, but it quietly dropped the word 'cider' from its packaging; it was simply 'Strongbow', a slightly sweeter alternative to beer.

And then, Magners happened.

Drinking is all about ritual. And the simple device of taking a pint bottle and a pint glass full of ice, pouring the cider over the ice and then topping it up from the remains of the bottle, captured the essence of the laid-back summer drinking the British love, but only experience fleetingly.

A generation of younger drinkers who had done the underage park-bench thing with alcopops came into pubs with few established preconceptions about cider, and saw

Magners as a thrilling new drink. Other brands followed, making cider much more about the chunky bottle than the pint. And it helped that, after decades of advertising depicting beer as a macho drink in a world where women were mere accessories, the simple, summertime image was refreshingly unisex.

The more fundamentalist extremes of the 'real cider' movement saw big, industrial, marketed Magners as Satan's own urine. But in fact it proved a lifeline for the entire British cider industry. Interest grew quickly in anything called cider. Everyone down to the smallest farm-gate cider maker saw increased business, and now the story in traditional cider-making regions is of orchards being planted rather than dug up.

Britain still has its white ciders and other industrial products that have had only the most fleeting relationship with an apple tree. But it also has scores of rejuvenated traditional farmhouse cider makers, a new generation

of ciderists rediscovering forgotten styles and neglected orchards, and an awakening sense of cider's gastronomic potential. 'Real cider' can be found in farm shops and delicatessens, as well as an increasing number of pubs, and is celebrated at real ale festivals, county shows and an emerging breed of specialist cider events.

Cider never did become Britain's national drink. But it now occupies an intriguing middle ground between the great British pint and strong, heady New World wine. Despite its long and in many ways unrivalled heritage, the British public knows and understands cider far less than other drinks, unaware that their country is home to some of the world's very best cider makers. Pub offerings represent only a tiny fraction of what cider can be – what it already is to those in the know. Contrary to the opinions of some large commercial producers and some passionate advocates of 'real cider', we believe the new relationship between the British and cider has only just begun.

OPPOSITE: Cider maker Tom Dunbar contemplates life at Glastonbury.

ABOVE: Falling apples at Sheppy's Orchard. No, Bill's not going to reveal how he got this shot.

# APPLE DAY THE COMMUNITY

One of the most famous rock musicians of the last 20 years is on his knees at the base of an apple tree. He's shuffling around awkwardly, circling the trunk, and as he does so, he's pouring a bottle of very expensive cider brandy onto its roots.

He's pulled far more outlandish drunken stunts than this in the past, as freely recounted in his best-selling autobiography. But today Alex James, bassist for indie legend Blur and latterly a successful cheese maker, is receiving holy approval for his actions. A local vicar stands above him, intoning a prayer of thanks as Alex crawls around the tree, emptying the last dregs. Michael Eavis, the man who created the Glastonbury Festival, looks on and applauds with a mixed crowd of fashion models and Somerset farmers (some of whom are dressed strangely alike).

It could only be Apple Day, Burrow Hill-style.

Julian Temperley's farm is not the only place Apple Day happens. There are now hundreds of events up and down the country, most of which manage without a single music legend. But this year, the two women who created this national event have chosen to spend it here. Sue Clifford and Angela King created the pressure group Common Ground in 1982, to promote what they call

'local distinctiveness' and help preserve the relationship between people and nature. They devised many ideas for doing so, and on 21st October 1990 they held the first Apple Day, taking over the piazza at Covent Garden to demonstrate the significance of the apple to British culture, landscape and wildlife.

'Celebration is a starting point for local action,' they say in their punningly but accurately titled *The Apple Source Book*. 'It lifts spirits, builds alliances and opens eyes.'

The book gives pages of ideas for organizing Apple Days, which now take place on the nearest weekend to 21st October every year. It notes that Apple Day can be anything from a small party at home to a festival attended by thousands. Events are held in village halls, schools, churches, pubs – anywhere that's important or symbolic to a community – as well as the Houses of Parliament.

'The first Apple Day poster had the names of all the apple varieties in a border around it,' Angela tells Bill and me after Alex James has completed his task. 'We've

ABOVE: Apple Day at
Burrow Hill.

OPPOSITE, ABOVE: Alex James swaps his bass guitar
for a bottle of cider brandy.

## 'CELEBRATION IS A STARTING POINT FOR LOCAL ACTION.'

stuck with it since then, because that's why we started it. We were aware of a culture that was disappearing. Lots of orchards were being grubbed up. The 1970s saw the rise of French Golden Delicious and the British industry decided it wanted its own monoculture as well to compete. So Apple Day was about preserving orchards, because they do many different things and have such a huge variety of species, most of them *down there*,' she stamps hard on the ground, 'because the soil remains undisturbed for decades. There's so much life here.'

The plan has worked. The latest edition of *The Apple Source Book* lists almost 3000 different varieties currently grown in the UK: culinary, eating and cider.

As we walk back to the farmyard for a refill of mulled cider (fortified with a shot of cider brandy), my wife says, 'Alex James just smiled at me.' There's an uncomfortable silence, as I contemplate a still young, handsome, famous multimillionaire smiling, unbidden, at my wife. Then she adds, 'I still like you better, though.'

RIGHT: A huge mound of apples brings out the child in everyone.

# BULMERS
## AND THE GREAT BRITISH COMMERCIAL BRANDS

Within the world's largest cider market, there's an eternal war being waged for the very soul of cider. In one corner is the Campaign for Real Ale (CAMRA), which has defined 'real cider' as a product that is entirely natural, that has not been carbonated, pasteurized, micro-filtered or made from concentrated juice. In the other are the huge commercial cider brands that this definition has been specifically designed to exclude from consideration.

But CAMRA's definition would also exclude many excellent ciders featured in this book, and it doesn't necessarily offer a guarantee of quality. Some of the best ciders we have tasted have been filtered and/or carbonated, and some of the very worst have been 'real' ciders in sore need of intervention (although we'd probably agree about the use of concentrate).

You can understand CAMRA's frustration when, just as with beer, the majority of drinkers in the UK think all there is to cider is cold, fizzy stuff that doesn't taste of much. Even though many people like their cider bland, it's frustrating if the giants get in the way of people looking for more interesting flavours.

The curious aspect of Britain's cider giants is that big hasn't always meant bad. It may come as a surprise to anyone who encountered Bulmers Cider for the first time within the last 10 years that the biggest cider maker on the planet has a distinguished and proud heritage full of premium products and royal warrants.

Bulmers was founded in Herefordshire in 1887 by HP 'Percy' Bulmer with the help of his brother, Frederick. Percy was ill as a child and never completed a formal education, which meant he couldn't get the kinds of jobs this wealthy vicar's son would expect. He decided to go into business on his own, and was inspired by his mother's brilliantly wise observation that if he started his own business he should do so in food and drink, 'because these things do not go out of fashion'. His father had a great interest 'in everything to do with the land', and Percy began making perry in an old stone mill. In 1888 the brothers moved to their first professional premises, and business began to grow.

The key distinction from their peers is that the Bulmer brothers were not farmers making cider as part of a wider food-and-drink concern, but entrepreneurs looking to build a business. They approached their task with a single-minded determination that reflected the drive to quality among the great Herefordshire houses of people like Lord Scudamore 250 years before them.

But with better communications and widespread press advertising, they had advantages over Scudamore and succeeded in building a market that stretched far beyond the Three Counties, and were soon selling big volumes in London.

Like Scudamore, they also looked to France for inspiration. Percy visited wine and Champagne makers in Reims and Épernay, and in

**MAIN:** Commercial cider-making has come a long way from the simple farm.

**RIGHT:** The evocative elixir imbibed in the famous tale by Laurie Lee was anything but commercial, but it defined the quintessential Britishness of cider for generations.

1906 launched his 'Super Champagne Cider de Luxe', rebranded in 1916 as 'Pomagne'. Anyone who drank Pomagne in its late 1970s/early 1980s incarnation before it disappeared from view will remember a sugary, fizzy drink that gained a reputation for the height of tackiness. So it's astonishing today to visit the Bulmers' museum in Hereford and walk through the endless cellars where thousands of bottles of this *méthode champenoise* cider were once matured. Pomagne was granted a royal warrant in 1911 and was served in the finest restaurants in London. In the early 20th century, cider was being described as 'the wine of the west', and Pomagne was its Champagne.

In 1974 Bollinger took British cider makers to court over the use of the word 'Champagne' to describe the product and won. No longer able to call it apple Champagne, Bulmers had already stopped using the bottle-conditioning method in the 1960s and switched to making it in massive 6000-litre fermentation tanks. The company went public in 1970, and even though the family retained a bulk of the shares, Bulmers began acting as all shareholder-owned companies must: maximizing dividends by a programme of perpetual growth and an eternal vigilance for any extraneous costs that might be cut. Expansion was rapid – more land was bought, more vats installed, and as technology progressed, big new canning lines and technical centres were installed. Soon, the wooden vats in which the cider was aged were replaced by huge stainless-steel tanks, apples by water and sugar solution.

By its own terms Bulmers was an astonishing success, exporting to over 60 countries. At home, its Woodpecker and Strongbow brands sold far more than the rest of their competitors put together. This success was driven by brilliantly judged (and retrospectively hilarious) advertising. The 1950s sex bomb Diana Dors told us coquettishly 'I never say no to a Golden Godwin' to help push the Champagne perry of the same name. Cartoon woodpeckers suggested we 'pull a bird tonight', 'give your bird one tonight' or 'get out of your tree'.

But from a cider lover's point of view, the quality of the cider deteriorated just as rapidly. One product, the extra-dry Bulmers Number 7, first produced in 1890, remained as a quality benchmark – which showed how bland everything else had become. It was quietly discontinued around the millennium.

Like all large-scale commercial cider makers, Bulmers is forced to make its product to a price point dictated by retailers rather than a quality specification. As retailers become ever more powerful and margins are continually squeezed, costs will continue to be cut from the brand.

There are degrees of compromise, of course. In a blind tasting, it would be hard to tell whether the likes of Woodpecker or its rivals, such as Blackthorn, have ever been near an apple. The introduction of Magners, which does taste as if apples have been involved in its manufacture, established a new 'premium mainstream' category. Relaunches of Bulmers Original and Gaymers Original joined Magners here and, later, so did Stella Cidre.

In 2010, the British government got tough on such so-called ciders, and introduced harsh new regulations mandating a minimum apple juice content if manufacturers wish legally to call their product 'cider'. That minimum level was set at 35 per cent. This means 65 per cent of commercial ciders you buy can consist of sugared water with artificial flavours and colours. Imagine what we would think of wine if it were made in a similar fashion.

The large mainstream companies could still make great cider if they wanted to. Gaymers in particular has a range of very good bottled ciders, but these are not widely promoted and are often difficult to get hold of. Bulmers still buys large quantities of fresh apples across

It's telling how quickly many drinkers moved from here to the so-called 'super premium' brands such as Thatchers, Westons and Aspall. While these companies are enjoying great success and now face challenges about growth versus product integrity, they remain closer to 'craft' cider in character than the rest of the mainstream.

At the other end of the market, there's been a big switch from mainstream cider to fruit-flavoured ciders, with Scandinavian imports Kopparberg and Rekorderlig enjoying massive success. Although it has changed now, the label copy on Rekorderlig may have confused people who believe cider is made from fermented apple juice by boasting that it was made with 100 per cent pure mineral water. It's difficult to taste any difference between these stylishly packaged products and the garishly marketed alcopops sold in the 1990s.

the UK and allegedly its fermented concentrate prior to being diluted tastes 'like fine Chardonnay'. The company still champions cider culture, and even if the drink is not what it was, it's difficult to find anyone in Hereford who has a bad word to say about them.

In 2003 Bulmers was acquired by the brewer Scottish & Newcastle, which was in turn bought by global brewing giant Heineken in 2010. The same year the Gaymers Cider Company, first established in East Anglia in the mid-19th century and then relocated to Somerset, was acquired by Magners' parent company C&C. The world's two biggest cider makers are now focused primarily on building successful drinks brands globally.

It's hard to imagine that discussions about cider-apple varieties are high on the agenda, or that glorious, bottle-conditioned 'English Champagne' will be reappearing anytime soon.

LEFT: Despite progress, the horse-drawn dray long remained a symbol of the old days. RIGHT: For years, cider has played a role as a poor man's Champagne. Bulmers once made ciders that really were as good.

Presenting Bulmers No.7 the extra dry, dry drink. As approved by your butler.

# THE AMBASSADOR
## HENRY CHEVALLIER GUILD AND ASPALL

The Campaign for Real Ale has a list of ciders it asserts are 'not real' due to the processes or ingredients they use. Many names on the list are obvious, but some are more surprising – none more than Aspall.

'We use sulphites in our ciders, which is one of the things they don't like,' admits Henry Chevallier Guild. 'But so did Clement Chevallier 250 years ago. How far back does this definition of "real" cider go?'

Aspall certainly has a cider-making heritage no other company can match. Clement Chevallier, an émigré from Jersey in the Channel Islands, founded the business in 1728, after an unsuccessful attempt to cultivate vines. He had a stone cider mill imported at huge expense from Jersey to his new home, Aspall Hall, in Suffolk, and this beautiful house, complete with moat, has been making cider ever since. This makes Aspall not only the oldest cider maker on record, but also Britain's longest established family-owned company. As cider gave way to beer in the late 20th century, the focus of the business shifted to cider vinegar – a market in which Aspall came to play a key role.

When the latest generation of Chevalliers, brothers Henry and Barry Chevallier Guild, took over the reins from their retiring father in 1993, they began to move the focus back to cider. In 2000 they reformulated their Premier Cru and relaunched it in a replica of a bottle from the 1920s. This premium strategy was already paying off when the Magners-inspired cider boom hit – and when it did, their sales quadrupled over five years.

Having followed a rapid programme of innovation, responding to everything that develops in the market, Aspall now has a portfolio that stretches from mulled and fruit ciders to Champagne-style double-fermented ciders, each of which is a premium version of any mainstream equivalent. There's an open attitude to experimentation, because anything that goes wrong can end up in the vinegar rather than being thrown away.

Their ciders are carbonated and microfiltered – both anathema to the real cider lobby. But are these the right parameters to be using for cider, from an organization that uses beer as its reference point? 'There needs to be a greater appreciation that, given it is fermented from fruit, cider at our end of the market has more in common with wine than it does with beer,' says Henry. 'The apple variety, fermentation temperature and blending are where the real artistry lies.'

The company has taken some difficult decisions to protect the integrity of its products. Its ciders remain 100 per cent apple juice, with lower-strength products achieved by back-sweetening fully fermented cider of around 7 per cent ABV with additional unfermented apple juice. And they are never pasteurized. Some enticing potential orders get turned down because they would require moving away from these principles.

Of the two brothers, Henry focuses on the cider business, and recently completed a three-year stint as chair of the UK's National Association of Cider Makers (NACM). Cider makers know and respect him around the world, and he's always somewhere near any conversation about creating better links between producers in different countries. Described in an interview by *Management Today* as an 'upper-crust hippie', Henry Chevallier Guild puts his talents to use as an easy-going facilitator for cider in the broadest sense. Not only is he an ambassador for Aspall in an increasing number of countries, he is an ambassador for cider – *all* cider – to anyone, anywhere, who has yet to discover its delights.

**Henry Chevallier Guild and Aspall**
Debenham, Suffolk
www.aspall.co.uk

ABOVE: Barry (left) and Henry (right) Chevallier Guild have made Aspall a popular and hugely respected cider brand.

# SOMERSET

'E leaning fair!' Our apple press is not quite the right shape. The wooden slats holding together a thick tower of pomace are starting to look lopsided as the hand-powered press slowly pushes down, slightly more to the left than it should be. But it's still upright, and ruby-red juice continues to trickle from the bottom of the press, so we carry on.

Here in Tom Dunbar's barn, the work is slow and laborious. It's a warm October night, which is good because the front of the barn is open to the elements. The entire community of the small village of Milton is here. Giddy children run among the hay bales, infected by the excited vibe from the adults who have gathered to make Kingsbury Episcopi's first community cider. Most of us take our turn on the ancient Breton press, pulling a long lever from side to side to turn the screw. Others prepare a table full of bread, farm-made sausages, and boxes of cider to keep the workers refreshed. Buckets of juice are taken and poured into a line of scrounged wooden barrels. It will sit there until late spring, when the cider will fuel the village's May Day celebrations.

Many cider books talk nostalgically about scenes like this, always in the past tense. Supposedly this is a way of life wiped out by progress and commerce. Except now, it seems to be back. Most of the people in this barn are young families. Somerset cider-making is in rude health.

In the popular British consciousness, Somerset *is* cider. It is cider's heart and soul, its spiritual home. To those who seldom leave the grey comfort of the city, the Somerset cider-drinking stereotype is a familiar one: the buck-toothed farmer in a smock, with a cider costrel (a very old style of drinking vessel) in one hand and a big grin on his face, a floppy, shapeless hat doing nothing to prevent his face catching the sun and glowing red – or maybe that's the drink, the 'zoider' as they call it down 'ere in Zomerzet. It's not a flattering image, but it's one that does crop up in old photographs.

Once you actually get down here, however, you're punched gently by an entirely different set of associations. Much of the best cider is made within a few miles of Glastonbury Tor, an unnaturally shaped hill that draws myth and magic around it. Christ was brought here by Joseph of Arimathea. It was home to Gwyn ap Nudd, Lord of the Underworld and King of the Fairies. King Arthur and Queen Guinevere were buried here. Honest, it's true. Ask anyone.

The 12th-century historian William of Malmesbury identified Glastonbury as Avalon, the 'Isle of Apples' where the sword Excalibur was supposedly forged. Somerset's landscape is for the most part very flat and only slightly above sea level. Here and there, rocky sandstone outcrops – less dramatic than the tor – rise out of terrain that spent much of the time under water until the church organized the digging of its characteristic drainage ditches. The shallow, rocky soil on these outcrops, at places like Wedmore, Baltonsborough and Martock, just happens to be perfect for apple trees.

Whatever your beliefs, there's something about the collision of landscape and people that works on a deeper level to create cider magic. The Glastonbury Festival is arguably the world's greatest. Among stronger substances, it is suffused by cider's spirit of joyful anarchy, which seems to hang year-round in the Somerset air. Julian Temperley's cider bus is one of the busiest bars at a very thirsty festival. It sits, gaily coloured, in the corner of his farmyard for the rest of the year.

If Britain were prouder of what it does well, Somerset would not (just) be ridiculed; it would be celebrated as the cider equivalent of Belgium in beer – a place of ancient tradition and wild fermentation that somehow just works. New American cider maker Greg Hall, accustomed to the analytical scientific approach he perfected as a brewer at Chicago's Goose Island, spent time in Somerset while touring great cider-making regions. We met him at a cider festival. 'Goddammit,' he told us (at least I think he did, because he's American), 'you guys don't analyse the juice content of the apple. You don't analyse the yeast. You don't measure the sugar content or the acid content. You just stick it in and hope for the best. And it works! I don't understand!'

I consider telling him it must be the fairies from Glastonbury Tor, but decide not to say anything.

While there are big players such as Gaymers and the rapidly growing Thatchers here, Somerset is all about the small farmhouse cider maker. This is where that tradition survived intact better than anywhere else, where cider is, for the most part, made just as Greg describes.

Even though there were some large landowners here, they let out their land on short leases to tenant farmers. Plots remained small and difficult to improve, so farms didn't expand like they did everywhere else. 'The king of Somerset is the hard-working small businessman or yeoman farmer,' Julian Temperley tells me when I ask him what makes the county so special. 'There's less social hierarchy. We don't doff our caps.'

Each of these small tenant farms has always had its own cider orchard. These orchards prospered when Britain emerged as a major sea power. Bristol was a key port where many ships of traders and explorers were laden with supplies. Cider kept far better than water at sea, and was eventually discovered to help prevent scurvy.

In the 19th century cider was popular as the farm worker's drink just like everywhere else. And after World War I, tenant farmers were given the option of buying their land cheaply, so the small farms with their orchards remained here when they were industrialized elsewhere. They sold cider at the farm gate – and many still do – unofficially, often off the books. And they would sell to a few local pubs.

The first threat to Somerset cider came as those pubs were 'tied' by big breweries. Increasingly farmers were not allowed to sell direct to one pub, but were invited to pitch to a brewery head office to supply hundreds, and then thousands. The Taunton Cider Company won a contract to supply pubs owned by the Yeovil brewery Brutton, Mitchell & Toms. When that grew, Taunton grew with them, and when it was swallowed up as part of Bass Charrington, which became the UK's biggest brewer in the 1960s, Taunton became a nationally distributed brand as other similar companies went out of business.

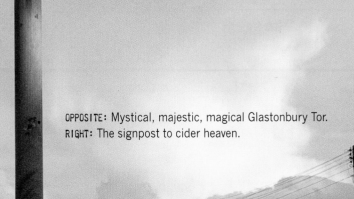

'E LEANING FAIR!
E LEANING FAIR
TO THE LEFT!
E'S PISSED,
LIKE US!'

OPPOSITE: Mystical, majestic, magical Glastonbury Tor.
RIGHT: The signpost to cider heaven.

MAIN: Roger Wilkins
shows that apple
pomace who's boss.

Other long-standing producers such as Sheppy's, Hecks and Perry's survived by a mixture of luck, determination and excellent cider. They also took advantage of Somerset's burgeoning tourist trade – Sheppy's has an excellent, award-winning museum and visitor's centre.

A more severe threat came when farmers were paid grants to grub up their apple trees and plant other crops instead. In 1894 there were 24,000 acres of apple orchards in Somerset; by 1973 there were just 2499. But Somerset County Council saw the county's heritage and character disappearing and began paying farmers to plant trees instead: 15,000 apple trees were planted between 1986 and 1996, for a reward of £10 per tree.

Many of those planted were old varieties that cider makers became increasingly keen to revive. 'The old Kingston Black is always recalled by farmers, but there are few trees left,' wrote one author in 1986. This perfect all-rounder for cider-making is now much in demand, and increasingly available.

The Yarlington Mill initially grew from a pip, or 'gribble' as they say round here, out of a wall near a water wheel. It was transplanted to the orchard with the intention of being grown to graft another variety onto, but before that happened it produced good yields of excellent bittersweet apples.

There are almost 200 Somerset cider-apple varieties, with new ones emerging. And interest in them is growing thanks to an unlikely saviour.

## 'THAT MAGNERS: 'IM AIN'T ZOIDER, 'IM'S FAR-KIN LU-CO-ZADE! BUT NONE OF US WOULD BE 'ERE NOW, WEREN'T FOR 'IM!'

Roger Wilkins is holding court. His old farm in Mudgley at Wedmore sits on one of the legendary cider-apple-growing areas. When you find it down a dead-end track, you feel like you're discovering an authentic survivor, an untainted example of the Somerset farmhouse tradition. And you are. It's just that you're not the first one who has. Countless TV crews have been here. Jamie Oliver loved it. The Clash's late Joe Strummer declared it his favourite

place on earth. Mick Jagger's brother lives next door, and apparently we only just missed Jerry Hall. Banksy is probably the author of the stencil on the back wall of the rudimentary drinking shed.

When Bill and I arrive, the regulars are less keen to be caught on camera than they were when Jamie Oliver came. Many of their wives don't realize this is where they spend their Sunday lunchtimes and they don't want to be busted.

## 'DRINKIN'?' ROGER SAYS BY WAY OF GREETING. WHEN WE NOD, HE ASKS, 'SWEET OR DRY?'

We opt for dry, and are given a half pint each without another word. Later, two attractive young women arrive, and our host transforms into a showman, telling us how cider can save the world, and how he recently received a visit from 'that woman who runs six o' them US states for that there O-ba-na' and advised her on deficit reduction. 'I may not be able to read nor write, but I can add up and take away!'

The cider is excellent. It has hints of cheese and vinegar that in larger quantities might make it the rough, intimidating scrumpy of which Somerset is so proud. But here, funky elements remain in perfect balance and the apple shines through, in something that's neither rough nor smooth. It's easy-going but demanding of your attention – just like the man who made it.

'Would you like any cakes or pastries with that?'

The café on Taunton train station platform is exactly the same as the one on every train station in Britain, selling the same limited selection of big brands. Just a few miles away from Roger Wilkins, Burrow Hill and Tom Dunbar's barn, the only cider on offer is Strongbow. Bill dropped me off minutes ago, but already the homogeneity and standardization of the real world makes a visit to Somerset feel like a dream. But like the end of any magical dream sequence in the movies, I look down to see I'm carrying a plastic container of Roger Wilkins' dry cider. As I refuse to be 'upsold' fatty snacks with my cup of tea, the continuing survival of Somerset cider-making feels even more miraculous.

OPPOSITE, TOP: Cider pressing in Tom Dunbar's barn. Note author with glass in hand when he claims to be working.
OPPOSITE, BELOW LEFT: Roger Wilkins holds court, setting the world to rights.
OPPOSITE, BELOW RIGHT: Roger Wilkins' barn decoration. Either this is Banksy, or someone who desperately wants everyone to think he is.

RIGHT: Just one of Julian Temperley's elegant and pretty Somerset orchards.

# THE PASSIONATE PROVOCATEUR

## JULIAN TEMPERLEY
### BURROW HILL CIDER AND THE SOMERSET CIDER BRANDY COMPANY

The first time I meet Julian Temperley, Bill introduces me as a beer writer. Temperley looks me up and down. 'Beer?' he spits. 'There's nothing to *write* about *beer*. Beer is what northern men drink before they go home to beat their wives.'

ABOVE:
Somerset Cider Co's 20-year-old brandy. The limited-edition bottle, designed by Damien Hirst, is collectable in its own right.

Over the next 40 minutes Julian Temperley talks to me, at me, in an unbroken monologue, a spontaneously fermented, wide-ranging lecture in which he gives me an overview of everything he thinks I need to know about cider. I often lose the thread, and then realize that this is because he is somehow developing three or four different points simultaneously. A lot of what he tells me is unprintable. He divides opinion, does Julian Temperley.

Some believe he is the archetypal loose cannon, too unpredictable and singular to push forward as a representative of his industry. They

argue that he does not work well with others. Others disagree, pointing to his determined struggle to win the right to call his distilled cider spirit Somerset Brandy, and win European PGI (Protected Geographical Indication) status for it. Or his campaign for farmhouse cider makers to be exempt from the proposed minimum unit price for alcohol, which would kill their business. Or simply that his energy and personality mean Somerset cider always has a media-savvy ambassador willing to make its case.

'Cider makers are a cussed bunch of bastards.' says Temperley. 'We don't like each other. We just hate everyone else more.'

RIGHT: Julian Temperley posing with his two favourite girls: Josephine and Fifi, his French-built stills.

Burrow Hill itself is an unnatural green dome with a single tree at the top. Like many of Somerset's geographical features it feels like part of a magical landscape: too convenient, too neat, to have occurred naturally. On one side of this hill, the Temperley family farm is piled high with unlikely objects large and small in corners between the barns and sheds. On my first visit, I spot an antique tractor, a caravan, a small dinghy and a double-decker bus. There's also a distillery, bonded warehouse, cider mill, barn full of ancient wooden barrels, office, and cider shop. One hundred and sixty acres of orchard containing 40 varieties of apples curves away down the hill.

Burrow Hill makes excellent ciders – even those who dislike Temperley are forced to admit that. He's a passionate defender of old traditions, blending his apples by sight, until he has a large pile that seems to have the right mix of colours. 'Industrial cider makers take their cues from lager, which I assume you know how to make,' he says. 'We farmers have to do things differently. We take our cues from wine. We need to be artisanal.'

His perry is also excellent – 'The horrible thing is that it has to end up on a middle-class dinner table' – but Temperley's real passion is clearly for his cider brandy, created by his distiller, Tim Edwards.

'Cider is everything that comes out of the orchard, from apples to brandy. Cider-making and distilling go together. You can't have one without the other. It would be like a dairy farmer who views cheese as an exotic concept. Brandy gives cider the respect it deserves.'

But the range doesn't end there. The brandy is blended with unfermented apple juice to create Kingston Black, an 18 per cent ABV aperitif, and Somerset Pomona, a 20 per cent ABV *digestif*. These in turn can be mixed with bone-dry, *méthode Champenoise* ciders to create sophisticated cocktails with names like 'Orchard Mischief'.

Temperley speaks plainly about cider, and yet his favourite word to describe its appeal is 'mystique'. He has an almost aristocratic bearing, yet one of the things he loves most about his native Somerset is what he considers its classlessness.

English cider is full of contradictions. Perhaps it's apt that Julian Temperley is one of its most visible figures.

'WE FARMERS HAVE TO DO THINGS DIFFERENTLY. WE TAKE OUR CUES FROM WINE. WE NEED TO BE ARTISANAL.'

**Burrow Hill Cider and
The Somerset Cider Brandy Company**
Pass Vale Farm, Burrow Hill
Kingsbury Episcopi, Martock, Somerset TA12 6BU
**www.ciderbrandy.co.uk**

A man wearing a facial disguise, a coat that looks like it's made out of 1970s wallpaper and a top hat with flowers and ostrich feathers on it advances towards us with a lit blowtorch, his eyes gleaming in the firelight.

# THE PAGAN RĪTE
# WASSAĪL!

There would be no point trying to run – we're up to our ankles in sticky mud. We'd be blind outside this circle of firelight. And we're in the middle of a field, miles from the nearest village. Not for the first time, I'm forced to reflect on the unlikely situations one can end up in while exploring the world of cider.

The man with the blowtorch raises it above my head and lights a torch I'm carrying. Soon there is a procession of us carrying yellow flames that give surprising illumination against the night. We follow a group of men dressed like the blowtorch carrier, visible by their colours and feathers, audible thanks to the bells around their legs. They lead us to an apple tree around which we form a circle of fire. The leader of the troupe pours cider around the roots of the tree, then places cake soaked in cider in its branches. The gaily dressed men sing songs, dance around the tree, and shout 'Wassail!' Then, from our circle several men step forward and fire deafeningly loud shotguns into its branches. Our work is done, and we process back through the mud to a wooden barn, where significant quantities of cider are drunk.

It's an unusual way to spend a wet Saturday night in January, a week after the Christmas decorations have

been packed away. But as cider's popularity spreads, so does the traditional wassail.

The name derives from *Wæs hæl,* a traditional Middle English greeting meaning 'Be in (good) health'. Before the introduction of the Gregorian calendar, January 17 was the Twelfth Night of Christmas, the night when wassailing traditionally took place.

The ceremony survived in the apple-growing counties of southwest England as a rite that ensures a good apple crop for the following year. Each of the seemingly bizarre elements of the ritual is part of waking up the trees from their winter slumber and driving evil spirits from their branches.

While these core principles and the purpose of wassail are consistent wherever it is held, each example offers different variations on the theme. Most have a 'wassail queen' from the local community. Some involve huge bonfires. Some are straightforward performances from morris dancers to an audience of spectators, while others are communal rites in which everyone plays a part. Some focus on children, on education and play, while others are riotous, emphatically non-child-friendly bacchanals.

ABOVE: The Leominster Morris Wassail at the Tram Inn, Eardisley.
RIGHT: A shy, retiring morris man with much-needed refreshment.

Like all the best traditions, wassail is rooted in the past but allows every community to impose its own stamp. It's growing in popularity because it is an unmediated, unbranded entertainment that links us back to the land and the passing of the seasons. And perhaps also because in the UK, academics have calculated that the third Monday of January – which always falls very close to wassail night – is the most depressing day of the year.

The arrival of credit card bills bearing the full cost of Christmas coincides with Christmas itself dimming in the memory and the point at which most new year's resolutions fail, and there are still months of winter to go. The modern wassail makes a glorious obscene gesture to these statistics, and celebrates our communion with nature and each other on one of the best parties of the year.

And does this chaotic circus of shotguns, dances, toasts and torches make any real difference whatsoever to the fate of the apple harvest that year?

Of course it does.

# HEREFORDSHĪRE

If Somerset is the heart and soul of British cider, Herefordshire represents its intellect and ambition. Home today to by far the world's largest cider maker as well as an intriguing array of smaller producers, Herefordshire has been at the centre of transforming cider-making from a part-time pursuit into an exact science since the early 17th century.

John Scudamore was born in his family seat of Holme Lacy, Hereford, in 1601. He was elected MP for Herefordshire at just 20 years old, and enjoyed a distinguished career as a diplomat, serving as ambassador to France for Charles I. When he was at home, he had a passion for apple cultivation and cider-making.

As well as being possibly the first man to create bottle-fermented drinks, Scudamore also introduced one of cider's most famous apple varieties, the Redstreak. It's variously claimed that he discovered it growing from a seedling at Holme Lacy, or that he brought it back from France, where he was inspired by the high standards of apple cultivation. Having propagated the apple, he encouraged the drinking of the resulting cider from tall, elegant stemmed glassware.

Scudamore became one of a growing number of men urging their fellows to consider cider as English wine, and to plant orchards on a grand scale as a sound business investment. In 1664 John Evelyn commented that 'All Herefordshire is become, in a manner, but one entire orchard.' Evelyn was a founder member of the Royal Society, and wrote this in a collected work called *Sylva*, a book on forestry best remembered for 'Pomona', a section on cider-making written by various contributors, most notably John Beale.

This enormously influential tract became one of many that gave principles for making superlative cider. Carefully bred apple varieties such as the Redstreak stood in stark contrast to the usual method of tipping in any old apples that weren't used elsewhere. Some ciders were only made with the first 'weeping' juice from the press, before the screw was turned. Apples were 'tumped': kept in piles in the orchard or in drying lofts where partial dehydration and saccharification – the conversion of some starches to fermentable sugars – increased the sugar content of the juice and therefore the strength of the cider. Keeving and bottle-conditioning were used to produce clear, sparkling ciders that were every bit as strong and fine as imported wines – and just as expensive.

This was a long way from the simple cider of the farmhouse, so much so that some writers attempted to draw a distinction between ordinary *cider* and fine *cyder*, but the two words are used too interchangeably to offer any clear distinction.

Unfortunately the tastes of the rakes and dandies in London's clubs wandered off elsewhere, and by the 18th century fine 'cyder', and the Redstreak apple along with it, had all but disappeared.

When the Bulmer brothers started their business in 1887, they signalled a return to rigour and high standards. Bulmers repopularized high-quality bottle-conditioned cider and perry for almost a century before succumbing to the very consistent but bland products its huge scale required. But farmhouse cider-making also remained popular in Herefordshire. Westons has been making cider longer than Bulmers, and is increasingly easy to find nationwide. Some suspect an imminent transition to a Bulmers-style big brand, but visit their place at Much Marcle and it's still very much a farm with an orchard at the back. Shiny new conditioning tanks are rapidly filling in one of the fields, but Westons prides itself on its giant oak conditioning vats – 88 are in use, the most ancient allegedly 200 years old.

It's all about ageing here. Even the most mass-market brand, Stowford Press, is conditioned for four to six weeks. Henry Westons Vintage matures in oak for six to nine months. The oak character varies across the range, offering something for mainstream palates without Westons turning its back on characterful, well-made cider.

Smaller cider makers are also thriving in Herefordshire as well as Gloucestershire and Worcestershire, the other two of the famous Three Counties, though here, 'small' is a relative concept. Dennis Gwatkin's cider farm focuses on single-varietal cider and perry, and matures everything in oak. He's a regular presence at food-and-drink festivals, immediately identifiable in a room full of foodies because of his long, shaggy hair and beard. Tom Oliver and Ivor Dunkerton, two of the region's most revered cider makers, are also farm-based, although their stories are quite different. Oliver grew up on the farm where his grandfather used to make cider, whereas Dunkerton is a former TV executive who moved out to the sticks three decades ago in search of the good life.

OPPOSITE: Long and slow, all through the dark winter months, the cider matures.

'We wanted to rough it,' Ivor tells Bill and me, as fruity, sharp Breakwell's Seedling apples are washed and conveyed into the cider barn behind us. 'We decided to buy goats to make cheese, but they turned out to be the wrong kind of goat. Then we grew Brussels sprouts; I hate sprouts. Then my wife, Susie, noticed a lot of apples lying around that Bulmers wasn't buying and we went on from there. I spoke to Jeff Williams, who used to work at the Long Ashton Research Station, and we did what he said: get to know your apples.'

He makes it sound simple, but then Ivor Dunkerton is a master of understatement. (At one point he tells us his son 'works in the rag trade'. He's actually the creator and owner of the Superdry clothing brand.)

There's now a car park at the farm for the regular visitors who turn up to see the pressing and buy a wide range of Dunkerton's fully organic ciders from the beautiful old Norman-style barn that serves as a shop. 'The previous owners were teetotallers,' says Dunkerton. 'They'd be horrified to see what we've done here, but they're long gone now. Shame; they were nice people. Villainous, but nice.'

You can visit all these cider makers and more on the Herefordshire Cider Route. The tourist office has mapped out and signposted a circuit that can be driven or cycled, starting in Hereford and taking in 16 cider producers. We pick up a leaflet for it in the Three Counties Cider Shop in the centre of Ledbury. A row of wooden taps on the back wall dispenses cider into containers you can buy and then bring back to be refilled. A chalkboard tells you what's currently on. Around the walls, the shelves are full of bottled ciders from Three Counties' producers.

The shop was the brainchild of Once Upon a Tree, a relatively new cider maker based at Dragon Orchard on the Marcle Ridge at Putley. Cider maker Simon Day works in partnership with orchardist Norman Stanier in a business that takes painstaking care of everything from how the trees are planted to how the finished ciders are sold. Day has a background in wine making, and his vision to create a cider that can go with every course of a great meal has led him to create a wide range of ciders from perry to England's only ice cider, and possibly the world's only ice pear cider. Packaged in beautiful 750-ml wine bottles, his ciders certainly don't look out of place on the dinner table. A handful of miles from Holme Lacy, the pioneering spirit of Viscount Scudamore is alive and well.

ABOVE: Apples are washed just before pressing.
OPPOSITE: Simon Day of Once Upon a Tree brings a wine sensibility to cider, reviving a Herefordshire tradition that goes back 400 years.

# THE COMPOSER TOM OLĪVER

When Tom Oliver graduated from agricultural college, he surprised his parents by announcing that he was not coming back to work on the family farm, but going off to find a career in the music business instead. And he succeeded, too, becoming an accomplished sound engineer for some legendary bands.

Today Tom is one of the world's most loved and respected cider and perry makers, but he never did give up the day job. I meet him in a hotel just around the corner from a major London concert venue, where he's grabbing lunch before the sound check for a gig by legendary Scottish folk-pop duo The Proclaimers, for whom Tom still acts as road manager and sound engineer.

'When I'm mixing sound,' he says, 'there's a balance that's just right. I can hear it, and I wonder why no one else can. And I get the same thing with cider, too. It's all about mixing to get the balance just right.'

Tom and his brother grew up on a farm that has been in the family since his great-grandfather's day. At one point it grew cider apples and perry pears, but between the wars the combination of a financial disagreement with Bulmers and a bad accident – 'That was it: he stopped drinking altogether after that; well, during harvest anyway' – persuaded Tom's grandfather to rip out the trees and plant hops instead.

When Tom returned to the farm in 1999 it was facing an uncertain future. Hereford's status as one of the two great hop gardens of England had suffered badly in the wake of foreign imports, and hops could no longer be relied upon as a cash crop. So Tom renewed an interest in cider. The drinks he had grown up with were no longer around, and he was alarmed by the decline of traditional cider-apple trees. He planted varieties to help preserve them – 40 perry trees and 60 cider-apple trees – and launched into a passion for orcharding.

He began making cider in 2001, and very quickly the orcharding had to take a back seat to fermentation and the discovery of an old passion re-expressed: working with talent, mixing it until it is perfect to his finely tuned senses. 'I don't at any time work to a pre-determined recipe,' he says. 'Every year as cider matures I ask, "What does this cider taste like it wants to be?" Does it want to be sweet or dry? I can already sense what the balance is going to be. Whether I like it or not, I get all this information from it. If it's neutral or bland, it's going to give me some volume. If it's hard and austere, it needs something to lengthen it. Mix bland and exotic, and you'll get something that works. My motto is always to take what the fruit gives, let it tell me what it's going to do best.'

This does mean his products vary from year to year, which doesn't please everyone. He tells me of a complaint he received about a collaborative cider he made with Chicago's Virtue Cider, the substance of which is that the cider was not *bad*, but that it wasn't what this particular drinker was expecting. 'He didn't come to it with an open mind,' warns Tom. 'That's always dangerous with cider.'

As well as keeping an open mind, Tom believes the secret to great cider is breathtakingly simple. He advocates that you do it properly, as it's supposed to be done, without looking to rush things, and allow the fruit to express itself, stewarding or wrangling it to its full potential. 'Trees and blending are the most important things,' he concludes. 'The rest is just banality.'

ABOVE: In case of emergency...

OPPOSITE: Tom Oliver in his element.

'WHAT DOES THIS CIDER
TASTE LIKE IT WANTS TO
BE? DOES IT WANT TO BE
SWEET OR DRY?'

**Oliver's Cider & Perry**
The Old Hop Kilns, Moorhouse Farm
Ocle Pychard, Herefordshire HR1 3QZ
www.theolivers.org.uk

Compared to its esteemed neighbours to the east and south, Wales might look a bit of a poor relation as a great cider-producing region. But the fact that it's worthy of mention at all, let alone in the same context as the West Country and the Three Counties, is testament to an extraordinary cider revolution that has seen Wales transform from an irrelevance in cider terms to one of the UK's three most important regions in little more than a decade.

# WALES

There are a few slim volumes and articles about Welsh cider in local history magazines, if you search hard enough. There was a flurry of them in the 1980s, and they all talk about Welsh cider-making in the past tense: something that used to happen and doesn't any more.

Wales shares the same climate as the UK's other great cider regions: near the west coast, benefiting from the mellow temperatures and generous rainfall of the north Atlantic Gulf Stream. The only problem is that much of the country is mountainous and completely unsuitable for apple cultivation. The big exception is the county of Monmouthshire in southeast Wales, where the steep-sided valleys give way to softly rolling green hills. The Usk and Wye river valleys have their own microclimates that avoid late frosts and harsh winters, and share the Old Red Sandstone soil consistency of neighbouring Herefordshire.

Look a little closer, and the relationship between Monmouthshire and Herefordshire makes it inevitable that the former should also be a notable region for cider. It's reminiscent of the relationship in beer between the regions of Bavaria in Germany and Bohemia in the Czech Republic – divided by a national border, they share not just climate and geography but also an attitude and passion for their product and the culture that surrounds it. The border between Herefordshire and Monmouthshire has always been more a dotted line than a solid one; for centuries, many in west Herefordshire actually spoke Welsh.

But Monmouthshire isn't just a hanger-on to the cider culture of its more famous neighbour: it is the centre of a separate Welsh cider identity that developed in quite different directions.

The earliest mentions of Welsh cider are just as sketchy as everywhere else in Britain. The first clear records are from the reign of Elizabeth I in the late 16th century, though it was probably being made much earlier. The cider was obviously of good quality because it was exported to Bristol, and even London on occasion.

But, for the most part, cider-making remained a small-scale but widespread concern, linked to the practice of refreshing travelling farm workers. When the great houses of Herefordshire began improving cider and bringing in larger-scale presses, in Wales each farm looked after itself, and cider became the default drink throughout this rugged, sparsely populated country. Many farms had their own orchards, and even those that didn't would acquire apples from elsewhere.

The Truck Acts that made payment in kind illegal didn't really seem to have much of an effect here. What

HAVING LOST ITS ANCIENT TRADITION COMPLETELY, WALES IS NOW BACK ON THE CIDER MAP WITH A BANG.

THE WELSH PERRY & CIDER FESTIVAL

2011

ABOVE: Welsh cider and perry. In Welsh cider and perry glasses.
RIGHT: Enough apples to keep Welsh cider maker Andy Hallet busy for a while.

really killed the Welsh cider industry was the mechanized industrial age. Farm machinery put an end to the need for itinerant workers. At the same time, the giant industrial cider makers of Herefordshire began offering Welsh farmers good returns for their orchard harvest and turned it into easy-drinking cider that was cheap and convenient for them to buy back.

By the 1970s Welsh cider had disappeared. But it wasn't away for long before the revival began. Ralph Owen, a manager on the Bulmers' estate, began making his own cider in 1976. In 1984 he moved to his own place in Badland, Radnorshire. Finding a neglected orchard of White Norman trees there, he began where he left off. Soon he was selling his cider commercially, and still does. He's a fixture at country shows and festivals with his ancient travelling wooden press, and even has his own cider house at the farm, which we're assured he even opens now and again.

Soon after, Mike Penney started Troggi Seidr in Monmouthshire, producing both cider and particularly outstanding perry with old Victorian kit. One or two others joined in, and then a whole spate followed around the turn of the millennium. Some farms selling apples to Bulmers were not getting the prices they once had and began to experiment making their own cider instead. Others were moved by a resurgent sense of Welsh identity to revive and celebrate lost Welsh apple varieties such as the 'Broom Apple' of Monmouthshire, and 'Pen Caled' from West Wales.

By 2003 there was such a buzz that Dave Matthews and Alan Golding of new cider maker Seidr Dai formed the Welsh Perry and Cider Society to bring the emerging movement together and share information. The society created an annual Welsh Perry and Cider Festival, which helped raise standards to such an extent that Welsh ciders were soon dominating awards at UK competitions and festivals.

Today there's a rich diversity in Welsh perry and cider. True to its history, there's a real artisanal feel to it. Many producers are small and part-time, foraging for forgotten cider apples in the corners of fields and hedgerows by

roadsides, supplying a few local pubs or festivals. Others are developing rapidly into more polished-looking brands that are gaining national attention. Gwynt-y-Ddraig, now the giant of Welsh cider, makes clean, crisp accessible drinks that are rapidly gaining popularity across the UK. Blaengawney cider maker Andy Hallett is exploring a range of different methods and styles, selling carbonated ciders under the Hallets brand name and still ciders as Blaengawney. Ty Gwyn was founded by two brothers disillusioned with the music business, who returned to their stepfather's farm – traditionally a Bulmers supplier – to create sparkling bottled ciders, including a particularly fine Dabinett single variety.

The Welsh Regional Assembly is keen to develop this land of farms, rolling hills and country inns as a noted gastro-tourism destination. Apart from the direct funding given to help cider makers develop their business, this is helping events such as the Abergavenny Food Festival (mid-September) become one of the best foodie events in the UK. Pubs such as the Clytha Arms, just outside Abergavenny, and the Blue Bell Inn in Halkyn, North Wales, use their fame and multiple awards to help promote fledgling cider makers. For such a scattered population in such a difficult country to navigate, Welsh cider shows astonishing energy and cohesion.

Having lost its ancient tradition completely, Wales is now back on the cider map with a bang.

OPPOSITE, ABOVE: The view from Blaengawney Farm, home of the Welsh Perry and Cider Festival.
OPPOSITE, BELOW: Andy Hallett of Blaengawney and Hallets cider. His under-the-counter specials are always popular.
RIGHT: It's not true that it rains all the time in Wales. These people are at a Welsh cider festival, wearing sunglasses.

# CIDER HOUSES

'What do you want to drink?' I asked my wife. 'You're having cider,' snapped the woman behind the stable-door serving hatch. 'Yes, I know,' I replied meekly, 'I just meant did she want medium or dry...'

Welcome – if we can call it that – to the Monkey House. This makeshift bar on a farm in Woodmancote, Worcestershire, wasn't officially called the Monkey House, but that's how everyone knows it now. The story is that after one particularly festive evening, one of the regulars arrived home late, battered and bruised. Concerned, his

wife asked if he'd got into a fight at the pub. 'No,' he replied. 'It was all those monkeys in the trees who attacked me on the way home!'

It's almost a stretch to refer to the Monkey House as a pub. There's no real bar. It doesn't sell beer. It keeps eccentric hours that suit the owner's whim, and customers mainly sit outside. It's not really a pub at all, more one of the last remaining examples of a dying British institution: the cider house.

There are very few true cider houses left now in the UK – some estimate as few as four. A cider house isn't just a pub that focuses on cider; it's a more informal institution somewhere halfway between a pub and a farmer's scullery or barn.

The first time the uninitiated usually hear of a cider house is the sad announcement of its closure.

Every time you hear the story it's the same: a tiny establishment, often linked to a farm, which had been in the same family for generations. It was run by a couple, who either remained childless or whose kids grew up and understandably moved away to find a career that allowed them to afford to have a home of their own. The couple grew old, one of them passed away, and usually the story is of an 81-year-old widow who still imposes her formidable personality on the place, but finds herself too infirm to continue or passes away herself, leaving no one to take over.

The appeal of the cider houses can also be their economic undoing: they are in hidden places, sell nothing other than cider, perhaps some soft drinks, pork pies and farm produce, and refuse to play by the conventional rules of commerce. For centuries they operated off the books, outside the law. They are, in some ways, a distillation of the pure essence of the British pub – an informal gathering of like-minded souls where alcohol is consumed and money changes hands, but it never feels like a retail establishment.

There remain perhaps a few more such places than we might think, although it would not be fair to suggest that they're open to just anyone. When a farmer puts a few rickety chairs in the barn where his barrels are stored, and may or may not have a licence to serve alcohol on the premises, arguing that the place is not open to the public, but a private concern for a few 'friends', who can say whether this counts as a cider house or not?

One thing's for sure: if you are ever in a rural part of England and someone invites you to an establishment that sounds like this, take them up on their offer while you still can. Just watch out for those monkeys; they can be dangerous.

ABOVE: The Monkey House didn't want us to take any pictures because they didn't have their hanging baskets out, but this place (Halfway House in Pitney, Somerset) is also nice.

**The Cider House (The Monkey House)**
Woodmancote, Defford
Worcestershire WR8 9BW
**01386 750234**

# UNITED KINGDOM CIDER SUGGESTIONS

## AMPLEFORTH ABBEY ORCHARDS
Ampleforth, N.Yorkshire
www.abbey.ampleforth.org.uk

### Cider Brandy
(40% ABV)

The monks of Ampleforth have been growing apples since 1802, but commercial cider production only began when control of the orchard was given to Brother Rainer in 2001. Matured for five years in oak, this enticing brandy is still young enough that the apples come through vibrantly, followed by a gentle, warm glow.

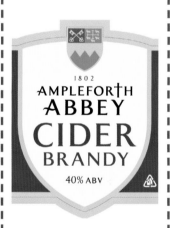

## ASHRIDGE
Totnes, Devon
www.ashridgecider.co.uk

### Vintage Brut (7.5% ABV)

Bottle-conditioned, buttery gold, with delicate apple and minerality on the nose. There's a wine-like structure and acidity that holds an almost chalky dryness and elegant fruit in perfect balance.

## ASPALL
Debenham, Suffolk
www.aspall.co.uk

### Imperial Cyder 2011 Vintage (8.2% ABV)

Strong aroma of cider fruit and hints of smoke, peat and rubber, thanks to the addition of muscovado sugar, as stipulated by the original 1921 recipe. The flavour is bruised apple, malty and tangy, with hints of grapefruit and peat again. There's a darkness beneath its deceptive drinkability, and a lingering, mellow finish.

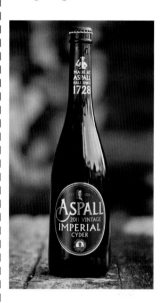

### Premier Cru
(7% ABV)

Using an intriguing mix of cider, culinary and eating apples, this is clean, elegant and quite characterful. Soft, dry, with nice acidity and moderate tannins; begs to be served in Champagne flutes.

## BLAENGAWNEY
Caerphilly, Wales
www.blaengawneycider.co.uk

### Hallets Real Cider
(6% ABV)

Deep orange, with an aroma of cooked apple with a hint of caramel. The flavour is full-bodied and muscular, with that pairing of ripe fruit and caramel notes developing further, joined by hints of melon and tropical fruit and a mild oakiness, finishing with a lingering fruitiness.

### Blindfold
(5% ABV)

A good wallop of cheesiness in the full-fruit aroma, followed by a palate that's full of fruity, citrusy sweetness with a slight caramel hint.

## BOLLHAYES
Cullompton, Devon
No website

### Dry Cider (8% ABV)

Bottle-conditioned, deep and richly coloured with a fruity aroma and a hint of leather. That leatheriness comes through surprisingly strongly in a cider that is uncompromisingly dry with little or no residual sugar, just tannin, oak and very dry apple skins, which is great if you like this kind of thing – and we do.

## BRIDGE FARM

East Chinnock, Somerset

www.bridgefarmcider.co.uk

### Bridge Farm Somerset Cider (6.5% ABV)

A regular fixture on the podium at cider awards. Orange and opaque; full-on fruit, farmyard aromas and a big, juicy body. One of the best small-scale Somerset cider makers, available in sweet, medium or dry. .

### Porter's Perfection (6.5% ABV)

A single variety from the Porter's Perfection apple, pressed using traditional rack-and-cloth methods on a century-old press. Huge fresh-apple aroma and a big, fruity taste. Sour edge and slightest tannic hint.

## BURROW HILL FARM AND THE SOMERSET CIDER BRANDY COMPANY

Kingsbury Episcopi, Somerset

www.ciderbrandy.co.uk

### Farmhouse Cider (6% ABV)

Famous as the drink of choice at the hugely popular 'cider bus' at the Glastonbury Festival, does everything you want a farmhouse cider to do. Matured in oak barrels, a classic 'scrumpy' with fresh-apple sweetness seasoned with wood and vanilla, perfectly supported by moderate tannins and acidity. One of those dangerous ciders you can't stop drinking.

### Kingston Black Apple Aperitif (18% ABV)

Such an obvious, brilliant idea: the Kingston Black is widely regarded as the perfect cider apple. Here the fresh juice of the apple is blended with cider brandy to give the ultimate, turbo-charged showcase of its balance of bitterness, sweetness and tannin. A perfect aperitif with an intriguing dry finish.

### Somerset Alchemy Cider Brandy (40% ABV)

Burrow Hill revived the tradition of Somerset cider brandy and now launches various vintages. Alchemy is the 15-year-old. Aged in a mixture of oak and Sherry casks, it has lost some of the fresh fieriness of younger expressions in favour of a smooth, mellow richness.

## CIDER BY ROSIE

Winterborne Houghton, Dorset

www.ciderbyrosie.co.uk

### Dorset Cider Draught (6.5% ABV)

Opaque orange-gold in colour, with a floral aroma of sweet apples and honey. The flavour is full-on juicy with tannic apples, slightly sour, with spicy, oaky and apple-skin hints.

## CORNISH ORCHARDS

Duloe, Cornwall

www.cornishorchards.co.uk

### Vintage (7.2% ABV)

A sugary, bubblegum, green-apple aroma gives way to flavours of fruity sweetness, rounded tannins and a rich, medium body with a faint sour tang. Tastes like a meeting of traditional farmhouse cider and crisp Granny Smiths.

## COTSWOLD CIDER CO
Coleshill, Oxfordshire
**www.cotswoldciderco.com**

### Coleshill House Cider
(9% ABV)

Bottle-conditioned, with an aroma of pear drops, vanilla and green apple. The flavour is crisp, green apple with hints of tart lemon, liquorice and cloves, with a tannic, earthy finish.

## DUNKERTONS
Pembridge, Herefordshire
**www.dunkertons.co.uk**

### Breakwells Seadling
(7.5% ABV)

A bold and unusual single-variety cider. Hazy, with a sharp, green-apple flavour followed by spicy, sour, rhubarb notes and a huge woolly, tannic finish.

### Perry
(7.5% ABV)

Clear and pale organic, sparkling perry with a delicate floral aroma. Beautifully balanced sweet fruit flavour with an elderflower tinge, a hint of honey and a long, smooth finish.

## GAYMERS
Shepton Mallet, Somerset
**www.gaymers.co.uk**

### Devon (5.8% ABV)

Gaymers' 'county range' of ciders proves big cider corporations can make good cider when they're not talking down to the mass market. Hints of wood and smoke on the nose and a rich, sweet, full apple flavour.

## GOSPEL GREEN
West Sussex
**No website**

### Sussex Cyder (8% ABV)

Bottle-conditioning gives a vibrant, Champagne-style fizziness, complemented by a fresh wine-like aroma with faint apple notes. The flavour is vinous, with dry apple but very little tannin.

## GWATKIN

Abbey Dore Farm,
Herefordshire

www.gwatkincider.co.uk

**Norman Cider** (7.5% ABV)

As the name suggests, made with apples originally imported from Normandy, and bears a passing resemblance to some French ciders. Big, ripe fruit and farmyard aromas; soft, juicy, sweet apple flavours with an acidic edge and a hint of cheese.

## GWYNT Y DDRAIG

Pontypridd, Wales

www.gwyntcider.com

**Gold Medal Cider**
(7.4% ABV)

The original cider from Wales' biggest producer, and the first Welsh cider to win a gold at CAMRA's national competition in 2004. Filtered and gently carbonated, it's a wonderful middle way between traditional farmhouse cider and commercial cider – easy and welcoming, but full-bodied with plenty of fruit, gentle tannin and acidity.

## HARRY'S

Long Sutton, Somerset

www.harryscidercompany.co.uk

**Harry's Medium Dry**
(6% ABV)

Deep amber, almost ale-like. An aroma of sweet, freshly pressed apple juice with bubblegum and orange-blossom hints. Ripe, juicy fruit, bruised apple and apple skins are matched perfectly by just the right amount of tannin.

## HAYE FARM

St Veep, Cornwall

www.hayefarmcider.co.uk

**Haye Farm Cider**
(7% ABV)

Medium farmhouse cider with a sweet and tart apple aroma, followed by a big, juicy delivery in the mouth and a tangy, tart, barnyard finish.

## HEALEY CORNISH CYDER
Truro, Cornwall

www.thecornishcyderfarm.co.uk

### Classic Reserve Whiskey Edition
(8.4% ABV)

Aged in whisky casks, this has taken on a deep caramel colour and a gentle peaty, smoky spiritousness. But the sweet, honeyed fruit still shines through in a powerful cider that's dangerously drinkable.

## HECKS
Street, Somerset

www.hecksfarmhousecider.co.uk

### Kingston Black
(8% ABV)

Single-variety from the mighty Kingston Black apple. Clean, crisp apple on the nose. Sweet, juicy and tangy with hints of wood, vanilla and citrus.

### Farmhouse
(6.5% ABV)

Hecks' sweet, medium and dry farmhouse ciders are matured in wooden barrels and dispensed on draught straight from the wood when you buy them. This has an apple aroma with a barnyard hint, an acidic undertone and dry finish. It is a frequent national award-winner.

## HENNEY'S
Bishops Frome, Herefordshire

www.henneys.co.uk

### Vintage
(6.5% ABV)

From this hugely respected cider maker, the 2011 vintage is tangy, full, slightly sour with mild tannin and a long, clean finish. A sophisticated cider.

## HOGAN'S
Alcester, Warwickshire

www.hoganscider.co.uk

### Dry (5.8% ABV)

Crisp, clean aromas give way to a palate that's deliciously crisp, sharp and tangy with not much tannin. Refreshing and light, but very satisfying.

## LYME BAY WINERY

Axminster, Devon

www.lymebaywinery.co.uk

### Jack Ratt Vintage
(7.4% ABV)

Award-winning scrumpy, named one of the 50 best food products in Britain in 2012. Intense fruit aroma with a hint of oak, full-bodied, smooth and juicy with good tannins and a crisp finish.

## LA MARE WINE ESTATE

St Mary, Jersey

www.lamarewineestate.com

### Branchage (6% ABV)

An aroma of apple skins and wet apple flesh, with flavours of tangy sweetness, soft tannin, oak, clove and cedar with a slight funk. Satisfying and juicy with a pleasantly sour finish.

## MINCHEW'S

Tewkesbury, Gloucestershire

www.minchews.co.uk

### Malvern Hills Perry
(7% ABV)

Pale and opaque, with an aroma of sweet pears. The flavour is medium-dry, slightly oaky, very juicy with gentle tannins. A typically great perry from one of the world's most respected producers.

## MCCRINDLE'S CIDER

Blakeney, Gloucestershire

www.mccrindlescider.co.uk

### Loiterpin (8.5% ABV)

A *méthode champenoise* perry that's aged on lees for 12 months. This gives it some big, funky aromas that suggest a challenging drink. So when the deliciously mousse-y palate is simple, crisp and biscuity, as if it's hiding the fruit just out of reach from you, the result is intriguingly and insanely moreish.

## NEW FOREST CIDER
Burley, Hampshire
www.newforestcider.co.uk

### Gold (3.8% ABV)

The beautiful fruity, perfumed aroma has a slight edge of funk, opening on to a palate that is a riot of melon, pineapple, apricot and fresh apple-juice flavours all balanced with a lovely soft tannin. An astonishing cider at such a low alcohol level, and a great advert for keeved cider as a distinct style.

## NOOK'S YARD
Northwich, Cheshire
www.nooksyard.com

### Cheshire Perry (6% ABV)

Slightly hazy with a hint of cheesiness behind the fresh-fruit aroma. On the palate it's dry and slightly smoky, tart and fruity at the finish. Manages to combine some interesting flavours with a clean freshness and delicacy that make it very drinkable.

## OLIVER'S CIDER AND PERRY
Hereford
www.theolivers.org.uk

### Oliver's Herefordshire Perry (5.4%)

A bottle-conditioned perry with a Champagne-style fizz. The nose is light and citrusy with alluring Christmas spice notes, and on the palate the flavour is rich and firm-bodied, with hints of spice, smoke and fruit, elegant and vibrant, with a dry, crisp finish that pulls you in all over again. Sensational.

### Oliver's Herefordshire Cider (Dry) (5% ABV)

Bottled-conditioned with a hazy orange colour, and the kind of aroma that captures you so completely you can almost forget to take a sip: musty, wet straw, mild camphor and barnyard funk set up an expectation of a formidable cider, and it's true to its promise, with a very complex flavour involving cedar and oak wood, hessian, cherry and apricot blended in with the dominant crisp apple. A truly great cider.

## ONCE UPON A TREE
Ledbury, Herefordshire
www.onceuponatree.co.uk

### The Wonder Dessert Pear Wine (12% ABV)

They weren't mincing their words when they named this, the world's first 'ice perry', although the makers refer to it, with some justification, as 'dessert pear wine'. A spirituous, *tarte Tatin* aroma, viscous, rich and smooth sweet pear on the palate with hints of apricot, quince and melon, and a lingering sweet finish that leaves you begging for more.

### Marcle Ridge (7.5% ABV)

When you taste them, it makes perfect sense that Once Upon A Tree's ciders are created by a wine maker. Aromas of apple blossom and a clean, dry cider with excellent balance and soft tannins.

## ORCHARD PIG
Glastonbury, Somerset
www.orchardpig.co.uk

**Charmer** (6% ABV)

Light and delicate with faint, fruity aromas, buttery sweetness and good tannins on the palate, with a short, crisp finish. Quite simple, but a satisfying alternative to anaemic mainstream brands.

## PERRY'S CIDER
Dowlish Wake, Somerset
www.perryscider.co.uk

**Premium Vintage Cider** (6% ABV)

A medium cider with fresh-apple character and baked, caramel sweetness. Big, juicy and tannic, this is a modern interpretation of a classic style from one of Somerset's oldest cider-making families.

## PILTON CIDER
Pilton, Somerset
www.piltoncider.com

**Naturally Sparkling Somerset Cider** (5.5% ABV)

A rare English example of a keeved cider. A vigorous, inviting aroma with loads of fresh, sweet apple on the nose makes sipping irresistible. A soft, mousse-like texture, bright sweetness and vivid fruit.

## PIPS CIDER
Dorstone, Hereford
www.pipscider.co.uk

**Medium Cider** (7.5% ABV)

Having grown apples for large producers for years, this family business launched its own Pips cider in 2010. The expertise with the fruit shines through. The medium is a blend of seven carefully chosen cider apples, which gives an incredibly moreish burst of flavour with a delicate tannin structure.

## RICHS FARMHOUSE
Highbridge, Somerset

www.richscider.co.uk

**Medium Dry** (6% ABV)

An acetic edge to the nose with a bit of funk. But then it's very smooth and silky on the palate, with a dry, tannic finish.

## ROSIE'S TRIPLE D
Horseshoe Pass, Wrexham

www.rosiescider.co.uk

**Perfect Pear** (6% ABV)

White-gold in colour, with a light nose of caramelized fruit. A big, full-bodied pear flavour is followed by a light, crisp, clean finish. You could drink a lot of this beauty.

## ROSS-ON-WYE CIDER AND PERRY CO
Ross-on-Wye, Herefordshire

www.rosscider.com

**Ross-on-Wye (Broome Farm) Traditional Farmhouse Dry Still Cider** (7% ABV)

Mike Johnson is revered by his fellow cider makers and has won the Pomona award for his contribution to promoting cider. Dry, light and smooth, with fruit developing on the palate and a soft, tannic finish.

## ROCQUETTE
Castel, Guernsey

www.rocquettecider.com

**Traditional Rocquette Cider** (6% ABV)

Guernsey's only cider maker produces a broad enough range to satisfy everyone on the island. This flagship product is fully organic. A spicy apple aroma, there's big sweetness on the first sip and then firm, robust tannin makes its presence felt, giving a long, dry finish.

## SANDFORD ORCHARDS
Crediton, Devon
www.sandfordorchards.co.uk

### Shaky Bridge (6% ABV)

Increasingly stocked in craft-beer pubs as an alternative to mainstream ciders, this is clear, inviting and lightly sparkling, but offers woody spice, gentle funk and a tangy, tannic twist for a proper grown-up cider that's still light and refreshing enough for pub drinking.

## SHEPPY'S
Taunton, Somerset
www.sheppyscider.com

### Goldfinch (7% ABV)

A tart, sour-apple aroma that promises crisp, sharp flavours. Moderate tannins come in to form a robust, dry cider with great structure and slight spiciness.

## TROGGI SEIDR
Earlswood, Monmouthshire
**No website**

### Perry (6.5% ABV)

Aroma of pear, nectar and a hint of elderflower. Does what only good perry can do, combining firm, refined structure with juicy fruit that's held in check and elegantly displayed. Big and complex, yet supremely drinkable.

## THATCHERS
Sandford, Somerset
www.thatcherscider.co.uk

### Heritage (4.9% ABV)

Thatchers' products have become more crowd-pleasing in recent years as they benefit from the upsurge of interest in something a little more refined than the main commercial brands. Heritage shows them at their best: a medium draught cider that's balanced and drinkable with good apple aromas and flavour, mild acidity and a dry finish.

## TY GWYN
Monmouthshire, Wales
www.tygwyncider.co.uk

### Dabinett (6.5% ABV)

This single-variety Dabinett cider is often described as 'medium' and demonstrates the inadequacy of that simple scale to describe a great cider such as this. Sweet apples on the nose, the taste is delicate and fruity, with a seriously spicy hint and a long, clean finish.

## WESTONS

Much Marcle, Herefordshire
www.westons-cider.co.uk

### Henry Westons Vintage
(8.2% ABV)

Westons ciders are aged in huge, ancient oak vats, and that character is evident here when you look for it. Green-apple sweetness is balanced by tannin, oak and vanilla for a cider that's clean, elegant and refreshing yet satisfying and rewarding.

## WEST CROFT CIDER

Brent Knoll, Somerset
www.burnham-on-sea.co.uk/ west_croft_cider

### Janet's Jungle Juice or JJJ (6.5% ABV)

A hazy, warm gold with a juicy apple and tropical-fruit-salad aroma, fresh fruit on the palate with the slightest cheesy hint and a pleasing dry finish. Full-bodied and yet ridiculously drinkable, it's a source of delight on the palate – and possible regret the following morning.

## WILKINS CIDER FARM

Mudgeley, Somerset
www.wilkinscider.com

### Farmhouse Cider
(6% ABV)

A legend of the cider world, it takes a big cider to live up to Wilkins' larger-than-life personality. Happily, his cider delivers as much character and personality as the man himself. A strong farmyard, cheesy hint suggests this is not for the faint-hearted, but the juicy palate delights and the dry, tannic finish pulls you in for more. Irresistible.

## WORLEY'S

Dean, Somerset
www.worleyscider.co.uk

### Premium Vintage
(6.2% ABV)

Buttery gold, with spicy, woody aromas. On the palate it's all about big, furry tannins, a little fruit and farmhouse funk. Classic Somerset style, rich and satisfying.

# ĪRELAND

# IRELAND

Ireland has a very strong association with one particular drink that is somewhat darker and chewier than cider.

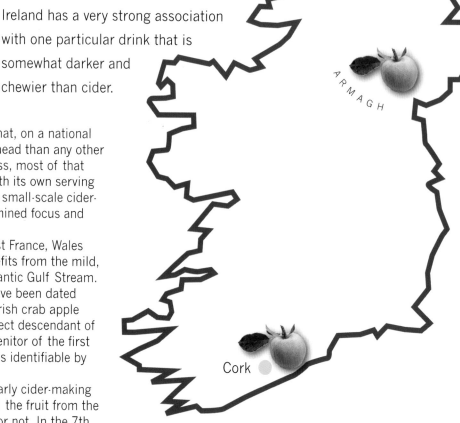

So it may come as a huge surprise that, on a national level, the Irish drink more cider per head than any other country in the world. As with Guinness, most of that cider is one singular, iconic brand with its own serving ritual. However, in the last few years, small-scale cider-making has come back with a determined focus and sense of purpose.

Just like northern Spain, northwest France, Wales and southwest England, Ireland benefits from the mild, wet climate created by the North Atlantic Gulf Stream. Apple pips found in County Meath have been dated back to 5000 years ago, and a wild Irish crab apple still occasionally found today is a direct descendant of the *Malus sylvestris*, the ancient progenitor of the first domesticated apple varieties, which is identifiable by its thorned branches.

Like everywhere else, records of early cider-making are lost in time, and we don't know if the fruit from the earliest orchards was used for cider or not. In the 7th and 8th centuries AD the ancient Brehon Laws classed the apple tree as one of the 'seven nobles of the woods'. These laws distinguished between wild and cultivated apples, and imposed huge fines for the heinous crime of cutting down an apple tree.

The first definite mention of cider-making appears in the 12th century, when a tribal leader from Ulster was praised for the quality of the cider made from his orchards. While this suggests cider-making was well established at the time (there's no indication that he was the *first* person to make cider), there are few other records until the civil surveys of the 1650s, which contain various references to orchards, and suggest that farmhouse cider-making was just as established here as it was in England and Wales.

By the 18th and early 19th centuries, Irish cider was being praised for its quality both at home and abroad. At one competition in Dublin in the late 18th century, the top prize was withheld until the winner could prove his cider wasn't in fact white wine in disguise, such was its quality.

Like so much else, cider-making almost disappeared with the great famine of the 19th century, but it was revived in the early 1900s with government assistance. A certain William Magner began making cider in 1934 in Clonmel, Tipperary, and the assistance of Bulmers of Hereford saw the company grow rapidly at the expense of farmhouse cider makers. In the second half of the 20th century, Irish cider became a one-brand market.

Whereas in many countries it was the arrival of Magners that prompted a revived interest in cider, in Ireland people were very familiar with it, and the same revival came directly from the broader growing interest in food and drink – where it's from and how it's made. A new generation of cider makers appeared and began to unearth traditional Irish apple varieties with enticing names such as the Bloody Butcher, Maiden's Blush, Greasy Pippin and Red Brandy. Over 70 such varieties have been saved and revived.

The newly formed producer group Cider Ireland has around a dozen members, every one of whom prides themselves on using exclusively Irish-grown apples and nothing but 100 per cent juice. The cider apples tend to be concentrated in three or four southern counties, and those in the north use culinary and dessert apples as well as traditional varieties.

A whole range of interesting, high-quality ciders has sprung up as if from nowhere in both Northern Ireland and the Republic. Just be careful about asking for them to be poured over ice.

OPPOSITE: The Irish cider revival is all about embracing the orchard, reconnecting with a natural old tradition.

# THE COLOSSUS MAGNERS/BULMERS

A time to create

MAGNERS
IRISH CIDER
Original

ENJOY MAGNERS SENSIBLY

When Magners appeared in the UK in 2005 to 2006 and revolutionized the world's largest cider market, its arch-rival, Bulmers, did nothing to dispel the confusion between it and the new interloper, relaunching Bulmers Original to look as similar to Magners as it dared, actively encouraging people to think the two were the same brand.

It's probably best to start at the beginning. When William Magner started making cider in 1934, he was one of many resurgent cider makers benefiting from the encouragement and advice of the department of agriculture, in a region noted for its outstanding apples. But Magner was a much shrewder businessman than the typical farmhouse cider maker, investing in his own press rather than relying on the travelling presses to visit farms. He also installed large oak fermentation vats, and his business grew quickly.

Magner quickly attracted the attention of Bulmers of Hereford when he persuaded his friend Éamon de Valera, president of the Irish Executive Council, to slap a shilling-per-gallon tax on imports of Bulmers to Ireland. Bulmers really was very keen to sell cider in

Ireland, and in 1937 agreed with William Magner the formation of a new company, Bulmer, Magner & Co, in which each had a 50 per cent share, and which would sell cider in Ireland under the Bulmers name.

Soon Irish Bulmers was selling two million gallons a year of cider and a soft apple drink, Cidona. In 1946, Bulmers bought out William Magner and renamed the company Bulmers Ltd Clonmel.

In 1964 after a costly court case over copyright, Bulmers sold its Irish operation, which eventually ended up in the hands of its rival, Showerings of Somerset. The sale included permission to use the Bulmers name in Ireland, but retained exclusive rights to the name everywhere else in the world.

In 1991 the Irish Bulmers launched a pint bottle and suggested people enjoy it with a glass of ice. It became hugely popular, so much so that many people believe drinking cider over ice is an established Irish tradition. But Mark Jenkinson of Cider Ireland is doubtful. 'When I was a kid you didn't get ice in pubs – it was a luxury for posh hotels and you'd have been looked at askance if you asked for it. It was common by the mid-1980s, and

Aren't Magners and Bulmers just the same?' It's is a question you hear in pubs up and down the UK and it's just one of cider's many mysteries and misunderstandings.

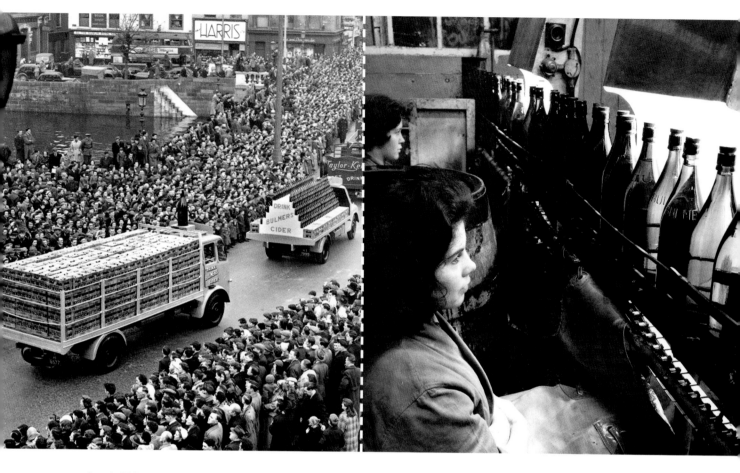

everyone drank Cidona, their apple-based soft drink, with ice in. So I think it came from there.'

In 1999 C&C, by now the holding division of Bulmers Ireland, was bought out as an independent company and decided to expand internationally. Coming up against the trademark exclusivity issue, it looked to the company's origins and renamed the product after its long-forgotten founder, William Magner.

So now, Bulmers in Ireland is the same drink, identical in packaging and flavour to Magners everywhere else. But Bulmers everywhere else is a completely different drink to Magners, as a side-by-side tasting will show.

The success of Magners in the UK, driven by the pint bottle and the glass-of-ice idea (and adverts that were filmed in orchards in New Zealand), stunned everyone. Drinkers loved it, competitors copied it, and Magners took the idea around the world.

While undoubtedly huge, Magners makes more of a play than most about its quality as a cider. It uses 17 named varieties of culinary, dessert and cider apples. The draught product, served without ice, has a greater proportion of sharp, tannic Dabinett and Michelin

apples. We'd like to tell you about Magners' juice content compared to its competitors, but the company refused to tell us anything about exactly how the product is made or what is in it.

Magners is now sold in 40 countries. C&C has also bought Woodchuck and Hornsby's – the two biggest cider brands in the United States – so it controls most of the North American cider market. Having started the cider revolution in the UK, Magners is on a determined path to become the world's favourite cider.

ABOVE FAR LEFT: Magners' launch advertising perfectly captured that idyllic summer cider mood.
ABOVE: After buying out William Magner, Bulmers Ireland grew rapidly to become a huge cider-making concern.

# IRELAND CIDER SUGGESTIONS

## ARMAGH CIDER COMPANY
Portadown, County Armagh
www.armaghcider.com

**Carsons Crisp** (4.5% ABV)

Made exclusively from freshly pressed apples with no additives or flavourings. Deep gold. Clean, sweet-apple flavours with a dry finish.

## CRAIGIES IRISH CIDER
County Wicklow
www.facebook.com/CraigiesCider

**Ballyhook Flyer** (5.8% ABV)

A blend of Dabinett, Katy and Bramley apples. A fresh, fruity nose, and dry palate with a bready hint.

## LLEWELLYNS
Lusk, County Dublin
www.llewellynsorchard.ie

**Double L Bone Dry Cider** (6% ABV)

Apples grown in their own orchards are picked and matured before pressing. Blending takes place just before bottling, and fresh apple juice is added to create a secondary fermentation in the bottle. As the name suggests, it's completely dry and crisp – and one for the cider connoisseur.

## LONGUEVILLE HOUSE
Mallow, County Cork
www.longuevillehouse.ie/artisan-produce

**Longueville House Cider** (5% ABV)

A blend of Dabinett and Michelin apples. Medium-sweet, but clean, dry, vivacious and refreshing. One of those ciders that simply seems to evaporate from the glass.

## MAC'S ARMAGH CIDER
Forkhill, County Armagh
www.facebook.com/pages/Macs-Armagh-Cider/148853781815654

**Mac's Dry Cider** (6% ABV)

With a mission to 'walk the walk and spread the *craic*', Mac's makes dry, sweet and 'lyte' ciders using only natural techniques and ingredients. The dry is fully fermented, absolutely bone-dry and tannic, with slight funkiness and hay.

## MACIVORS
Portadown, County Armagh
www.macivors.com

**Traditional Dry Cider** (5.6% ABV)

Full-bodied and complex, fresh and fruity yet elegantly structured, this won silver in the Best Cider Above 5% category in the 2013 International Brewing Awards.

## MCCANN'S

Portadown,
County Armagh

www.mccannapples.co.uk

**Apple County
Traditional
Country Cider** (6%ABV)

Very pale gold, with a
sweet, eating-apple nose.
That sweetness continues
in the mouth, with just
a hint of straw and a
pleasant, countering
tannin, then finishes
cool and dry.

## STONEWELL

Kinsale, County Cork

www.stonewellcider.com

**Medium Dry Irish
Craft Cider** (5.5% ABV)

Sweet Golden Delicious,
floral aroma, and that
sweetness continues
on the palate, with faint
notes of spice, countered
and contained by a nice
acidic edge.

## TEMPTED?

Lisburn, Armagh

www.temptedcider.co.uk

**Medium Dry Irish
Craft Cider** (5.7% ABV)

Made with Bramley and
dessert apples in the
Kentish style, meaning
there's big, eating-apple
aroma, crisp acidity and
low tannins with a gently
dry finish.

## TOBY'S
## HANDCRAFTED CIDER

Orchard County, Armagh

www.tobyscider.co.uk

**Toby's Handcrafted
Cider** (6% ABV)

Bottle-conditioned,
with a zesty, fresh-apple
aroma and a hint of
bready yeast, a palate of
fresh, green eating apple,
hints of citrus and a long,
dry finish.

# REST OF EUROPE CIDER SUGGESTIONS

## DENMARK

Not the largest cider-producing country in Scandinavia, but certainly the most interesting. The tradition here dates back to the Vikings, who may have produced cider in order to preserve the produce of the apple tree. There's a distinct Norman influence here now, the journey of the Norsemen having gone full circle.

### COLD HAND WINERY
Randers, Jutland
www.coldhandwinery.dk

**Malus X Feminam**
(20% ABV)

A special mix of ice cider and apple *eau de vie*, aged for eight months in wine casks. You just know that's got to be special and it doesn't disappoint: an intense, baked-apple aroma gives way to a gentle alcohol burn on the palate, balanced with fresh acidity and apple sweetness, with honey and caramel notes. Outstanding.

### FEJØ CIDER
Fejø
www.fejoecider.dk

**Fejø Cider Brut** (6% ABV)

Deep orange with a barnyard funk and acidic aroma. There's good fruit on the palate but there is a lot more going on – an almost vinegary acidity, funk and wood all somehow resolve into a long, dry finish.

### KERNEGAARDEN
Fejø
www.kernegaarden.dk/index.php/cider

**Æble Cider Demi-Sec**
(5% ABV)

Naturally fermented and bottle-conditioned in the Normandy style. Yeasty, cooked apple aromas with a little vegetal funk, followed by a tangy, crisp fresh flavour with hints of wood and asparagus, and a great mousse. A classy take on the French style.

## ITALY

### ECOMELA
Verzegnis, Udine
www.ecomela.it

**Mosct** (4.5% ABV)

A painstaking re-creation of a traditional product that was a popular family drink in this fruit-growing region until it died out in the 1950s. Fresh, natural and elegant, with acidity to the fore and nice tannin complementing the fruit.

## NORWAY

### HARDANGER SAFT – OG SIDERFABRIKK
Lekve Gard, Ulvik
www.hardangersider.no

**Hardangersider**
(10.5% ABV)

Apples have been cultivated in the Hardanger region since the 14th century, and their juice is protected by a European protected designation of origin (PDO). This entirely natural cider has apple skins and a hint of funk on the nose, a medium-sweet apple flavour and a long and dry finish.

## POLAND

### CYDR IGNACÓW
Bledów
www.cydrignacow.pl

**Cydr Ignaców** (5.5% ABV)

This is a good example of the new face of Polish cider. It is traditionally made during the autumn using freshly pressed juice from several apple varieties grown in orchards in Ignaców, a small village in the district of Grójec, in the middle of the largest orchard in Europe. It's matured in the winter and spring. Pale straw in colour, it contains no artificial flavors or dyes. The aroma is fruity, fresh apple with a slight pear note. In the mouth it is medium-dry but fresh, with a delicate sweetness and a pleasant peach-fruit finish. It goes well with food.

## SWEDEN

Cider is huge in Sweden, but unfortunately we haven't found anything so far that's as good as the rest of the ciders in this book. Big brands **Kopparberg** (www.kopparbergs.se) and **Rekorderlig** (www.rekorderlig. com) are international sensations, but with added fruit flavours and artificial sweeteners they bear little resemblance to cider. When a brand boasts on its bottle labels about the quality of the water used in the product, you have to wonder why they call themselves ciders at all – they're effectively alcopops in disguise.

Sweden's largest cider is **Herrljunga** (www. herrljungacider.se) and the smaller **Briska** (www.briska. se) claims to be a 'craft' cider on the basis of its longevity as a family-run cider maker. But having tasted them, sadly we find them little different to their more internationally famous counterparts.

## SWITZERLAND

### CIDRERIE DU VULCAIN
Le Mouret, Fribourg
www.cidrelevulcain.ch

**Trois Pépins** (5% ABV)

This organic cider promises the marriage of three fruits. Quince gives it a floral nose, and lively acidity balances the sweetness from both apple and pears.

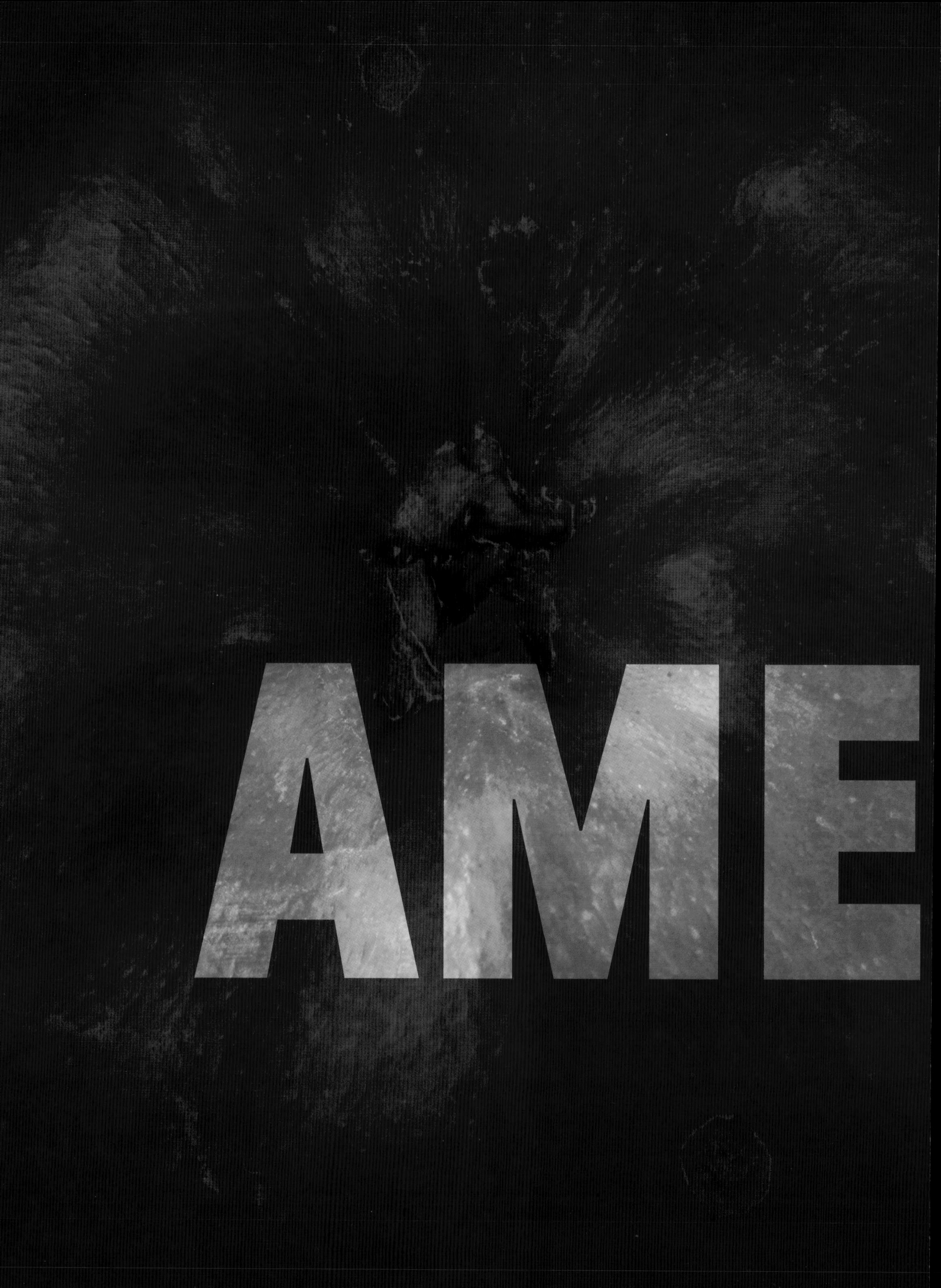
AME

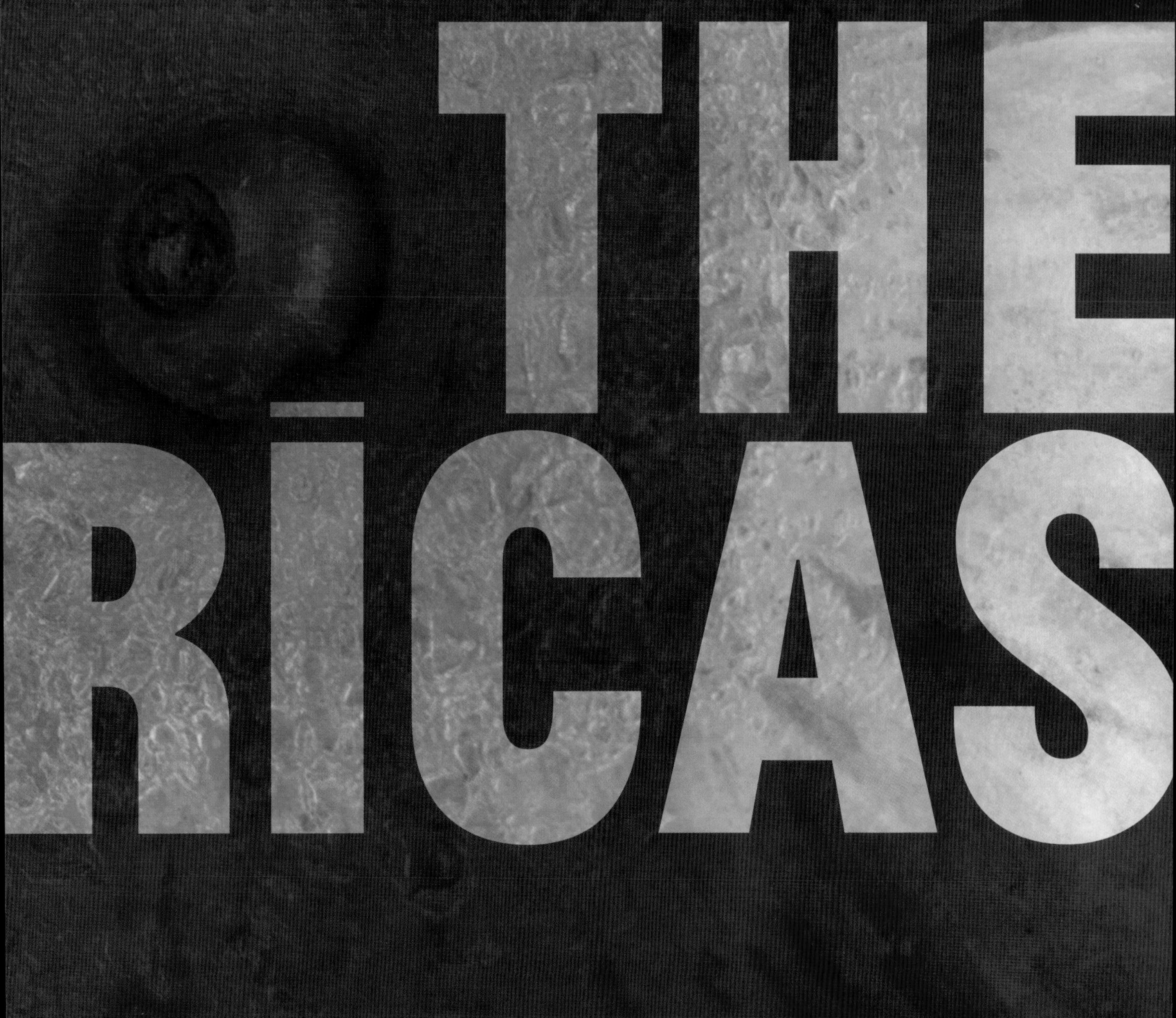
THE
RICAS

HARD CIDER

A Rural Favorite!

COPYRIGHT 1907, A. B. WOODWARD CO., N. Y.

# UNĪTED STATES

# UNĪTED STATES

The problem with asking for a glass of cider in the United States is that you can never be quite sure what you're going to get. The United States federal government defines cider (for tax purposes) as 'a beverage made from fermented apples of not more than 8 per cent alcohol'. Seems clear enough. However, in Pennsylvania, for example, cider is legally defined as an 'amber golden, opaque, unfermented, entirely non-alcoholic juice squeezed from apples'. And this is what most people understand cider to be.

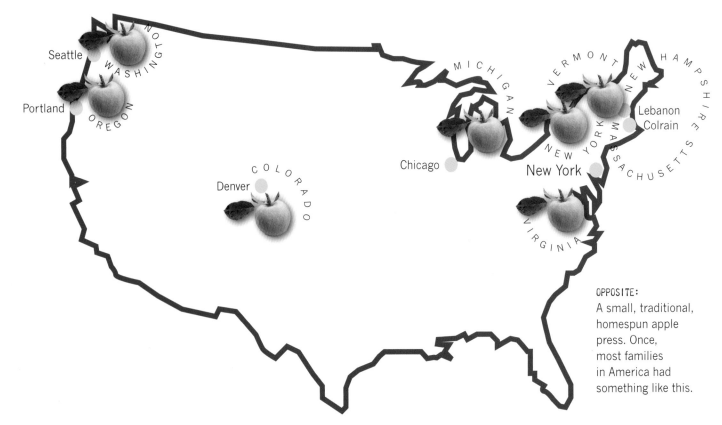

OPPOSITE:
A small, traditional, homespun apple press. Once, most families in America had something like this.

Cider has been twisted into new shapes by America's laws and social history as much as apple trees have been altered by its climate. Like so much in America, cider's story is one that marries extreme frustration, bizarre twists and turns, and thrilling wonder.

Today, fans and producers have to explain to curious novices what cider is, usually contextualizing it as the equivalent for apples of what wine is to grapes. What few Americans realize is that cider is the drink that built their nation, an alcoholic beverage of unsurpassed significance which has suffered a Stalinist airbrushing from history – an injustice that is only now beginning to be corrected.

The only apples indigenous to the American continent were viciously tart crabs. The earliest Virginia colonists brought grafted Old World trees with them, but these fared poorly in the harsh winters and random late spring frosts of their new home. The apple only really took hold when planted from seed. Seedling trees were therefore planted within years of the first colonies being established in the eastern seaboard. While early vines for wine also failed miserably, thanks to the apple's propensity towards infinite genetic variety, some seedling trees, or 'pippins', found the new environment to their liking, especially after the colonists brought honeybees from Europe to help them pollinate.

From these random seedlings, America's own indigenous apple varieties were created. As author Michael Pollan writes, 'In effect, the apple, like the settlers themselves, had to forsake its former domestic life and return to the wild before it could be reborn as American – as Newtown Pippins and Baldwins, Golden Russets and Jonathans.'

People like John Chapman (page 174) helped propagate these raw, new varieties from the eastern seaboard across the continent. The cultivated orchard was a reminder of home, part of a settled and productive landscape, and signified the domestication of the wild.

Early American varieties were largely inedible and used exclusively for making cider. Alcoholic refreshment was necessary even to Puritans: a safe alternative to water in uncertain lands where the hops and barley required for beer proved much harder to adapt. It was a rare homestead that did not have a stand of trees with which to make its own cider each fall, to be laid down in the cellar to help get the whole family through the harsh winter.

America's second president, John Adams, drank a tankard of hard cider for breakfast every day – and lived to the age of 91. Even children drank cider for breakfast. Orchardist Tom Burford believes that Americans drank as much cider per capita in the 18th century as they do sodas or soft drinks today.

Within the random spread of seeds and resultant varieties, each time someone found and named an apple that was tasty and suited the environment, it was enthusiastically propagated. Agriculture employed 75 per cent of the population, and over 1000 cultivated apple varieties were recorded in 1850 – the vast majority being cider apples. The mid-19th century saw an apple gold rush as people looked for emerging stars. Finding the next Golden Russet could mean fame and fortune.

In 1840, William Henry Harrison was elected president after famously convincing the populace that he was the homespun candidate of the 'log cabin and hard cider'. From its birth through to the end of its troubled adolescence, America was the world's cider nation.

The change began in the 1870s, when the mass influx of Germans fleeing political unrest coincided with a migration away from farms and into cities. Lager beer, the German national drink, was also an urban beverage, in contrast to cider's homespun farming heritage.

Later, as the temperance movement successfully demonized all forms of alcoholic drink, orchardists turned to more edible varieties. In 1900, horticulturalist Liberty Hyde Bailey pointed out that 'the eating of the apple (rather than the drinking of it) has come to be paramount'. The apple-growing industry sought to create associations between the apple and health, giving us the slogan, 'An apple a day keeps the doctor away'.

Prohibition is often blamed for finally killing off America's cider tradition. Inedible cider apples became worthless (unless you could keep them out of sight), and cultivation turned to edible varieties. What had been previously known as sweet cider – unfermented apple juice – came to be known as cider, period.

But it has been argued that it was the *end* of Prohibition that put the final seal on America's cider

tradition. After 13 dry years, America was thirsty. Beer could be produced within a few weeks, but it was going to take five years to re-cultivate the lost cider-apple trees. The nation couldn't wait that long. And in the meantime, America's soft drinks industry had sprung up to satisfy the taste for something sweeter. With rail transport opening up the country to create a single market, popular culinary varieties pushed quirky cider apples out of the way. The Red Delicious apple may have been great to eat but, according to Tom Burford, it was 'one of the worst apples cider can be made with', and a new generation of drinkers declared Red Delicious cider 'the worst drink they had ever put in their mouths'. The American cider industry survived Prohibition in a critical state, but was dead by the mid-1940s.

Commercial 'six-pack' ciders offering a straight substitute for beer re-emerged in the 1970s. Crude and sweet, they had to position themselves as 'hard' cider against the unfermented juice that had appropriated the name. It didn't catch on; imagine being forced to describe wine as 'hard grape juice' and you can appreciate the dilemma cider faced.

But over the decades that followed, true cider began to reappear, hesitantly at first. Proselytizers like Stephen Wood introduced Old World apple varieties. Others developed better ciders from culinary varieties. And people began to discover what were now dubbed 'heirloom' varieties: the last survivors from the old settlers' tradition, ivy-clad and forgotten in fields, on roadsides and at the margins of orchards.

Today, cider production is thriving around New England, the Great Lakes and the Pacific Northwest. We cover each of these regions in detail. But cider is now on sale in all 50 states, and producers are establishing themselves across the country. The cider revival owes much to the craft-beer movement. Like American craft beer, it draws influences from around the world and from its own forgotten past and combines them with modern-day rigour and a quest for excellence. For many who missed the start of the craft-beer boom, it's a second chance to be in at the beginning. Right now, America still defers to Old World tradition and expertise. But some of these new cider makers are already winning competitions in Europe, beating their idols.

With the United States Association of Cider Makers (USACM) being formed even as this book went to press, it won't be very long before American cider regains and surpasses its former glory.

RIGHT: Cider is just one of the products on offer at a top-notch North American farm stand.

ZESTAR!

CHAMPLAIN
ORCHARDS

APPLES
and
CIDER

CIDERS
FARMHOUSE
NEW OAK
HONEY PIE
SCRUMPY LITTLE WOODY
SWEET HEART
POMONA

SWEET CIDER

GALLONS $650
HALF GALLONS $375

SNACKS

RACLETTE Cheese Plate $8

# THE FOLK HERO JOHNNY APPLESEED

America may be a young country, but it has made up for this by meticulously recording, celebrating and often mythologizing its past.

Within the American creation myth are various figures: real people who have grown in stature ever since their deaths to become giants of the past—part fact, part fiction, but all-American historical superheroes. Men like Davy Crockett and Daniel Boone. And Johnny Appleseed.

Kids learn about Johnny Appleseed in school. There are Disney films and storybooks and songs about his life, which describe how this humble, saintly man, always kind to animals, walked barefoot along the wild frontier, carefully and selflessly planting apple trees so that when tired and hungry settlers arrived in their covered wagons, nature's bounty was waiting for them.

What tends to be omitted from such accounts is the inconvenient truth (from the point of view of a children's story) that Johnny Appleseed planted cider apples, satisfying the thirst, rather than the hunger of the exhausted frontiersman.

Johnny Appleseed was born John Chapman in 1774 in Leominster, Massachusetts. He trained as an orchardist, before heading out to Ohio – at that point, the frontier between America and uncharted wilderness. It's true that Chapman lived a simple, austere life, preferring to sleep outdoors, enjoying the company of Native Americans, children and animals over that of adults. Many accounts describe him as wearing a burlap sack and a tin pan for a hat. It's also seemingly true that he was kind to all and preached an evangelical, inclusive Christian message. One biographer summed it up when he said Chapman had a 'thick bark of queerness around him'.

But he was also a shrewd businessman. Each year, he collected apple seeds from the hard-cider mills of Pennsylvania and headed out West to the Ohio frontier. He seemed to have an uncanny knack of knowing where the next settler's advance would be. He picked his spot

and planted nurseries, fencing them to protect them from animals, sometimes tending them himself, other times moving on. When the settlers arrived, he would have two- to three-year-old saplings waiting, which he sold for six cents apiece.

There was always a demand. To discourage idle land speculation, settlers were required to plant at least 50 apple or pear trees to obtain a land grant. Given that apple trees needed to be looked after and required up to 10 years to bear fruit, an orchard was a symbol of permanent settlement. With the proceeds, he would move on, buying more land and planting more nurseries. By his death in 1845, he owned 1200 acres; this barefoot eccentric was a very wealthy saint.

So how do we know he nurtured trees for cider apples? Simply because he planted apples from seeds rather than grafting them. Apples have an extraordinary tendency towards genetic diversification. Any apple seed will create a tree dramatically different from its parents. The only thing these trees would have had in common is that they would have produced fruit that was, in the words of Henry David Thoreau, 'sour enough to set a squirrel's teeth on edge and make a jay scream'. Such apples are good only for making 'hard', fermented cider.

On the wild frontier, good drinking water could be hard to come by. And, cider and its distilled big brother, applejack, warmed against the cold nights and took the edge off the hardness of frontier life.

Cider was the drink that pushed America westwards, and Johnny Appleseed was its propagator. By planting and nurturing so many seeds, those that took, combining their individual genetic codes with their new surroundings, created potentially thousands of new species of all-American apple. While some proclaim him as a Christian saint, to writer Michael Pollan Johnny Appleseed was more of a Pagan god: the American Dionysus.

# THE IN-BETWEENERS
## AMERICAN 'MAINSTREAM' CIDERS

It's a rainy grey day when we arrive at an even greyer industrial unit to meet Woodchuck cider. It's not a huge building – about the size of a successful micro-brewery – but in the cider world Woodchuck is a colossus, making six of every 10 ciders drunk in the United States.

Dan Rowell, Woodchuck's chief financial officer, doesn't talk like the corporate drones we've met in some industrial cider concerns. For one thing, he talks about apples and flavours rather than brands and positioning. 'I grew up in Vermont, and as a kid I used to pick apples at Steve Wood's place,' he tells us. 'Of course, now Steve thinks of us as commercial cider.'

Maybe. But it was Steve who insisted we should visit Woodchuck as part of our tour.

Woodchuck is referred to as 'cider beer' by many of its customers, and it's telling that most other large-scale 'six-pack' cider makers arrived on the scene with beer as their point of reference rather than orchards or wine.

While this is not necessarily a barrier to making good cider, it does seem to come with a different mindset: most larger-scale commercial producers use concentrate, and many add water and other flavourings, even if they are at pains to point out that these are 'natural'.

But we're in quite a different world here than that of the UK, home of the world's largest mass-market cider brands. The original idea behind Woodchuck when it was founded in 1990 was to replicate the UK's Woodpecker cider. Woodchuck soon changed into something 'more suited to the American palate', but the company does still import Strongbow from the UK. Tellingly, Woodchuck compares favourably with the UK version, because the minimum level of juice required before you can legally call something 'cider' is higher in the United States than in the UK. It has been seriously suggested by people who know their cider that certain products from some of the world's largest brewing corporations, which list their

The largest cider brands in the United States aren't yet that large, meaning they still at least pay lip service to craft values.

**LEFT:** Woodchuck product waiting to be dispatched.
**BELOW:** Woodchuck, America's largest cider maker, still tries to retain a homespun feel.

**The Woodchuck Cidery**
153 Pond Lane
Middlesbury, VT 05753
**www.woodchuck.com**

ingredients as 'apple concentrate, dextrose and water' and then pay bloggers to write about how nice they are, are so awful that they have been designed deliberately to put people off cider and neutralize a threat to the easy-drinking end of the beer market.

However, other large brands, such as Crispin and Hornsby's, and offerings from brewers such as Harpoon and Samuel Adams, are not as cynical and drift into a territory Steve Wood has labelled as 'hybrid' – clinging to some of the principles of craft even as their larger scale means they cannot produce on a truly artisanal basis. Many are excessively sweet, but this is what the more mainstream American palate currently expects. Crispin's tastes more like sparkling apple juice than cider, but at least it tastes like apples have been involved in its manufacture. Angry Orchard's Traditional Dry contains so much sugar that it hardly resembles cider at all. But its Crisp Apple is much better.

As with any innovation-hungry market, there's a tendency towards rapid product proliferation. But limited editions, wood-aged versions and flavoured ciders such as Woodchuck's ginger or pumpkin variants do feel more interesting than the more typical fruit flavours elsewhere.

If you wanted to be kind to America's mass-market cider makers, you could say they are providing a bridge between the sickly sweet mainstream and the more interesting craft sector. (There's certainly evidence that such a migration happened in the UK.) If you wanted to be more critical, you could say they're stealing the imagery and mystique of craft and wrapping it around inferior products.

Either way, the commercial ciders in the United States are not as bad as those elsewhere. Given that, after a certain point, the character of cider declines in inverse proportion to the size of the producer, they're simply not big enough to be truly awful. Yet.

# THE EAST COAST

The story of American cider begins in the beautiful green hills of New England.

From an American perspective, this is where it all began. Apples as we know them were not native to North America; the first orchards were planted from seed by the Massachusetts Bay colonists within a year of them landing, and these wild apple varieties were initially used exclusively for cider. A Mr Holyoke of Harvard College noted in his diary of 1743 to 1759 that he put 16 barrels of cider into his cellar one autumn, and later went back to add spirit to the cider, 'to give it greater authority'.

Cider was much easier to make in an untamed land than other drinks, and even when beer arrived cider remained much cheaper. By 1767 the average Massachusetts resident drank 35 gallons of cider a year – a calculation that includes children. The cider mills of New England, New York and Pennsylvania provided the seeds that propagated apples across the nation. New York City acquired its famous nickname from being at the heart of such bounty.

While the temperance movement killed off such enthusiastic drinking, it's hard for even the most powerful legislature in the world to ban the naturally occurring process of fermentation in a state running with so much apple juice. Reminiscing in 1973, writer Vrest Orton revealed, 'Many of us who live in rural New England still buy a 36-gallon keg of sweet cider in the fall, let it ferment, and then bottle it, with a smidgen of sugar in each bottle, and come up with what the French call Champagne cider and what we call sparkling cider – a rousing good drink.' It's hard to imagine how Prohibition could have prevented this.

In the northern Berkshires of western Massachusetts, the misty forests are too dense for even the most ardent Prohibitionist to purge them of apples, and old colonial varieties such as Baldwin and Cox's Orange Pippin still grow on ancient trees wrapped in ivy. Here, Judith Moloney of West County Cider walks barefoot through the rain-sodden grass like Johnny Appleseed to greet us with the words, 'Hello, young Englishmen.' We like her immediately. Over a light lunch of corn chowder with 'some oyster mushrooms we found out near the dump', she tells us that people here never stopped making cider, even if it was supposedly just for personal use. 'In this town people

'IN THIS TOWN PEOPLE KNOW WHO MAKES GOOD CIDER, AND WHO JUST MAKES CIDER, AND OVER THE YEARS THERE HAS BEEN A LOT OF UNOFFICIAL BARTER.'

know who makes good cider, and who just makes cider, and over the years there's been a lot of unofficial barter.' Her own ciders, mainly single-varieties made from these heirloom trees, look and taste like fine wines.

There's a similar sense of permanence at Slyboro Ciderhouse in Granville, New York. In 1990 husband-and-wife team Dan Wilson and Susan Knapp took over this exquisite farm, all rust-red slats and white piping with lichen-dusted roofs from locally mined slate. Dan's parents bought it in 1974 and Mickey Spillane (Dan's uncle) used the old coaching house as a peaceful writing retreat.

Dan and Susan began experimenting with cider-making in 2001, and in 2007 they opened their cider house to the pick-your-own groups who come for eating apples each fall. Most of their products are above seven per cent alcohol, which means they are categorized for duty purposes as fruit wines. But the similarity goes beyond alcohol levels. 'New Yorkers love shopping local, which means they really should be drinking cider, not wine,' says Dan. 'We have seven pourers working full-time in the height of the season. They have to explain to people what cider is. People love it when they taste it, and then go, "What grape did you say this was again?"'

Growing conditions can create a lot of uncertainty. New England has long winters that have a habit of reappearing with late frosts to kill off the spring blossom and destroy any chance of a harvest. The local pests are problematic, too. Porcupines just love cider apples – but not the ones that have dropped. Their tracks resemble a drunken bowling ball ploughing through the long grass, and when they get to a tree they leave a trail of devastation, stripping off branches as they climb to get the fruit.

We see one when we visit Eden Ice Cider in northern Vermont. It walks on its hind legs, carrying an apple contemplatively in its front paws. It's unbearably cute, like a little old man in a lavish cloak. Just as well it's not we sentimental 'young' Englishmen who are tasked with shooting him tomorrow.

LEFT: The stunning view from one of Farnum Hill's orchards in New Hampshire.
BELOW: Judith Moloney of West County Cider, in her farmhouse kitchen.

Eden is only a few miles from the Canadian border, and emulating ice cider from Quebec was an obvious thing to try when Albert and Eleanor Leger relocated here from New York City in 2007. They are propagating heirloom blends, creating an American take on ice cider, pushing cider to its full extent.

There's incredible variety in this region. But behind everything is the presence of Stephen Wood, owner of Farnum Hill Cider and Poverty Lane Orchards. Through him, New England is once again propagating new apples in the New World, thanks to his endless passion for bringing across Old World cider apple varieties and sharing them with as many people as he can.

It has been slow work getting people to understand what Steve and his acolytes are trying to do. For a long time, their products were stuck on the bottom shelf at liquor stores, next to cheap wine coolers. But the courting of wine journalists and Manhattan restaurants is gradually repositioning cider as a low-alcohol alternative to wine rather than a sweeter 'six-pack' faux beer. Packaged in classy 750-ml bottles, discussed in terms of varietals and vintages, this 7 to 8 per cent ABV product suddenly becomes a responsible, moderate drinking option rather than heady rocket fuel. If beer is the main point of reference on the West Coast, cider is all about the wine comparison in the east.

The Beer Judge Certification Program of America (BJCP) is so enthusiastic about creating categories and classifications for fermented beverages that it has defined various ones for American cider. One of these is a 'specialty' named 'New England Cider', the only category with a geographical appellation, which is defined as being made with 'characteristic New England apples for relatively high acidity, with adjuncts to raise alcohol levels', and the rather sublime comment that there are 'no known commercial examples of New England Cider'. Only the BJCP could come up with a category for something and then assert that this category does not exist.

At the risk of getting into a fight with these pioneers of 'Quantum Cider', we found a few products that fit the description. But they are neither exclusive to the East Coast, nor do they reflect the full range of cider produced there.

Cider is moving far too quickly right now to be classified in such a way. And while comparisons with both wine and beer are useful up to a point, cider increasingly demands to be discussed on its own terms.

BELOW: The invitation from Champlain Orchards is too good to resist.
OPPOSITE, ABOVE: Fitz inspecting the crop at Farnum Hill.
OPPOSITE, BELOW: The Cider Barn at Farnum Hill and Poverty Lane – come and buy cider, or just pick your own apples.

POVERTY LANE ORCHARDS

You might expect the most venerated craft-cider producer in America to have harsh words for what he calls 'macro' cider makers. But Steve Wood loves to confound expectations. 'All cider makers, big or small, imported or domestic, are important,' he is fond of saying. 'Any one of them could be instrumental in spreading the word about cider and helping revive a drink we almost lost.'

Wood is a charismatic, totemic presence on the American cider scene. To some extent, every other cider producer follows him, is influenced by him or reacts to him and he inspires many a rumour. 'How did all these English cider apple varieties suddenly appear in the US?' asks one of his admirers and close friends. Did Steve *really* smuggle scion wood samples through border controls that are very fussy about agricultural produce by whittling them to look like pencils sticking out of his pocket? On the record, there's neither confirmation nor denial.

Wood began his career as a culinary apple orchardist at Poverty Lane, Lebanon, New Hampshire. But he quickly realized that with endlessly improving communication networks in the world and harsh winters at home, he would soon be unable to compete with the big commercial apple varieties from Washington State and abroad.

So, in the early 1980s, he took a trip to visit friends in the southwest of England and became fascinated by some of the curious cider-apple varieties growing there. Somehow, scions from these trees appeared back in New Hampshire, and Steve began experimenting with quirky apple trees as a hobby. When some grafts took, he began making cider, 'throwing away most of it', until he was making stuff he was happy to sell. For Steve Wood, it's all about the quality of the apple and what it can do.

We don't get to meet Steve when we visit Poverty Lane in the 2011 harvest season because he is in hospital, crippled by a very painful bad back. Flying high on absurdly powerful painkillers, he phones us from his sickbed. He explains that, in 2010, Farnum Hill lost 90 per cent of its crop due to a warm spring that brought the blossom out early, only for it to be killed by a late frost. They had to buy apples in from elsewhere, and Steve, proud of his own cultivation, refused to put his Farnum Hill brand name on the resulting ciders. Named 'Dooryard' instead, they still taste absurdly good.

For someone so influential and authoritative, Steve Wood is surprisingly warm and shockingly generous. He freely distributes grafts from his cider trees across the United States, doing everything one man can to help rekindle the tradition.

'Steve was the great-grandfather of the cider renaissance in the US,' says Sue Knapp of Slyboro Ciderhouse. 'Everything I hear in years of conversation with him is a yearning for the cider industry to take root properly. He doesn't want to be a one-off anachronism.'

Back at Poverty Lane, there's a quote from Steve printed out and pinned to the wall, which backs this up: 'We practically have to kneel on people's chests and pry open their mouths to get them to drink this stuff. And then they generally like it.'

It's possible that America's cider renaissance might just have happened without Steve Wood. But it's impossible to imagine that it would have looked as robust and exciting without him at the helm.

'WE PRACTICALLY HAVE TO KNEEL ON PEOPLE'S CHESTS AND PRY OPEN THEIR MOUTHS TO GET THEM TO DRINK THIS STUFF. AND THEN THEY GENERALLY LIKE IT.'

**Farnum Hill Cider**
Poverty Lane Orchards
98 Poverty Lane
Lebanon, NH 03766
**www.povertylaneorchards.com**

OPPOSITE: Steve Wood of Farnum Hill, proud of his elegant ciders.

# THE RESURRECTIONIST
## STEVE WOOD
### POVERTY LANE ORCHARDS

# THE GREAT LAKES

With its huge skies and flat landscape laid out in giant grids punctuated by strip malls, Michigan doesn't look like the kind of place you would find a burgeoning cider culture. So initially it comes as a surprise to find that there are over 30 cider makers here – more than in any other state.

Dig a little deeper, and the momentum of Michigan hard cider becomes less surprising. While Washington, 'The Apple State', grows two-thirds of America's total apple crop, the vast majority of that fruit is sold to be eaten. When it comes to processing and squeezing for juice and other products, Michigan is some way ahead. It supplies around 60 per cent of all the apple slices for commercial apple pies, and the vast Gerber baby-food operation buys 95 per cent of all its pears in the state. There are 7.5 million apple trees in commercial production, covering 36,000 acres of Michigan's farmland.

Michigan's problem is that, of all the different uses of the apple, processed apples are the most vulnerable to the increased competitive pressures of a globalized economy. For some apple growers, America's renewed interest in cider arrived just in time.

Jim Koan runs an organic orchard just outside the town of Flushing, where the famous Newton Pippin was first discovered. A white-bearded, sun-beaten man with faithful dogs seemingly attached to his feet, he settles into a rocking chair on his porch and gives us an unconventional pitch. 'I don't like making cider. I like growing apples,' he barks. 'But I can't compete with the

big commercial growers. The only way I can pay my bills is to ferment my apples.'

He also has his own take on the fall and rise of American cider. 'The problem started when they gave women the vote, which we call the temperance movement,' he says, conflating what many might feel are two separate issues. 'They figured we had the devil in us when we drank, so they went around chopping down all the apple trees. But we deceived 'em by switching to beer: it was easier to disguise. Now cider is coming back again, but it's very different from what our ancestors had. American tastes have – I won't say "evolved" because that is a bad word – changed. They've inundated us all our lives with fizzy pop, and now Americans just want bland and sweet!'

The quality of Koan's cider suggests he's not being entirely straightforward about his supposed lack of passion for cider, although it's certainly sweet enough for the 'changed' American palate.

Other cider makers in the region believe there is the potential to re-educate that palate in the delights of the 'heirloom' cider-apple varieties left behind by previous generations of drinkers, and that hard cider can take its place within a profitable farm-based business. This is a region where coming out to a farm to buy cider, among other things, is a fun day out for all the family. The cider season coincides with the run-up to Halloween, when all nature's fruits are ripe for picking. Cider mills sell the fresh, unpasteurized apple juice that has been referred to as 'cider' for the best part of a century, as well as doughnuts, toffee apples, honey, and groaning shelves full of local produce.

Parmenter's Northville Cider Mill has been such a business since 1873, but only (re)started making hard

BOTH PAGES: Graphic representations of cider in all its forms attest to the importance of cider in the Great Lakes region.

cider in 2003. 'We had too much apple juice and some of it was going off, so we decided to ferment it,' says cider maker Rob Nelson. Using a large proportion of eating apples, he creates light, crisp cider, which is blended with other fruits such as cherry juice or apple to create drinks that resemble Belgian *kriek lambic* beer or rosé wine rather than cloying commercial alcopops.

There's also a hungry spirit of adventure in the region that pushes way beyond ideas of cider, both old and new. With its bank of draft taps on the wall behind the bar, the Vander Mill cider mill and winery in Spring Lake has the feel of a young craft brewery, even though it has to contend with wine legislation. It has an almost hyperactive approach to new products. All ciders are fermented with ale yeast. Michigan Wit combines the characteristics and ingredients of cider with those of Belgian wheat beer, while Cider Masala is made with Indian chai spice and Totally Roasted contains vanilla and homemade cinnamon-roasted pecans. A boat ride away on the other side of Lake Michigan, Æppeltreow is bringing both traditional and inventive ciders to the state of Wisconsin, mixing French, English and old American influences, and also exploring a range of apple brandies.

Meanwhile, just down the road in Chicago, there's a sign of things to come. The city's Goose Island Beer Co has become one of the most famous names in craft brewing over the last 20 years. In 2011, it was acquired by the world's biggest brewer, Anheuser-Busch Inbev, for nearly $40 million (£26m). Master brewer Greg Hall decided to invest his cut of the proceeds in building Virtue, a new cider company that aims to combine modern craft technology with Old World tradition to bring a new take to old cider styles. Hall's high-profile

and previous success have provided yet another boost to cider's rapidly growing profile.

Back over in Michigan, to the west of the vast farmland, the glaciated, fractal shores of Lake Michigan are middle America's playground: kayaking or boat trips in the summer, snowmobiling or skiing in the winter, or just trips to the beach or enjoying the scenery. A visit to a cidery makes a novel change from the region's many wineries.

Tandem Ciders sits on a hilly road near the lake's edge, a fairy-tale American rural scene. It looks like a traditional American farmstead crossed with a gingerbread house: all white wood with green-and-gold trim, flower beds by the door and a bright-red tandem affixed high on the front wall. Orchards stretch up a gentle slope to the south. Inside, on the plain bar, the cider pumps are flanked by a small reading lamp on one side and a jug of sunflowers on the other. If women ruled the world, all pubs would be this beautiful and inviting.

It's designed to remind the owners, Dan Young and Nikki Rothwell, of their time spent in English pubs – which may come as a shock to people who know English pubs intimately. Dan and Nikki must have happened upon some special places in their 2003 tour around England astride a tandem, which began as a pilgrimage to British beer, but ended with them discovering cider, and planning their new business on their return. Tandem ciders are made using American heirloom varieties, and are good enough to attract a very pub-like bunch of regulars to the tasting room as well as tourists.

'Here, take a T-shirt,' says Dan as we leave. 'We like good-looking people to wear 'em. If we go out of business I'll call you for the 17 dollars.'

We're not expecting that call anytime soon.

'NOW CIDER IS COMING BACK AGAIN, BUT IT'S VERY
DIFFERENT FROM WHAT OUR ANCESTORS HAD. AMERICAN TASTES
HAVE — I WON'T SAY "EVOLVED" BECAUSE THAT IS A BAD WORD —
CHANGED. THEY'VE INUNDATED US ALL OUR LIVES WITH FIZZY
POP, AND NOW AMERICANS JUST WANT BLAND AND SWEET!'

# THE PLAYGROUND

## UNCLE JOHN'S FRUIT HOUSE WINERY AND DISTILLERY

If there's one cliché that plagues North America more than any other, it's about how BIG everything is. Europeans joke that American tourists constantly boast about how buildings/mountains/fields/cars (delete as applicable) are much bigger at home. But when those Europeans venture to the States, they are awestruck by the immensity of the skyscrapers, distances – and especially the breakfasts.

The huge expanses of Michigan make Bill and me feel like we've shrunk to hobbit size on the plane. By contrast, Mike Beck has such a large presence and charisma that he gives a fairly good impression of owning the whole state; his vast farm-cum-theme-park in St John's, Michigan, is the cider world's answer to Disneyland and indicates an immense passion and skill for cider-making. There's space for 7000 cars in the parking lot. In the peak season, between Labor Day (the first Monday in September) and Halloween, Uncle John's caters for up to 20,000 visitors per day. This is a family destination, not just a cider mill and winery. People drive miles to come and pick their own pumpkins, strawberries or blueberries, go on funfair rides, or get lost in the corn maze. Uncle John's gets through thousands of caramel apples, and sales of its irresistible homemade doughnuts peak at 350 dozen per hour. But this is no cheap, plasticky theme park full of empty calories. Everywhere you look, the emphasis is on educating generations of children who live in an increasingly virtual world about farm produce and nature.

Mike Beck has been helping the family-farm business sell non-alcoholic cider since he started helping his brother with the juice mill at eight years old. He knows his apples, and is proud of Michigan's prominent role in the apple-processing industry. 'Steve Wood came out here and said we should be taking out what we had and planting English and French cider varieties to make hard cider,' says Beck. 'I realized we had unique varieties held over from America's cider tradition – varieties like Winesap, Northern Spy, Rhode Island Greening and Baldwin were still grown widely across the state. I knew we could make great cider from what we already had.'

Beck convinced the Michigan Apple Association to obtain a grant to help develop hard-cider production, and was instrumental in creating the Michigan Cider Makers' Guild, which was established in 1999. Today, Beck makes a variety of ciders as well as perry, Pommeau and cider brandy: a range of Old World drinks with New World fruit and philosophy. People who bring the kids to choose a pumpkin and enjoy a doughnut invariably wander into the winery side of the business and discover these ciders. Every year, Uncle John's is introducing thousands of people to cider for the first time.

Beck also hosts the Great Lakes Perry and Cider Festival. On the September weekend of our visit, Uncle John's becomes a cidery playground that's as exciting and educational for adults as it is for children the rest of the season. Pretty much all of Michigan's cider makers attend, joined by their counterparts east, west and north, and there's also a good selection of ciders and cider makers from overseas. Some are packaged like craft beers, others like fine wines. All the cider makers are desperately keen to talk about their products to a mixed crowd, whose numbers are swelling dramatically from one year to the next. 'You get the sense that there's a whole cider subculture here, just waiting to take off,' says one cider maker from Canada.

'At one time we had a rich heritage of cider in America,' says Beck. 'I would like to see it come back. I will assist in any way I can to make it happen.'

ABOVE: The mastermind of Uncle John's cider – Mike Beck, with his wife, Dede.

> **Uncle John's Cider Mill**
> 8614 North US 127
> St Johns, MI 48879
> **www.ujcidermill.com**

ABOVE: Uncle John's humongous cider mill. You can't miss it.
BELOW: That's what they call it in the United States!

'I REALIZED WE HAD UNIQUE VARIETIES HELD OVER FROM AMERICA'S CIDER TRADITION — VARIETIES LIKE WINESAP, NORTHERN SPY, RHODE ISLAND GREENING AND BALDWIN WERE STILL GROWN WIDELY ACROSS THE STATE. I KNEW WE COULD MAKE GREAT CIDER FROM WHAT WE ALREADY HAD.'

# THE PACĪFĪC NORTHWEST

Wherever you go in the world of cider, comparisons with craft beer are never far away. Sometimes the comparison is illustrative and inspiring; other times it gets in the way of the full picture of what cider can be.

It's the dominant conversation in the Pacific Northwest, the region where cider is experiencing an off-kilter, hyperactive boom quite unlike anywhere else. This area was, and is still generally regarded as, the cradle of the craft-brewing revolution that has now swept the world. Everywhere you go, cider people tell you that right now it feels just like beer did 10 or 20 years ago. This is hardly surprising – and it's not just a lazy 'cider is the new beer' search for the next big thing. The conditions that gave rise to one are perfect for the next: namely, the place itself, and the people who choose to live here.

The Yakima Valley in north-east Washington State grows around three-quarters of all America's hops, which made the region a natural magnet for brewers. It also contains a third of all Washington's vineyards and is the second-largest premium wine producer in the United States and grows 65 per cent of all of America's apple crop.

The soil in this high desert valley is fertile and rich, but the mountains to the east, with dense rainforests on their western flanks, mean little precipitation falls on this side. Misty Douglas firs are instantly replaced by golden gorse and rough scrub as you cross into the valley.

But in the early 20th century, a great irrigation project drawing from the Yakima River opened up the valley to farming. There's one more hour of sunlight per day here than in California, and the annual growing season is longer. That means hops, grapes and apples grow bigger and bolder than they do elsewhere.

The Campbell Orchards have stood at the northern end of the valley since Craig Campbell's grandfather moved to the town of Tieton from a depressed Midwest in the 1920s. Craig began planting cider varieties in 2008, and now the Tieton Cider Works produces an astonishingly diverse array of ciders.

Which brings us to the other element that makes this region so extraordinary. In a country built upon the spirit of quest and adventure, the northwest is full of people who couldn't find what they were looking for anywhere else. As the last part of the US to be colonized, symbolically and practically, it is the home of mavericks, dreamers and creatives. The same sense of experimentation that created new beers styles here has inevitably inspired cider.

Tieton's range includes apricot cider, apple-cherry cider, ice cider, perry, cyser (a cyder/mead hybrid) and dry-hopped cider. The latter may sound like a terrible idea, and like many of Tieton's other products it would be – if it were in the wrong hands. But in the valley that grows all the hops as well as all the apples, it makes perfect sense.

Tieton's range is typical of the sense of wild experimentation in the northwest. This is a melting pot, where cider is the latest revelation to a population that takes its food and drink very seriously. 'Cider is popular because it's gluten-free, and in the northwest *everyone* is gluten-intolerant,' says Jenny Dorsey of the Northwest Cider Association, which currently boasts around 20 members. Both Jenny and her colleague, Dave White, came to cider from coffee, where they train baristas and judge international competitions. Cider may be new, but everyone making it has previous expertise: brewers, wine makers, orchardists and foodies all come together in a collegiate atmosphere to swap ideas and create a riot of cider innovation.

ABOVE & OPPOSITE: The Pacific Northwest combines the world's best cider bars with jaw-dropping valleys that grow most of America's apple crop.

'WE THOUGHT WE WERE
BRINGING BACK THIS
LOST FRONTIER DRINK,
AND THEN WE FOUND OUT
IT WAS STILL HERE.'

Some cider is gimmicky, and not all of it is good. But the urge to innovate is accompanied by a serious commitment to quality. A few hours' drive north from Tieton is East Wenatchee, way up in the high desert. Here, Snowdrift Cider Co has been making English-style cider and perry since 2008. In 2012, its products swept the board at an English cider competition, so its owners can be forgiven for thinking that they are perhaps transcending their influences.

'In the UK there's no irrigation system and not as much monitoring of nutrients and so on, so you get stressed trees,' argues Snowdrift's Peter Ringsrud. 'Up here we have much harder conditions, there's very little water and it evaporates quickly, so we have to manage the whole growing process much more carefully.'

The combination of tougher *terroir* and more careful management means that the fruit here is different. The northwest has moved on from making cider with eating apples and uses a mix of bittersweet and bittersharp French and English cider varieties, and 'heirloom' varieties descended from what the first European pioneers brought over. The sugar content is higher and the tannins softer than their Old World counterparts meaning northwest ciders have big but clean flavours.

The problem now is meeting demand. Apple trees take years to grow, and all around the northwest cider-apple varieties are being planted or grafted. Peter Mulligan of Bull Run Cider just outside Portland, Oregon, talks about 'a mad dash to fruit propagation' in the region – his own company has grafted 3000 trees in two years. 'If it takes five years, that's what it takes,' he says. 'But today people need something to help them feel that life is good, and there's an attraction in taking a raw product and making something of it.'

This idea that cider is part of 'The Good Life' is manifest out on the Olympic Peninsula, west of Seattle. Among the wineries and dairies, inns and cafés that constitute a burgeoning network of hippy-scented agri-tourism trails, cideries are popping up everywhere, each one evidently the fulfilment of someone's dream.

Bear and Nancy Bishop created an immaculate homestead and orchard hewn from a patch of virgin rainforest. Calling on his background as a forest firefighter, Bear keeps pests down while remaining fully certified organic by protecting the trunks of his trees and then taking a flamethrower to the ground beneath them – hence the name of his business, Alpenfire.

Just down the road, Keith and Crystie Kisler wanted to create a lifestyle that blended the wild and the human and linked them to the land. The farm came first, and then came Finnriver cider. 'We thought we were bringing back this lost frontier drink,' says Crystie, 'and then we found out it was still here.'

Washington State may be where all the apples grow, but Oregon, and Portland in particular, has the larger cider makers. This offbeat, out-of-kilter city remains the craft-beer capital of the world, and a city of food-and-drink obsessives more broadly. At the Portland Nursery's annual Apple Tasting, hundreds of people – young and old, families, couples and groups of friends – queue for hours to taste and evaluate endless tables of apple varieties. Local cider makers such as Wandering Aengus carefully list each variety that goes into their ciders on the bottle labels.

The rivalry between Portland and Seattle is a gentle one, but it spurs each to outpace the other. Most of the pubs in either city now stock at least one craft cider on tap, and bottle lists are growing. It would be undiplomatic of us to have an opinion on which city we think is best; they share a buzzing cider culture with great drinks at its heart.

One thing is for sure, though: just as it did in beer, the Pacific Northwest is destined to set the agenda in cider in years to come.

ABOVE: Harvest time at Tieton. All cider apples must be handpicked.
OPPOSITE, ABOVE: The Yakima Valley: fertile soil, long hours of sunshine and manmade irrigation create the perfect apple-growing conditions.
OPPOSITE, BELOW: Life is good out on the Olympic Peninsula, where locally made cider plays an important role in gastronomic tourism.

# THE ORCHARDĪST

## KEVĪN ZĪELĪNSKĪ, E.Z. ORCHARDS

'Apples are like your kids. You don't have to remember their names; you know who they are and when they're going to be troublesome.' Kevin Zielinkski paces between rows of trees, pointing out different varieties, taking apples and cutting into them, showing us the seed patterns, stroking their skins, paring slices and handing them around to taste. He explains which ones are doing well, which give him concern. Despite the incessant rain we are lucky to be here with Kevin during harvest season. The colours and aromas of fruit that's almost ready to pick make this his favourite time of year.

E.Z. Orchards has been a farm and orchard business since 1929, growing apples, pears and peaches. Zielinski is the third generation of orchardists on site, and in 2000 he was offered some scion wood of French cider-apple varieties. They yielded their first fruit in 2003, and he began experimenting with cider-making.

He was not to be rushed. Each year, he divided the juice four ways, and experimented with different yeasts and fermentation techniques. By 2007, he had a product he was happy with: a French-style cider fermented at low temperatures for five or six months, with no added yeasts, no sulphites and no pasteurization. Before fermentation, the fruit was placed in cold storage for several months, increasing the intensity of its flavour. He repeated the procedure the next year, applied for a commercial licence, and E.Z. Orchards launched its first vintage in 2009.

'I make cider in a slow way, using old methods, tried and true. It's part of a slower lifestyle, where things are not as rushed,' Zielinski tells us as we stand in a marquee on the edge of his orchards, huddled against the rain. This is where children come for their non-alcoholic cider and free doughnut after visiting the petting zoo and pick-your-own pumpkin patch just outside. E.Z. Orchards doesn't allow visitors to pick their own apples, however: 'It's too painful to see them yanking the fruit from my trees.'

Zielinski gives us a tutored tasting of the three vintages that exist so far. The 2011 is lively, structured and crisp, like a fine, dry Champagne, drinking far higher than its 6 per cent ABV. The 2010 has more evident fruit, but the crisp acidity at the end makes it very moreish. 2009 was a wetter season, a slower fermentation, and the resulting cider is richer, a buttery sweetness countered by slight musty farmyard and sour notes that remind us not only of aged Normandy cider but also Belgian Abbey ale.

Each is amazing, but in a different way, which lends total credence to applying the concept of vintages in the first place. 'The process is simple, but fruit is the most important thing. I'm an orchardist, the fruit is what I relate to the most,' says Zielinski. 'I want to see the apples shine through.'

Occasionally, music documentaries show some old footage of the Rolling Stones playing a 1964 British pop TV show, Jagger strutting and imperious, the whole band impossibly cool. Then B.B. King took the stage, and this imperious group transformed into young, wide-eyed fans, just like everyone else, sitting at the side of the stage and gazing up at one of the legends who first inspired them. Earlier we were with a bunch of young cider makers who were justifiably proud of their creations. But when Kevin Zielinkski's name was mentioned, they underwent the same transformation as the Stones before their idol. 'He's the man,' they each said. 'I'll never be able to make cider as good as he does.'

In the Pacific Northwest, Kevin Zielinkski is the cider maker's cider maker.

LEFT: Looks like wine, tastes like cider – very, very good cider.
OPPOSITE: Kevin Zielinski, at home.

**E.Z. Orchards**
5504 Hazel Green Rd
NE Salem, OR 97305
www.ezorchards.com

# THE ALADDIN'S CAVE
## BUSHWHACKER CIDER PUB

The original aim was simply to set up a cider-making facility in downtown Portland. That's why Jeff Smith, who had been making his own cider for a few years, saw nothing wrong with locating his new business in a nondescript industrial unit, a concrete oblong with a rolling glass shutter at one end.

But as he built his facility, Jeff was keenly aware that he was surrounded by craft breweries which, as a rule, included a tasting room where the public could come along and try the product on the premises. That seemed like a good idea, so he decided to do the same.

Smith strikes you as someone whose enthusiasms run riot, who is constantly thinking of the next thing. So, as soon as the tasting room was built, with its bar and tall, glass-fronted coolers, he decided it might be a good idea to sell other ciders, too. By late 2010, the tasting room at the Bushwhacker cidery had somehow mutated into modern America's first cider-only pub.

By 2012, Bushwhacker was stocking over 180 bottled ciders, with a constantly rotating selection of six on tap. Bushwhacker's own ciders are constantly represented, as is pretty much every other cider maker in the Pacific Northwest. But the range goes far beyond that.

'We're just starting to build the cider category here in the US,' says Smith, 'so I wanted to stock anything you can get in Oregon.' It's a testament to this adventurous melting pot that 'anything you can get in Oregon' is already by far the best selection of ciders from around the world that we've ever seen. The fridges are crowded with ciders from Normandy, Asturias and the Basque country that are not available anywhere in the UK. There's even a wide array of British ciders that you only see in Britain within a few miles of the places they are made.

It's all very reminiscent of what the craft-beer scene was like in Portland a decade ago, and Smith believes cider is the next logical step. 'People are getting tired of over-hopped beers. This is a genuine alternative, and it's not gimmicky. Well, most of it isn't,' adds the man who is smoking some of his apples in the Edelweiss Deli just across the parking lot.

Bushwhacker is certainly popular. In keeping with great cider pubs everywhere, the building is unfussy and simply decorated. Food is kept to a basic minimum of peanuts, potato chips and pickled eggs. There are two dartboards and regular live bands for entertainment. There's a tiny handful of beers if you look hard, but really, you only come here if you want to drink cider, and many people do – the bar is crowded every night.

'Many people underestimate cider,' says Smith, 'The palate is changing and Americans no longer just want the sweet commercial brands. That's why we've gone from stocking 34 to over 180 ciders in just two years.'

Our delight at experiencing the place is tempered by a hint of jealousy that Smith has managed to bring together the whole world of cider before we did. Bushwhacker's website boasts that it is 'the future of cider'. I would think this was a bold claim if I hadn't already written in my notebook, 'This is a bar from the future.'

'PEOPLE ARE GETTING TIRED OF OVER-HOPPED BEERS. THIS IS A GENUINE ALTERNATIVE, AND IT'S NOT GIMMICKY.'

OPPOSITE, ABOVE: The best selection of cider in the world? We haven't seen better...

OPPOSITE, BELOW: This selection has obviously met with the approval of the clientele.

**Bushwhacker Cider Pub**
1212-D SE Powell Blvd
Portland, OR 97202
www.bushwhacker.com

# UNĪTED STATES CIDER SUGGESTIONS

## 2 TOWNS CIDERHOUSE
Corvallis, Oregon
www.2townsciderhouse.com

**Serious Scrump** (11% ABV)

Described as a 'scrumpy-style' cider, it's actually much cleaner and less funky than traditional farmhouse cider. Made mostly with culinary apples, which give it a massive dessert fruitiness with a hint of bubblegum. Very drinkable, with hardly a trace of that hefty alcohol.

## ALBEMARLE CIDERWORKS
North Garden, Virginia
www.albemarleciderworks.com

**Old Virginia Winesap** (7% ABV)

Winesap is a colonial variety described in 1817 as 'one of our best cider fruits', creating a cider that is 'vinous, clear and strong'. Albemarle needed no further encouragement to create this single-varietial. Medium-sweet, spicy and floral with hints of honeysuckle and melon, a soft earthiness and a tart finish.

## ALMAR ORCHARDS
Flushing, Michigan
www.organicscrumpy.com

**JK's Scrumpy Hard Cider** (6% ABV)

Lightly carbonated with a strong aroma of apples laced with dates and figs. Dark orange, the sweet-apple taste reminds us of the cider lollies we used to get from the ice-cream van.

## ALPENFIRE ORCHARDS
Port Townsend, Washington
www.alpenfirecider.com

**Pirates Plank 'Bone Dry' Cider** (6.9% ABV)

Dubbed 'bold, brash, tannic, no-apologies cider' by its creators, who use English cider-apple varieties to create a scrumpy-style cider that is utterly, chalkily bone-dry.

**Glow Rosé Hard Cider** (6.8% ABV)

Described An apt name for an orange-red cider that really does seem to glow from within, thanks to Hidden Rose, the rare, red-fleshed fruit from which it is made. Soft, rich apple aromas. Soft tannin balances a sweetness slightly reminiscent of ice cider. A fascinating result from one apple variety.

## ANGRY ORCHARD CIDER COMPANY

Cincinnati, Ohio

www.angryorchard.com

### Crisp Apple (5% ABV)

One of the best of the more mass-market ciders. A blend of eating apples means it's much sweeter on the palate than most traditional ciders, but there's good, fresh, ripe-apple flavour and great drinkability.

## CARLTON CYDERWORKS

McMinnville, Oregon

www.carltoncyderworks.com

### Citizen (6.75% ABV)

Blended from over a dozen traditional cider apple varieties, including Kingston Black and Yarlington Mill, fermented to dryness and then sweetened slightly with organic cane sugar, it remains dry, tannic and astringent, with good earthy, apple flavours.

## CASTLE HILL CIDER

Keswick, Virginia

www.castlehillcider.com

### Celestial (8.6% ABV)

Made with traditional heirloom apples which give earthy, spice and citrus notes on the nose, a bone-dry, structured body and a bright, clean finish.

## CHAMPLAIN ORCHARDS

Shoreham, Vermont

www.champlainorchards.com

### Vermont Semi-Dry Hard Cider (6% ABV)

From an orchard that does everything you can possibly imagine with its apples, this flagship cider has lots of fruit, with citrus and honey notes balancing a sharp astringency.

## CLEAR CREEK DISTILLERY
Portland, Oregon
www.clearcreekdistillery.com

### Eau de Vie de Pomme
(40% ABV)

Made from Golden Delicious apples harvested in Oregon, then aged for at least eight years in French Limousin oak barrels, this is as far away from the rough 'applejack' of the Old West as you can get. Pale and delicate, with an incense-laced nose that combines the wood and apple perfectly. Gentle, smooth and seductive on the palate, North America's finest apple brandy.

## COLORADO CIDER COMPANY
Denver, Colorado
www.coloradocider.com

### Glider Cider (6.95% ABV)

Fermented dry with a touch of fresh juice added back to increase the fruit in the body, but still very crisp. Created by a disillusioned brewer, beer's loss is cider's gain.

## EAGLEMOUNT
Port Townsend, Washington
www.eaglemountwineandcider.com

### Quince Cider (8% ABV)

Quince are gnarly, ripped and hard to work with, the street-gang member of the fruit world. But tamed, and blended with apples, they create a cultured melange of fleshy, green, salty and spicy fruitiness. If you don't like quince jelly, don't worry – you'll love this.

### Perry (8% ABV)

It's easy to be sniffy about the idea of perry made from dessert fruit, but this blows away any preconceptions. Gentle carbonation, lightly sweet, and just a little buttery, it's gorgeous and seriously easy-going.

## EDEN ICE CIDER
West Charleston, Vermont
www.edenicecider.com

### Heirloom Blend (10% ABV)

Unlike most Canadian ice ciders, this is made with a blend of heirloom cider apples rather than culinary varieties. Sticky sweetness on the nose is joined by fresh acidity on the palate. Vibrant, young and fresh, yet has structure and elegance.

### Orleans Herbal
(15% ABV)

According to his wife, Eleanor, Albert Leger just can't stop tinkering. That's good, because it led to this intriguing apple wine: fresh-pressed cider is concentrated by the cold and then has *brettanomyces* yeast and a variety of herbs added to create an aperitif with a fresh, zingy aroma and dry, savoury palate. Perfect just as it is, over ice or in cocktails.

## EVE'S CIDERY
Van Etten, New York State
www.evescidery.com

### Bittersweet (10% ABV)

Created from a blend of French, English and American cider apples, this tries to be the best of all worlds and just about succeeds. Big, ripe-fruit aromas with suggestions of spice and butterscotch, then a palate that concentrates fruit, more dry spice, tannin and faint acidity.

## E.Z. ORCHARDS
Salem, Oregon
www.ezorchards.com

### Willamette Valley Cidre, 2010 Vintage (5.7% ABV)

Based on Normandy-style cider, this arguably surpasses its influences. Great fruit on the nose persists throughout with hints of jellied fruit, spiciness and earthiness, balanced by clean tannins, lifted by perfect soft carbonation, and rounded off by great acidity which makes it very moreish. One of the very best ciders in the United States – or anywhere else.

# FINNRIVER

Chimacum, Washington

www.finnriver.com

### Fire Barrel Cider

(6.9% ABV)

Made from bittersweet cider apples and then aged in Bourbon oak barrels. A sweet, spicy nose leads onto a caramel, candy-like sweetness entwined with notes of smoke, spice and vanilla. There's so much going on, it's a nice surprise when it finishes nice and dry.

### Spirited Apple Wine

(18.5% ABV)

This sweet cider is fortified with apple brandy to produce a seductive, sticky aperitif that manages to avoid being cloying, and has surprisingly little alcohol burn for its strength. They say it shows the sexy, sultry side of the apple. We say it's difficult to disagree.

# FOGGY RIDGE

Dugspur, Virginia

www.foggyridgecider.com

### Serious Cider (7% ABV)

A mixture of English and American cider varieties creates a trade-off of tannic dryness and sharp acidity. Crisp, refreshing and tart.

### Foggy Ridge's First Fruit (7% ABV)

A blend of heirloom apple varieties. Bright and slightly sweet with a refreshing, tart finish.

# ORIGINAL SIN

New York, New York

www.origsin.com

### Newtown Pippin

(6.7% ABV)

The favourite cider apple of both George Washington and Thomas Jefferson deserves its own single varietal. Here it makes a dry, clean, fruity, refreshing cider fit for a president.

## POVERTY LANE ORCHARDS AND FARNUM HILL CIDER

Lebanon, New Hampshire
www.povertylaneorchards.com

### Semi-Dry (7.4% ABV)

The most popular cider among Farnum Hill's range for those encountering cider for the first time. Balances crowd-pleasing, full-bodied fruit with dryness, complexity and a nice tart astringency.

### Kingston Black Reserve (8.5% ABV)

It's a little lazy simply to quote the tasting notes the cider maker gives, but when they come up with something like 'redolent of muskmelon, orange peel, flowers, bittersweet apple, romance', it's too good not to share. More neutral tasters agree that it's lightly spicy with apple-skin notes and is dry, finishing tart.

## REVEREND NAT'S HARD CIDER

Portland, Oregon
www.reverendnatshardcider.com

### Apricot Hard Cider

(6.9% ABV)

A great example of a combination that sounds like a gimmick that shouldn't succeed, but does so in style. Demonstrates that sometimes dry, fully fermented cider forms a beautiful cradle to hold other flavours.

## SLYBORO CIDERHOUSE

Granville, New York
www.slyboro.com

### Old Sin (8% ABV)

A blend of spicy Russet and floral McIntosh apples sweetened with a dash of ice cider creates a fruity but surprisingly dry refresher that's shockingly drinkable for its strength. The cider maker's favourite.

### Night Pasture (8% ABV)

Named after Slyboro's oldest orchard, where farmers grazed their livestock at the end of the day, this blend of eating- and cider-apple varieties is beautifully light and delicate, and very close to a crisp white wine. Begs to be served with fish.

## SNOWDRIFT CIDER CO

East Wenatchee,
Washington

www.snowdriftcider.com

### Orchard Select

(7-8.3% ABV)

The faintest funky whiff on the nose gives way to rich, deep, tropical-fruit flavours. A little sweet, a little sharp, yet still light and delicate, with nagging hints of pineapple pulling at the corners of your palate. Like a wedding breakfast on a Caribbean beach.

### Perry (7-8% ABV)

The best perry produced outside England, or even outside Herefordshire? Starts dry and astringent with a Champagne fizz, then develops layers of luscious fruit, with perfect touches of wood and tannin. Totally within the classic Herefordshire style, but cleaner and with more fruit. Outstanding.

## TANDEM CIDERS

Suttons Bay, Michigan

www.tandemciders.com

### Pretty Penny (5.5% ABV)

A blend of over 30 heirloom apples sounds like it might get muddled, but it works here: crisp and slightly sweet, and very moreish.

### Smackintosh (5% ABV)

Blend of McIntosh and heirloom varieties. Huge sweet aroma carries through to the palate, balanced by fresh tartness.

## TIETON CIDER WORKS

Tieton, Washington

www.tietonciderworks.com

### Apricot Cider (6.9% ABV)

The genius of this combination is that apricot skins are acidic, and therefore dry, even though the flesh is sweet, so it's a world away from cloying sickly commercial fruit ciders. Vivid apricot aroma on the nose carries through to good flavours of both fresh and dried apricot, with the sweetness balanced by a nice tartness.

### Yakima Valley Dry Hopped Cider (6.9% ABV)

It sounds like it shouldn't work, but boy, does it work! Unlike some other hopped ciders, the hops don't jump out like an uninvited guest. They blend completely to create a completely new drink with a sake-like dry minerality on the nose, followed by fruit that develops slowly and beautifully.

## UNCLE JOHN'S FRUIT HOUSE WINERY

St John's, Michigan
www.ujcidermill.com

### Hard Cider (6.5% ABV)

Crisp, appley and grapey, if the gentle pinprick of carbonation was any more assertive you might mistake this for Champagne. Subtle yet full-flavoured, a perfect aperitif or accompaniment to cheese.

### Apple Brandy (45% ABV)

Aged in a mix of American and French oak barrels, this brandy has subtle fruit on the nose and exceptional smoothness on the palate with hints of spice and leather, and a toasty oak finish.

## WANDERING AENGUS CIDERWORKS

Salem, Oregon
www.wanderingaengus.com

### Golden Russet Single Varietal (9.8% ABV)

A single-varietal made from Wandering Aengus's favourite heirloom apple, which is more than up to the job. A full-on nose with dollops of honey and a hint of farmyard character, with lots of fruit accompanied by strong, tart acidity.

### Wanderlust (7.5% ABV)

A semi-dry blend of Newtown Pippin, Golden Russet and 15 different heirloom varieties, there's a citrus aroma with notes of pear and lemon on the nose, followed by great fruit, a touch of caramel, a gentle but bright acidity and a lovely dryness at the end.

## WESTCOTT BAY

San Juan Island, Washington
www.westcottbaycider.com

### Traditional Dry (6.8% ABV)

Dry and crisp but with a hint of sweetness and great apple character. A firm favourite in North American cider awards.

## WEST COUNTY CIDER

Colrain, Massachusetts
www.westcountycider.com

### Pippin (5.5% ABV)

Cultivated from trees that were supposedly Yarlington Mill and Tremletts, the apples had an acidity that those varieties don't possess, leading Judith Moloney to believe they are nameless pippins grown from rootstock. They still make very fine cider: fermented to dryness with an acidity that just offsets it. It's a complex, yet very quenching cider.

### Baldwin (6.4% ABV)

Baldwin was a popular cider apple in the 18th century, and Judith Moloney rescued it from ancient, ivy-covered trees in a nearby abandoned orchard. Crisp, slightly sweet, firmly structured and very beautiful.

CANADA

# CANADA

With its cold climate and short growing season, Canada may not immediately strike you as an obvious centre of cider excellence.

But think about it: Canada has been shaped by Britain and France – two of the world's greatest cider-producing countries. This former colony has absorbed influences from both parent countries, and turned that chilly climate to its strong advantage.

Prohibition hit Canada just as it did the United States, but it was more fleeting. While it still damaged cider, some surviving domestic brands date back to the early 20th century, and these held their own for decades until the recent boom saw sales jump 55 per cent between 2005 and 2009 alone.

The bulk of the market consists of mass-market brands, both home-grown and imported. Strongbow is popular and Magners, poured over a glass full of ice, created a stir here just as it did in the UK. This proved very handy for mass-market domestic brands: many of these 'pub ciders' can be very sweet, and serving them over ice makes them more palatable to a wider audience.

One reason for the sweetness of mass-market brands is the type of apples they use. The vast majority of Canadian ciders are made from culinary apples. Varieties such as McIntosh (which computer firm Apple thought sounded kinda catchy), Empire, Spartan, Golden Delicious and Mutsu (also known as Crispin) are popular in school lunch boxes as well as in cider.

But there has been a dramatic growth in small, craft cider-making, too. Fermenting these apples fully produces stronger, more wine-like ciders with less cloying sweetness: a better balance with the crisp acidity many of these varieties possess and very little tannin.

Apples can grow all across Canada, but variations in climate mean they thrive on the coasts, along the Lawrence River and by the Great Lakes. Here, the growing season is a little longer, and there are more days of warmer temperatures than in the deep interior.

There are four major cider-making regions, similar to each other in some respects, but each with its own personality. Of all of them, Québec deserves special attention.

RIGHT: Domaine Pinnacle in midwinter – harvest time if you're growing the right sort of apples.

## Québec

While there are great ciders across Canada, Québec is the province that has grabbed the headlines. The first apple tree was planted in 1617, nine years after Québec City was founded. French settlers brought a strong Norman influence, and cider orchards were common by the end of the 17th century. The British conquest of 1760 halted cider's rise, as the British empire's trading policy favoured gin from England, whisky from Scotland and rum from the Caribbean. Beer from London's first industrialized breweries grew at cider's expense.

In 1807, *Le Canadien* newspaper argued that Québécois cider production should be encouraged, because it was 'superior or at least equal to that of Europe and the United States' and could help reduce the consumption of more harmful spirits. This concern with the damage caused by strong alcohol culminated a century later with Prohibition. In an 1898 national referendum, 51 per cent voted for Prohibition on a national level. Québec voted 81 per cent against. Fearful of upsetting the Québécois, the federal government allowed provinces to make their own decisions on this.

Québec was the last province to introduce Prohibition, in 1919. But it did so with a popular exemption for 'beers, ciders and light wines', which remained on sale. Then something extraordinary happened. Prohibition was hugely unpopular, and was repealed after just two years. A state monopoly, the Commission des Liqueurs de Québec, was established in 1921 to sell alcohol. But because of an administrative oversight, cider was not included in its remit. Bizarrely, as alcohol became legal, cider became technically illegal in Québec province.

It took 50 years for this bungle to be corrected, and cider was finally legalized in 1970. The Québécois were thirsty, and there was a liquid gold rush to bring cider to market. Unfortunately, this meant that the product was dire. The most famous brand, Grand Sec d'Orléans, evoked memories of Prohibition-era moonshine with TV ads that implied it had been made by gangsters. The taste confirmed this impression. Within 10 years an initial explosion of a million gallons per year plummeted to just 360,000.

Regulations surrounding food and drink in Québec are voluminous. There are two types of cider licence: artisanal and industrial. The 1970s ciders were industrial, and the first artisanal licences weren't granted until 1988. With a generation turned off cider seemingly for life, there was little interest in what they were doing.

And then, in the early 1990s, ice cider appeared. Here was an ultra-premium, desirable drink, completely new, and (arguably) exclusive to Québec. In the mid-noughties, when interest in cider began to take off more broadly, Québec had a unique angle.

There has been spectacular growth since. There are 600 apple growers in the province of Québec, and at least 65 artisanal cider makers. The Normandy influence is still there. With McIntosh and its descendants making up the vast majority of cider apples, even low-alcohol, carbonated 'pub ciders' feel closer in both body and spirit to wine than beer.

Some products, fully fermented, are genuinely almost indistinguishable from crisp white wines. Others have a decisive apple character, but an elegant cider of 9 to 11 per cent ABV, served in a wine bottle, from a *domaine* places us decisively in wine territory.

Québec can often be quite insular in its outlook. One cider maker, whose products are outstanding, proudly showed me a new thing he's been working on: a 5 per cent ABV, sparkling cider served in clear 330-ml bottles, designed to compete with beer. 'It won't taste like beer, though, because it's still cider, made from apples,' he explained patiently. 'But the idea is it will compete with beer.' He looked at me. 'What do you think? Is there perhaps a market for such a product?' 'I think there might be,' I replied. This insularity comes with a high degree of protectionism, designed to boost local food-and-drink production at the expense of multinational brands. Many are often frustrated by bureaucracy and red tape. But the policy has undoubtedly created a unique and precious food-and-drink culture in the province.

The regulations surrounding cider production are typical. Every aspect of style, definition, and production is carefully controlled. For example, if you want to sell cider in Québec, it must be made with 100 per cent juice from apples freshly picked at full maturity. Each time I express approval of this high standard to cider makers, they give me a look that says, 'But of course. How else could you possibly make cider?'

There is a strange quirk here as well, though. Traditional Québécois cuisine was formulated in the days of fur trappers, and typically has a high fat or lard content to help people get through the long, cold winter. The most common word people use to sum it up is 'dirty', always said with a sense of embarrassed satisfaction.

A typical example is *poutine*, a dish consisting of fries, cheese curds and gravy. The very name sounds like something that kills you softly, gently laying its head on your shoulder as it squeezes your heart. The Québécois are desperate to talk to foreigners about *poutine* because they want other people to understand and suffer, to loathe it as they do, and to find it as irresistible as they do. At *Au Pied de Cochon*, a Montreal restaurant where bookings must be made weeks in advance, men dressed as car mechanics serve a version of *poutine* topped with *foie gras*. It's dirty, greasy-spoon food done haute-cuisine style. And it pairs phenomenally well with a bright, vivid ice cider – a super-premium, sophisticated product at the top of most people's price range. When you taste them together, Québec makes perfect sense.

RIGHT: There's gold – and green and red, too – at the end of this Canadian rainbow.

## British Columbia

Cider has a long history in British Columbia, or 'BC'. The Growers Cider Company was established in 1927 to showcase Canadian wines and cider to the world. Mass-market brands can be dubious to the unsuspecting palate, with a lot of syrupy sweetness and sometimes not a lot of apple in the ingredients mix. But ciders from Vancouver Island's Merridale Estate, Sea Cider, and Duke's Cider from Kelowna's Tree Brewing take influences from Germany, France and especially the UK to create ciders that pay tribute to the originals. Heirloom-apple varieties such as Northern Spy, Winter Banana and Winesap have been rediscovered, and BC craft cider shares significant characteristics with Washington and Oregon over the border in the United States.

## Ontario

There's a real energy here, as demonstrated by the foundation of the Ontario Craft Cider Association in 2012. Cider is made mainly from culinary apples, but plenty of French and British bittersweets and bittersharps, such as the classic Yarlington Mill, Dabinett and Kingston Black, are now being propagated for blending. Grant Howes of County Cider says, 'The soil is quite Burgundian here, with lots of limestone. So the English apple varieties taste different, but the tannins are the same.'

## The Maritimes

Nova Scotia's Tideview Cider sits in a special microclimate. 'The high ridge of the North Mountain separates the Annapolis Valley from the Atlantic Ocean,' says cider maker John Brett. 'So we get a long, cool, gradual spring, warm summer and mild winter.' This creates perfect conditions for growing a wide variety of apples, and Brett believes the acidic soil gives them an extra bite you don't find elsewhere. These temperate conditions are common across Nova Scotia and New Brunswick, encouraging a host of cider start-ups over the last decade.

SPIRIT TREE

ESTATE CIDERY

www.spirittreecider.com

# ĪCE CĪDER/CĪDRE DE GLACE

Cider has always inspired inventiveness. The Normans were distilling it from at least the 15th century, the Spanish probably even earlier. Experiments with blending varieties are second nature to orchardists.

In the pioneer days in North America, cider was often 'freeze-distilled' to make a drink known as applejack. Water freezes before alcohol, so if cider is left out in the freezing cold, chunks of ice can be removed to leave behind a more concentrated liquor.

'This experiment I made satisfactorily the last winter,' wrote William Coxe in 1817, 'I can truly say that it was an excellent, vinous, strong, pure liquor... of twice the strength of good cider, and promises with age to improve to a high degree of strength and perfection.'

So you could say that ice cider is nothing new.

But you'd be wrong.

The difference between applejack and modern ice cider is that with the former, finished, fermented cider is concentrated. (In the wrong hands, this process can produce some pretty nasty alcohols.) Ice cider, meanwhile is made by concentrating the juice before fermentation. The differences in flavour and texture are dramatic.

The first ice cider was created in 1990 by Christian Barthomeuf, a French émigré who originally tried his hand at ice wine. German *Eiswein*, a dessert wine created by leaving grapes to freeze on the vine throughout winter, has a long history. The Inniskillin winery pioneered the technique in Ontario in 1989, and Barthomeuf, feeling that his adopted province did winter better than anywhere else, created Québec's first offering soon after. But while the Québec climate was perfect for the freezing part of the process, it wasn't that great for growing the grapes in the first place. So Barthomeuf decided to apply the same techniques to apples. In 1994 he worked with his neighbour François Pouliot to launch the first commercial ice cider.

Its popularity spread rapidly. As it did so, two quite different production methods emerged.

## Cryoconcentration

The most widespread method of ice-cider production involves ripe apples being picked in the autumn and kept in cold storage. At the end of December the fruit is pressed, and the fresh juice is stored outside in large containers. In temperatures averaging around −15°C, the water in the juice freezes, and clear striations of colour become visible as freezing water sits at the top, and a more concentrated 'must' – which remains liquid, thanks to its high sugar content – sinks. The bottom 20 to 25 per cent is extracted and fermented at low temperatures for up to eight months. The high sugar concentration gives

a liquid of between 8 and 12 per cent ABV that's still intensely sweet. But the process also produces higher concentrations of malic acid, which creates a wonderful balance in the finished cider that prevents it from ever becoming cloying. Ice ciders produced this way have an intense fruit character, bursting with fresh apple skins, with hints of tropical fruits such as mango and peach. 'Compote' is often used to describe the intense, fruity sweetness and acidity that combine to create a perfect alternative to dessert wine.

## Cryoextraction

The purest way of making ice cider is to find the rare apples that remain on the tree into the dead of winter. Québec is full of such forgotten varieties, sitting in people's gardens and by roadsides. With many, if they ever had names they were forgotten long ago. These apples invariably have a different character from domesticated culinary varieties, and there's an art to their blending. On the bough, the apples dehydrate in the sun, which naturally concentrates the sugar and acid just like cryoconcentration. But in addition, the elements 'cook' the apple. The frozen, shrivelled fruit is pressed in January and, again, ferments for up to eight months. The resulting ice cider has a similar fruit intensity to cryoconcentration, but resembles baked rather than fresh apples, and also offers deep caramel, hints of raisin, butterscotch and Madeira that somehow evoke dessert wine and barley wine simultaneously. These ciders are often referred to as *récolte d'hiver* ('winter harvest'), which is somewhat catchier than cryoextraction. Christian Barthomeuf argues that this is the only true ice cider.

The reaction from people drinking either for the first time is never less than extraordinary. Ice cider dazzles the palate. It's like drinking starlight. When I run tastings, people demand more, accusing me of lying when I say the tall, slim, half-bottle which emptied in moments was all I had. (To be fair, I *am* lying. I like to keep some back for myself.)

Québec has covered ice cider in rules and definitions. While these may not be tight enough for Barthomeuf, they're sufficient to keep Québécois ice cider distinct from the growing number of international imitations. The sugars in the juice must be concentrated to 30° Brix (percentage sugar by weight), and that concentration must happen naturally. 'There are only two ingredients in ice cider,' says François Pouliot, 'apples, and the

Canadian winter.' After fermentation the final product must have a residual sugar level of 130 grams per litre, and must be between 7 and 13 per cent ABV. There can be no added sweetness or other adjuncts. Not that you'd need them.

It's important that the integrity of what we might call the 'méthode québécois' is protected. But at the same time, it would seem a shame to deny the rest of the world these incredible flavours. So in this book we are drawing a distinction between Québécois products made with natural freezing, which we will call *cidre de glace*, and those made by freezing juice industrially, which we'll simply call 'ice cider'.

*Cidre de glace* doesn't come cheap – cryoconcentration or 'autumn harvest' variants start at $25 CAD per 375-ml bottle, and *récolte d'hiver* will often be almost double that. Given that there are up to 7 kg of apples in each tiny bottle, and that it takes a year to make, the price make sense.

In 2000 Christian Barthomeuf joined François Pouliot's main rival, Domaine Pinnacle. Pouliot's La Face Cachée de la Pomme and Domaine Pinnacle together account for around three-quarters of ice cider sales in Québec, with Domaine Pinnacle the larger of the two. This farm on the south-facing slopes of Mount Pinnacle dates back to 1859 and is rich in a drinks heritage that current owner Charles Crawford is adding to, pushing

ice cider in new directions. He was the first to create sparkling ice cider, with a gentle carbonation that enlivens the citrus, apple and caramel notes. He's blended ice cider and apple brandy to create Réserve 1859: a rich, caramelized *digestif* that tastes like sitting in front of a wood fire. And there's Coureur des Bois, which blends ice cider with maple syrup to create an aperitif liqueur that is surely the most Québécois product imaginable.

Christian Barthomeuf eventually left Domaine Pinnacle to set up his own place, Clos Saragnat, where he pursues his passion for obscure apple varieties and leaves the more commercial end of the market to the two businesses he helped create. His innovation has spawned an entirely new drinks category, with many variations he probably disapproves of. But *cidre de glace* has stunned critics and drinkers around the globe. When restaurants and wine writers who rave about it insist on calling it 'apple ice wine', you know a battle has been won, and the image of cider transformed.

ABOVE: The apples at Domaine Pinnacle, being 'cooked' in temperatures of minus 15°C.

IT'S LIKE
DRINKING
STARLIGHT.

# THE ĪCEMAN LA FACE CACHÉE DE LA POMME

François Pouliot does not claim to have invented ice cider. 'That was my mentor, M. Barthomeuf,' he says. But he played a huge role in developing it and popularizing it around the world.

Pouliot had a successful career directing music videos, but in his late twenties he wanted a change, and in 1989 – the year ice wine was first made in Québec – he decided to buy a farm and plant vines to make his own. He wanted to create something representative of the local *terroir* that he could take to film festivals, a product from home that he could proudly offer as an alternative to Champagne.

'I looked for land with orchards, and assumed that if apple trees grew there, the land must also be right for vines,' he says. 'I found this place. But M. Barthomeuf urged me not to cut down the apple trees.'

In 1994, Pouliot worked with Barthomeuf to create the first commercial *cidre de glace*. It was good enough to persuade him to keep the trees and forget about vines. When orders started to arrive from France, what began as a hobby quickly became much more serious. More trees were planted and leased from nearby farms.

Worried about the apples falling from the trees, Pouliot devised the cryoconcentration method of ice cider-making, picking the fruit and storing it until it froze in midwinter, then pressing it. But he clearly prefers the winter-harvest method, constantly searching, like his mentor, for apples that don't fall when winter arrives.

The quality of his ciders is beyond doubt. But Pouliot is also a brilliant marketer and salesman, a true showman. With his shaved head and designer facial hair, he looks far younger than his 50-something years, and the design sensibilities that made him a successful video director permeate the business. The designs for Neige, the core ice-cider brand, are stunning in their own right, making the bottle and its packaging as desirable as the liquid within.

The very name of the business (in English, 'the hidden face of the apple') is both a statement of intent and an invitation to be seduced. These are products that promise to reveal apples – and cider – in an entirely new light.

Pouliot is also very quick with a neat sound bite. When we taste *Neige Récolte d'hiver* together he says, as if unrehearsed, 'The apple that Eve tasted must have tasted like that.' I suspect he uses this line when he takes his products to international wine tastings and competitions. On tasting it, the world's leading wine critics say things like, 'I'm not gonna spit that one.' After one event, the head winemaker from Château d'Yquem approached him and offered a straight swap: a case of his own wine for a case of *Récolte d'hiver*.

The tasting room at La Face Cachée is packed with pictures, cuttings and menus from when visitors such as President Obama and Prince William and Kate Middleton were served *Neige* on state visits. It has also graced the wine lists of restaurants such as elBulli (Spain) and The Fat Duck (England).

He might not have time to visit film festivals any more. But François Pouliot has succeeded in creating a Québécois product that makes Champagne seem a little... *ordinary*.

PREVIOUS PAGE: *Cidre de glace* in its element: winter at La Face Cachée de la Pomme.
ABOVE: François Pouliot reaches for the stars.
OPPOSITE, ABOVE: La Face Cachée in its prime.
OPPOSITE, BELOW: It doesn't snow all the time.

**La Face Cachée de la Pomme**
617 Route 202,
Hemmingford (Québec), Canada J0L 1H0
**www.lafacecachee.com**

'I'M NOT GONNA
SPIT THAT ONE.'

# CANADA CIDER SUGGESTIONS

## ANTOLINO BRONGO
Saint-Joseph-du-Lac, Québec
www.antolinobrongo.com

### Cryomalus 2009 (9% ABV)

An object lesson in *terroir* and working with nature, guiding it to produce something it can't do on its own. Fruit compote with a hint of honey on the nose, followed by sweet, luxurious, honeyed richness on the palate. Served in 15 different Michelin-starred restaurants in Paris alone.

## CLOS SARAGNAT
Frelighsburg, Québec
www.saragnat.com

### L'original (10% ABV)

You'd expect the original ice cider to be pretty good, and there aren't enough words to describe the complexity and brilliance of everything that's going on here. Almost every sip evokes a fresh set of associations. Aromas of dried apple skins, caramel and a hint of maple wood, chewy and thick yet light and acidic, with suggestions of Sherry and Madeira.

## THE COUNTY CIDER COMPANY
Picton, Ontario
www.countycider.com

### Waupoos Premium (6.5% ABV)

Made with a blend of late-harvest and European cider apples. Billed as semi-sweet, but there is also sourness and a hint of grassiness on the nose. Crisp and nicely balanced, with a clean, refreshing finish.

## LA CIDRERIE CRYO
Mont-Saint-Hilaire, Québec
www.cidreriecryo.com

### Cryo de Glace Prestige (10% ABV)

Deep, dark, amber colour. Baked apples on the nose and then an explosion of flavour which offers cinnamon and caramel, intense sweetness that never becomes overbearing, and a hint of kiwi fruit towards the end.

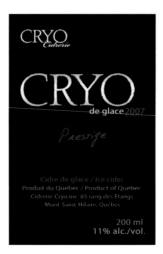

## DOMAINE LACROIX
Saint-Joseph-du-Lac, Québec
www.vergerlacroix.ca

### Le Lacroix Signature (10% ABV)

A perfect example of why the 'cryoconcentration' method of ice-cider production should be celebrated. Intensely fruity and vividly fresh, it may not have the complexity of winter-harvest varieties but it enchants and thrills the palate.

### Feu Sacré (16% ABV)

The sugar concentration is attained by boiling the juice over maple-wood fires rather than freezing, leading to a less complex product than ice cider, but one that is still worth investigating. Smooth and very sweet, a Sherry-like nose, with strong caramel and hints of vanilla and fruit. Warm and comforting.

## DOMAINE LAFRANCE
Saint-Joseph-du-Lac, Québec

www.lesvergerslafrance.com

### Jardin d'Éden (12% ABV)

Dry, lightly fruity and delicately fragrant, to an untrained palate this is indistinguishable from a Riesling-style white wine. That may not be to everyone's taste, but it's a stunning example of cider's diversity and range.

### Cuvée Lafrance Méthode Champenoise (11% ABV)

A *cidre fort* ('strong cider') made with eating apples and matured using the traditional *méthode champenoise* and Champagne yeast. Absolutely bone-dry, with a Champagne-style biscuit, appley aroma. A multiple award-winner.

## DOMAINE PINNACLE
Frelighsburg, Québec

www.domainepinnacle.com

### Verger Sud Cider (11% ABV)

A still cider made from the fruit of the southern orchard, this evokes summer lunchtimes. Very pale, fresh and crisp, minerally with good acidity. Has been known to fool wine tasters.

### Cidre de Glace (12% ABV)

Rich, gloopy, smooth and syrupy in the best-possible way. Something so luxurious should be sickly, but instead it's complex and incredibly balanced – a perfect harmony of sweetness and gentle acidity.

## DU MINOT
Hemmingford, Québec

www.duminot.com

### Crémant de Glace (7.5% ABV)

The intense sweetness of ice cider is balanced by a slight caramel note and the whole is utterly transformed by carbonation into something luxurious, sophisticated and vivacious. Sparkling ice cider really is an absurdly ingenious idea.

## LES ROY DE LA POMME
Saint-Georges, Québec

www.lesroydelapomme.com

### Clair de Lune (6.8% ABV)

Made with added strawberries and raspberries, whose flavours come through clearly on the nose and on the palate, where the sweetness is perfectly balanced by crisp apple acidity.

## LES VERGERS DE LA COLLINE
Sainte-Cécile-de-Milton, Québec

www.lesvergersdelacolline.com

### CID Original (5% ABV)

This notable ice-cider producer proves that it's also possible to raise the game in 'pub cider'. Made with McIntosh and Spartan apples, this is light and delicate, slightly perfumed, and gives local Irish pubs a sparkling, satisfying alternative to mass-market draught ciders.

## LA FACE CACHÉE DE LA POMME

Hemmingford, Québec

www.lafacecachee.com

### Neige Récolte d'Hiver (8% ABV)

One of the first winter-harvest *cidres de glace*, and one of the very best. The aroma has less apple than its counterpart, but is richer and fruitier. On the palate, it's smooth, mature, spirituous, with hints of dates and figs.

### Dégel (12% ABV)

When the 'must' that will become *cidre de glace* separates, only the bottom 20 per cent is used. So François Pouliot decided to see if he could do anything with the next 20 per cent. The result is an apple wine that has echoes of *cidre de glace* without the same intensity. Loaded with apple skins and apricots, it's zingy, crisp and fresh with a long, clean finish.

## LEDUC-PIEDIMONTE

Rougemont, Québec

www.leduc-piedimonte.com

### McKeown Draft (6% ABV)

The McIntosh apple in this quenching cider gives it an unmistakable apple-juice character. If it were not for this, the slight note of incense on the nose, citrus character, fruity body and clean, dry finish would make it indistinguishable from an acidic white wine. Not bad for a 'pub cider'.

### La Brunante (8% ABV)

The same base cider as McKeown draft is dosed with ice cider and served Champagne-style. So you get a crisp dryness weaving around ice cider's confit fruit, all enlivened by *méthode champenoise* bubbles. There are no real points of reference for this hugely exciting combination.

## MICHEL JODOIN

Rougemont, Québec

www.micheljodoin.ca

### Cidre Rosé Mousseux (7% ABV)

Made with 100% Geneva apples which have red flesh giving a perfectly natural shimmering pink cider. Complex floral and berry aromas, with a gentle apple and berry sweetness and firm acidity on the palate.

## SEA CIDER FARM AND CIDERHOUSE

Saanichton, British Columbia

www.seacider.ca

### Rumrunner (12% ABV)

Home-grown heirloom varieties are hand-pressed then fermented in rum barrels. The result is a great balance of sweet, dry and acid accompanied by warming woody, nutty and caramel notes.

### Pippins (9.5% ABV)

Newtown Pippin apples add structure to a blend of other heirloom varieties for a cider that has everything: sweet-and-sour fruit on the nose with a slight hint of funk, great apple and citrus flavours with a chalky dryness and crisp, acidic finish.

## SPIRIT TREE ESTATE CIDERY
Caledon, Ontario
www.spirittreecider.com

### Traditional Pub Cider
(6% ABV)

A faithful re-creation of a West Country-style scrumpy, up to the point where it is gently carbonated. There's a characteristic farmyard funkiness here complementing a perfect balance of sweet and dry, but the overall effect is still light enough to welcome anyone more accustomed to mass-market offerings. A cleverly judged stepping-stone to more complex offerings.

## TIDEVIEW
Anapolis, Nova Scotia
www.tideviewcider.ca

### Heritage Semi-Dry
(8% ABV)

Sparkling and pale gold, the pour immediately suggests quality fizz. There's sweet apple upfront with a hint of peach, followed by juicy acidity, a touch of earthiness and a dry finish, all delivered with seductive, Champagne-style mousse.

## TWIN PINES ORCHARDS & CIDER HOUSE
Thedford, Ontario
www.twinpinesorchards.com

### Cyser (11.2% ABV)

Cyser, a fermentation of apples and honey, is popular in North America but is in fact a re-creation of an ancient Mediterranean drink. When all that sugar ferments to dryness you get a high level of alcohol, a subtle, earthy aroma and a palate that has mead notes but is dry and clean overall.

## UNION LIBRE
Dunham, Québec
www.unionlibre.com

### Cidre de Feu (15.5% ABV)

Not an ice cider, but a similar product made in a very different way. Deep amber, with aromas of honey, baked apple and sweet fruit with hints of honey and walnut. On the palate it's smooth, sweet, seductive and caramel-laced.

### Cidre Apéritif (16.5% ABV)

Another pioneering *cidre de feu*, with a complex fruit nose and big, juicy fruit compote on the palate.

# ARGENTĪNA AND CHĪLE

# ARGENTĪNA

'What you should know is that the Argies are a very sociable people,' says my friend Julia Mazarro excitedly. 'Most of us have Italian and Spanish blood, as well as a bit of Irish mixed in with everything else. We will *always* find an excuse to get together and celebrate.' And when Argentinians celebrate, they drink enough cider to make their country one of the world's five largest cider-drinking nations by volume.

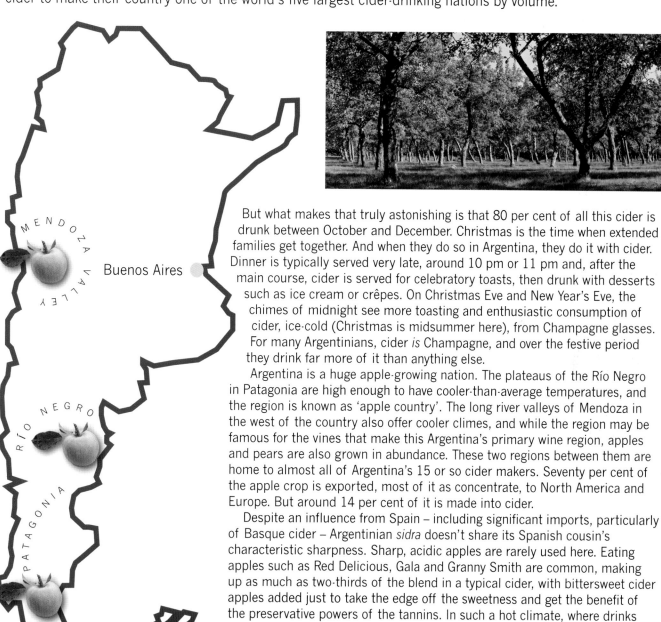

But what makes that truly astonishing is that 80 per cent of all this cider is drunk between October and December. Christmas is the time when extended families get together. And when they do so in Argentina, they do it with cider. Dinner is typically served very late, around 10 pm or 11 pm and, after the main course, cider is served for celebratory toasts, then drunk with desserts such as ice cream or crêpes. On Christmas Eve and New Year's Eve, the chimes of midnight see more toasting and enthusiastic consumption of cider, ice-cold (Christmas is midsummer here), from Champagne glasses. For many Argentinians, cider *is* Champagne, and over the festive period they drink far more of it than anything else.

Argentina is a huge apple-growing nation. The plateaus of the Río Negro in Patagonia are high enough to have cooler-than-average temperatures, and the region is known as 'apple country'. The long river valleys of Mendoza in the west of the country also offer cooler climes, and while the region may be famous for the vines that make this Argentina's primary wine region, apples and pears are also grown in abundance. These two regions between them are home to almost all of Argentina's 15 or so cider makers. Seventy per cent of the apple crop is exported, most of it as concentrate, to North America and Europe. But around 14 per cent of it is made into cider.

Despite an influence from Spain – including significant imports, particularly of Basque cider – Argentinian *sidra* doesn't share its Spanish cousin's characteristic sharpness. Sharp, acidic apples are rarely used here. Eating apples such as Red Delicious, Gala and Granny Smith are common, making up as much as two-thirds of the blend in a typical cider, with bittersweet cider apples added just to take the edge off the sweetness and get the benefit of the preservative powers of the tannins. In such a hot climate, where drinks are consumed so cold, sweetness is the order of the day. Cider is normally served sparkling – mainstream *sidra* is carbonated, while *sidra natural* is bottle-conditioned and naturally sparkling.

ABOVE: In a hot country, the high plateaus still provide perfect apple-growing *terroir*.

The only problem with having such a strong association with one particular time of year is that it can seem a bit odd to drink cider the rest of the time. 'Most times when we find something to celebrate we do so with cider,' says Julia, a fan of both beer and cider. But ask for a cider in a bar during the rest of the year and you'll get a strange look. Increasingly, cider is also seen as a downmarket drink – when the economy is doing well, people switch to Champagne instead, and lately beer and wine have stolen some of cider's thunder.

That's why the biggest producers are giving cider a makeover: on the one hand trying to play up its similarity to wine and on the other borrowing from cider's European renaissance and launching new products in 330-ml and 660-ml bottles as well as the old, established Champagne-style bottles. Slicker labels, and the *de rigueur* pour over ice, are being pushed by TV campaigns at the expense of the slightly dated wine-style label and gold-foil look.

For the moment, Argentina, along with France, remains one of the few countries in the world where cider is seen as something that's going out of fashion rather than coming back in. This may well change, given current efforts, but for the time being, cider makers here must sometimes wish it could be Christmas every day.

## SÁENZ BRIONES
Buenos Aires
**www.saenzbriones.com.ar**

The clear market leader in Argentina, offering a full range of products from traditional Champagne-lite-style ciders to more modern, recent launches – this is the company trying to revive cider and make it a year-round product.

**Gran Sidra Real Etiqueta Negra** (No ABV)

Sweet and light, with rich fruit aromas and slight hints of tannin and acidity.

## SIDRA CORTESÍA
Uco Valley, Mendoza
**www.sidracortesia.com**

**Cortesía Silver Cider**
(4% ABV)

Made with Red Delicious, Granny Smith and Royal Gala apples, sweet and delicate, with an intense apple aroma.

## THE GIBRALTAR BAR
Perú 895, San Telmo
Buenos Aires
**www.thegibraltarbar.com**

**Griffin Dry** (4.9% ABV)

A favourite pub with expats and travellers, a few years ago it enlisted the help of a Mendoza cider maker to create its own cider more in line with British tastes. Still on the sweet side, but significantly crisper and drier than the Argentinian style.

# CHĪLE

In the same way as Argentina, Chile remembers its Spanish links – and cider's popularity is evidence of this.

Santiago

LOS LAGOS

Apples are grown on family estates, harvested in March and April and made into cider in large facilities, such as the following.

**Gran Sidra Antillanca** (www.sidrantillanca.cl) in the Los Lagos region, proudly proclaims itself to be the southernmost cider in the world.

**Sidra Punucapa** (www.punucapa.cl) is in Chile's major apple-growing region where cider is one of the main products in the economy, and has grown from being a craft producer into a major supplier of Champagne-style cider for the festive holidays.

# AUSTRALIA AND NEW ZEALAND

# AUSTRALIA AND NEW ZEALAND

In our ever-shrinking world, it doesn't take long for the shock waves from an explosion in one country to travel to the other side of the planet. The cider-mania ignited by the 2006 'over ice' sensation in the UK hit Australia and New Zealand within the following 12 months. Since 2008, cider has grown (from an admittedly small base) by around 40 per cent every year. Market analysts reckon per capita cider drinking in Australasia will overtake Western Europe by 2015. In a region where sales of alcohol overall are stagnating, cider is leaving all other alcoholic drinks standing.

Apart from capturing the imagination of drinkers famous for their love of ice-cold drinks in very hot weather, cider appeals to producers because of a very favourable duty rate compared to other drinks. So with beer drinking at its lowest ebb for 60 years, brewers large and small are jumping into cider with both feet.

The biggest ciders in Australia are Strongbow, Bulmers and Mercury, all owned by Carlton & United Breweries. But in the last few years they've been joined by new launches from very respected craft-beer brewers. Sydney brewer James Squire has launched Orchard Crush; Tasmania's Little Creatures has Pipsqueak Cider; and Matilda Bay (also owned by Carlton) is doing very well with the charmingly named Dirty Granny (made with Granny Smith apples, see?) Wine writer and hobbyist cider maker Max Allen found 80 cider makers in production in Australia in 2012: up from 40 in 2011. The market in New Zealand is also buoyant, growing by over 10 per cent a year.

But there's a growing frustration among drinks writers and cider aficionados that among that impressive number, few are making what they call 'real' cider. Most of them (even the micro-brewers) are making cider with apple concentrate, water and sugar, even as they then wrap these products in homespun, natural imagery replete with descriptions such as 'genuine' and 'handcrafted'. Even more annoying is that, riding a trend

that's all about a love of locally sourced produce, much of the concentrate is imported from as far away as China.

Within this booming cider market, craft producers who make cider from freshly pressed apples are still in their infancy. But they are ambitious and keen to grow. In 2011, a group of artisanal cider makers came together to form Cider Australia, a new trade body that seeks to champion 'real' cider and educate people about what it is, and why it's different. In New Zealand, the Fruit

OPPOSITE, ABOVE: Cider is a sociable business for Tasmania's William Smith & Sons.
OPPOSITE, BELOW: Father Ian and son Andrew carry on a family business founded by William Smith in 1888.

Winemakers Association, founded in 1985, has now become the Fruit Wine and Cider Makers of New Zealand.

Their definition of 'real cider' here is refreshingly straightforward compared to the more convoluted ideas suggested in the UK. A product made from apple concentrate, sugar and water is not real cider. A product made with freshly pressed apple or pear juice, with as few additional ingredients as possible, is.

'Educating drinkers and changing perceptions of what cider is remain the big challenges,' says Coady Buckley of Melbourne's Ciderhaus, a bar promoting authentic German-style *Apfelwein*. 'There is very little real cider fruit in Australia or New Zealand, at least on a commercial scale. The vast majority of products are sweetened artificially.'

Many cider makers have struggled to persuade people that true cider should be dry and crisp rather than alcopop-sweet. But to help this process, Cider Australia has instituted an annual cider competition, open to all

cider makers. This has received a good response and plenty of coverage over its first few years. After the 2012 awards, the organizers told the press that it was as much about the future of Australian cider as the present, and aimed to identify an 'Australian style' of cider that could ultimately be exported.

We already have a few clues as to what that Australian-style cider might be like. Cider in Australia and New Zealand has a longer history than many people realize. Cider maker and author Tony Thorogood has found records of a Reverend Samuel Marsden writing about making cider in Parramatta, New South Wales, in 1803. Cider was also being made on Tasmania's east coast in the 1820s. Many gold-rush areas also happened to be good apple-growing areas, and there are various accounts of cider being made, often by crude mortar-and-pestle methods, to slake the thirst of miners throughout the 19th century. The mid-20th century saw brands such as Kellybrook and Mac's Cider occasionally rival beer in popularity, and many apple-farming areas such as Orange and Batlow in New South Wales had semi-official cider-making operations catering for private customers. Some

boasted examples of fine Champagne-style ciders, but the easy commerciality of Strongbow eventually won out everywhere and Australian cider was dumbed down.

New South Wales and Tasmania, and the districts of Hawke's Bay, Nelson and Central Otago in New Zealand, are all famous apple-growing regions, with the mild climate and thin, granite soil that apple trees love, and much fruit is produced for export. But this fruit has to be perfect, free from blemishes. This leaves a lot of unsellable fruit that can be turned into cider.

Many of these districts are also renowned for their wine, and it is wine makers who are leading the charge into craft cider that's a little more characterful than the breweries' products. They bring a wine maker's sensibility to cider, using precise controls and cultured yeasts to turn eating and cooking apples such as Pink Lady, Granny Smith and Golden Delicious into crisp, refreshing ciders balancing sweetness with an edge of acidity that are perfectly suited to the local climate.

There are many cider fans who, while enjoying these products, also yearn for something with the tannic structure and funky buzz of English or Normandy styles. Over 35 true cider-apple varieties have been identified in Australia and New Zealand, including legends such as Kingston Black, Yarlington Mill and Bulmer's Norman. Their presence supports the claim of a long cider-making tradition Down Under, but they remain in tiny quantities.

'What's really interesting about these varieties is that they behave very differently here than in their land of origin,' says Coady Buckley. In Victoria's beautifully lush Harcourt Valley, an hour's drive north of Melbourne, Drew Henry has been making cider mainly with eating apples since the mid-1990s. But his small collection of Kingston Blacks grow so large and full of juice that he claims they produce a cider that can ferment to 11 or 12 per cent ABV in some years – way more than any apple could produce unassisted in the UK.

As in various other New World countries, there's a race now to propagate more cider fruit alongside the drive to educate drinkers on what real cider is. But our prediction, based on who is making it, and what the fruit is like, and the culture it exists within, is that Australian and New Zealand cider will develop along similar lines to that of New England in the United States: big and wine-like, crisp and refreshing, and increasing in complexity as new apple varieties are nurtured and explored. We can't wait.

ABOVE: Clive and Lynne from Red Sails checking ripeness.

# AUSTRALIA AND NEW ZEALAND CIDER SUGGESTIONS

### BRESS
Harcourt Valley, Victoria
www.bress.com.au

**Harcourt Valley Cider Bon Bon** (10% ABV)

The high-strength and crisp, acidic, wine-like character betrays Bress's roots and influences. But be warned: this crisp, refreshing cider goes down much quicker than wine.

**Harcourt Valley Cider Brut** (10% ABV)

A blend of 85% cider apples and 15% perry pears. Tangy apple-skin aromas and a fresh, sweet, clean taste.

### HENRY OF HARCOURT
Harcourt, Victoria
www.henrycider.com

**Duck & Bull** (9% ABV)

Bottle-conditioned, and one of the few Australian ciders genuinely made with cider apples, including Kingston Black and Yarlington Mill, by one of the pioneers of Australian cider. Tart, dry and crisp.

### KANGAROO ISLAND CIDERS
Kangaroo Island, South Australia
**No website**

**Colony Cove** (5.4% ABV)

Medium-dry and slightly cloudy, combining crispness with full, ripe, apple flavours.

### LOBO
Lenswood, South Australia
www.loboapple.com

**The Royale** (4.2% ABV)

Bottle-conditioned and matured for six months, with full, spiced-apple aromas and rich fruit flavours given structure by firm tannin.

### NAPOLEONE & CO CIDER
Coldstream, Victoria
www.napoleonecider.com.au

**Methode Traditionnelle Pear Cider** (5.4% ABV)

The Australian climate seems to suit pears particularly well, and this perry has been named Australia's best. Bottle-conditioned, citrusy, floral and fresh, with a full sweetness on the palate.

**Methode Traditionnelle Apple Cider** (5% ABV)

Bottle-conditioned, made with a blend of Australian eating apples. Perfumed and aromatic, with good sweetness and just a hint of soft tannin.

## NATURAL SELECTION THEORY
Adelaide Hills, South Australia
www.naturalselectiontheory.com/cider

### Apple Cider (7.2% ABV)

Fully organic and fermented with wild yeast, this is cloudy and full-bodied but surprisingly well-balanced, with gentle acidity and soft tannin.

## PECKHAM'S
Moutare Valley, New Zealand
www.peckhams.co.nz

### English Apple (5.8% ABV)

Deep orange and full-bodied, beginning sweet and then developing an assertive tartness.

## RED SAILS
Middleton, Tasmania
www.redsails.com.au

### Cider Gold (6.5% ABV)

Bottle-conditioned and naturally fermented Breton-style cider. Rich apple and honey aroma, full, dry, rich fruit flavour followed by a sensationally smooth and clean finish.

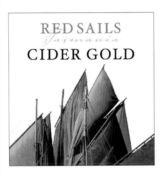

## ST. RONANS
Yarra Valley, Victoria
www.stronanscider.com.au

### Méthode Traditionelle Pear Cider (7% ABV)

A gold medal-winner at the 2012 Australian Cider Awards. Produced using the *méthode traditionelle*, with a light sweetness, spicy floral notes and a very slight funk.

## SEVEN OAKS CIDER
Mornington Peninsula, Victoria
**No website**

### Seven Oaks Sweet Champagne Farmhouse Cider (12% ABV)

Bottle-conditioned and using traditional cider apples. Lots of ripe apple-skin taste, rich sweetness, wonderfully complete and round.

## SEVEN SHEDS
Railton, Tasmania
www.sevensheds.com

### Sparkling Dry Cider (8.1% ABV)

Uses traditional cider varieties, including Yarlington Mill, Bulmer's Norman and Kingston Black, to create a pale, cloudy and very dry sparkling cider, with a great food-friendly edge of tart bitterness.

## SMALL ACRES CYDER
Orange, New South Wales
www.smallacrescyder.com.au

### Sparkling Perry (7.5% ABV)

Bottle-fermented, pear aromas with a hint of leather. Surprisingly tart before the sweetness develops, followed by a clean, crisp, medium-dry finish.

### Pomona Ice (8.5% ABV)

Rich, sweet-apple flavours and aromas with a citrusy zing, and clean and crisp finish. Less heavy than Quebec ice ciders, which makes it a perfect aperitif in this warmer climate.

### Somerset Still (7% ABV)

As the name suggests, a decent take on British West Country scrumpy, featuring earthy, green-apple flavours with lots of tannin and acid laced through the fruit, and a crisp, dry finish.

## TOWNSHEND BREWERY
Upper Moutare, New Zealand
www.townshendbrewery.co.nz

### Sitbee Cider (5.8% ABV)

English-style cider, naturally fermented and pale gold in colour. Dry and gently sparkling.

## THE TWO METRE TALL COMPANY
Hayes, Tasmania
www.2mt.com.au

### Poire (7% ABV)

Cloudy perry with intensely concentrated and farmhouse-style tangy pear flavour, and a rich but dry-finishing pear-juicy texture.

## WILLIE SMITHS
Huon Valley, Tasmania
www.williesmiths.com.au

### Organic Apple Cider (5.4% ABV)

Fully organic and inspired by French-style cider. Deep orange; juicy citrus-fruit aromas with hints of wood and earth, and then a surprisingly fruity, not-too-heavy body with a clean, crisp finish.

## ZEFFER BREWING CO
Matakana, New Zealand
www.zeffer.co.nz

### Slack Ma Girdle (7% ABV)

Sweet apple, honey and tropical fruit on the nose, then full-bodied, tart-apple flavour with hints of citrus and spice and a dry finish.

# REST OF
# WORLD

# REST OF WORLD

From its beginnings along the northeast Atlantic seaboard, cider spread to the New World with the colonial ambitions of each of the three great cider-making nations: Britain, France and Spain.

From this axis, cider is now spreading around the world, but, in most of the places we haven't yet covered, the market is tiny and dominated by the types of mainstream brands we've already described in their home countries.

Some countries are worth noting simply because within a few years they will be very big cider markets. Others, meanwhile, are starting to create fascinating new traditions of their own.

We haven't gone into as much detail here, and some of the products, while worth noting, don't yet make the cut as great ciders. In other cases, we simply haven't been able to get hold of the ciders for this book – but hope to for the next edition.

## SOUTH AFRICA

The world of cider is full of paradoxes, surprises and misunderstandings, and South Africa is a perfect example of this.

In the second-largest cider market in the world after the UK, 'cider' doesn't even exist as a specifically defined drink. In one of the world's largest apple-growing countries, there are no cider varieties grown. And, although cider has only been commercially available since the 1980s, the two main brands – Hunter's and Savanna, both owned by the same company, Distell – produce almost nine out of 10 ciders drunk in South Africa, and are the second- and third-largest brands in the world, respectively, after Bulmers of Great Britain. And somehow, somewhat improbably (and yet also somewhat inevitably), some interesting craft-cider producers are starting to emerge.

The drinks that industry experts call flavoured alcoholic beverages (FABs) and everyone else calls 'alcopops' are huge in South Africa, partly because cider is classed as one – Hunter's and Savanna are the second- and fourth-largest brands in the South African alcopops market. This means producers can legally use anything they like (within reason) and call a drink cider, because there is no separate regulatory definition of what cider is.

Despite the enormous freedom this provides, Savanna and Hunter's aren't too bad compared to some mass-market brands elsewhere. They proudly claim to be 'real cider' because they are made from fermented apples (even though they use some concentrated juice), as opposed to various cheaper malt-based beverages that try to pass themselves off as cider. They taste a bit bubblegummy and artificial, but they are dry and crisp when they could be excessively sweet. And they're spearheading a cider market that's in healthy growth – much more so than drinks generally here. Hunter's first launched in 1988 and Savanna in 1996, so their rise to fame has been undeniably impressive.

Both brands source their apples from the Elgin Valley in the Western Cape, known internationally as the place 'where the apples come from', and home to the famous (or infamous, depending on your point of view) soft drink Appletiser. Its rolling green hills teem with orchards, vineyards and olive groves, and supply 60 per cent of South Africa's apple crop.

Some of the fledgling craft-cider producers here were orchardists who turned to cider as a way to use windfalls, in a market where apples with blemishes are worthless. Others were wine makers who saw the abundance of fruit surrounding them and came to an obvious conclusion.

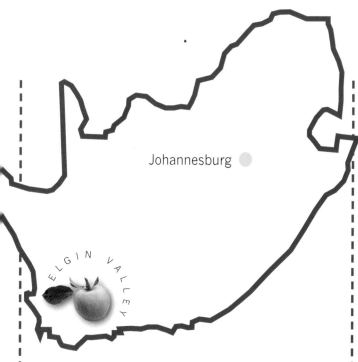

ELGIN VALLEY

Johannesburg

With no bittersweet cider apples to speak of, they're exploring the balance of sweetness and acidity in dessert and culinary apples such as Golden Delicious and Granny Smith, and finding just enough tannin in sweet varieties such as Braeburn and Rokewood. Fermentation and production techniques are heavily influenced by wineries. Natural yeast is separated, and wine yeasts are added for a clean fermentation in stainless-steel tanks – though some are experimenting with wooden barrels.

William Everson began making cider in 2009. He ferments his cider in large stainless-steel tanks with oak staves in the bottom, and leaves it to mature on the wood and the lees to let it soften before carbonating and bottling. His product is already being sold in some of the top bars and restaurants across Cape Town.

'I've had many a visitor from the UK, Ireland, France and the USA saying it's the nearest they have tasted to real ciders in Europe,' he tells us proudly.

So is he optimistic about cider in South Africa? 'It's currently very small. It's difficult trying to get people to try "real" cider for the first time in South Africa,' he says. 'I'd love to start some kind of craft-cider association, but we're still in the process of developing our own website. But I do look to beer for inspiration. A year ago, there were five craft or micro-brewers in South Africa. Now there are 25!'

With South Africa's fondness for apple-based drinks, it can only be a matter of time until cider follows suit.

ABOVE, RIGHT: The stunning Elgin Valley in the Western Cape, home of South Africa's orchards.
BELOW, RIGHT: Harvest time at Poplar Grove Farm, Villiersdorp.

# SOUTH AFRICA CIDER SUGGESTIONS

### ASH CREEK FARMS
Maluti, Eastern Free State

www.ashcreekfarms.com

www.redstonecider.co.za

**Red Stone Cider**
(4.5% ABV)

Natalie Meyer learned how to make cider from the internet as a way of using up all the apples on her farm. Extensive trial and error has produced a light, refreshing cider with nice fresh acidity that continues to improve.

### TERRA MADRE
Elgin, Western Cape
**No website**

**Terra Madre Pommes Classique** (8.7% ABV)

A bottle-conditioned Normandy-style cider that aims to rival Champagne and created an instant buzz after its 2011 launch. Big apple aromas with a funky hint, solid body and a long, dry finish.

### THE DRIFT FARM
The Drift Farm, PO Box 55, Napier, 7270, Western Cape

www.thedrift.co.za

**James Mitchell Gone Fishing Cider** (5.8% ABV)

This family-owned farm is more famous for its heirloom vegetables, but cider maker Mark Stanford wanted to create something that recalled the stuff made by his great-grandfather, after whom the cider is named. English in style, it's sweet and tart, with flavours of wood and apple skins, and a crisp, refreshing finish.

### WILLIAM EVERSON WINES
Klipkop, Grabouw 7100, Western Cape

www.eversonscider.com

**Everson's Cider** (8% ABV)

*Garagiste* wine maker William started to experiment with cider in 2009. A blend of five culinary and dessert apples and ageing on wood staves has produced a light but structured cider with good apple and some wood on the nose, soft acidity and a long, dry finish.

### WINDERMERE FARM
Grabouw, Western Cape

www.windermerecider.co.za

**Windermere Cider**
(7.5% ABV)

After importing and grafting a few European bittersweet varieties, Windermere originally began selling cider in the mid-1990s, but found South Africa 'wasn't ready' for a cider in this style. They started again in 2012 with a cider styled after German *Apfelwein*, which is light and fruity with fresh, green aromas.

# REST OF WORLD CIDER SUGGESTIONS

### CHINA

China is the world's largest exporter of apples, much of which ends up as concentrate being used by the big western cider brands. So it's inevitable that as the economy explodes, cider shows steady year-on-year growth. Cider is drunk at business meetings, weddings and banquets, and is hailed for its health and digestive benefits. **Changyu Pioneer Wine Co** (www.changyu.com.cn) has over half the domestic market with its Changyu Sparkling Cider.

### INDIA

As the Indian economy grows, people are looking for new and interesting products, and they look to what's happening in the West. In 2007 the Green Valley cider company launched India's first cider, **Tempest** (www.tempestcider.com), which is made in the cooler climate of the Shimla Hills. Cider is sold heavily on its health benefits here, with Green Valley claiming that it is 'wholesome for our bodies', a remedy against kidney stones and rheumatism.

### JAPAN

Japan may seem like one of the more surprising countries to be producing cider, and it is certainly a very young drink here, being made in small volumes. But the best ciders are some of the most intriguing and enjoyable we've tasted. There's often a sake-like hint to them and they are best thought of as apple wines.

### MASHINO WINERY

Mashino Matsukawa, Nagano Prefecture

www.mashinowine.com

**Apple Wine** (10% ABV)

Very pale and clear, with sake's clean sharpness and a touch of alcohol spirit. On the first sip, you're not sure what to make of it. On the second, you realize you're head over heels in love with it. An extraordinary drink.

### ST. COUSAIR

Iizuna, Nagano Prefecture

www.stcousair.com

**Cidre** (6% ABV)

Bottle-conditioned and very pale, like a light perry, with a faint, tequila-like aroma. The flavour is crisp and tangy Granny Smith with hints of Sherry, asparagus and a slight cheesy touch. And then the finish explodes with big tequila and Sherry spirituousness followed by a dusty, mouldy tang – all of which is far more enjoyable than it might sound.

### RUSSIA

Cider was once popular in Russia but died out in the Soviet era. Now, in the wake of Russia's burgeoning craft-beer scene, a small number of people are keen to revive Russian cider and it is gaining in popularity, particularly in Moscow.

### YABLOCHNY SPAS

Moscow

www.en.yablochny-spas.ru

**Apple Cider St. Anton Semi-Sweet** (5% ABV)

A determined attempt to revive a real cider tradition. Fresh and sweet, with strong acidity and a slight hint of farmhouse character.

# CĪDER
# AND
# FOOD

# THE PRINCIPLES OF CIDER WITH FOOD

One of the greatest triumphs of lazy thinking in the world of gastronomy is the idea that wine is the only suitable partner with food. People who think this are simply following convention rather than actually considering the way flavours go together – and it's surprising how many people do.

We have no quarrel with wine – we drink a lot of it – but it is not the only answer. Any honest sommelier or wine critic will admit that. Compared to wine or even to beer, very little has been written about the relationship between cider and food, and yet it has long been used both in cooking and as a preferred accompaniment to meals in all the established cider-making regions. The basic principles that guide it are the same as those for any other drink, and a bit of common sense and lateral thinking produces some beautiful flavour combinations.

Cider is made from apples, so whatever matches well with apples will also suit cider. For example, just as apples go well with pork, cider can do no wrong with it, either. Whether as an ingredient in Somerset pork sausages, a cooking liquid for Spanish chorizo or an accompaniment to crisp pork belly at a New England barbecue, pork and cider are a perfect match.

That slice of apple on the side of a cheese plate? The cows that produce Montgomery Cheddar graze in fields next to cider orchards. *Terroir* says they must go together, and they do, sublimely. Cornish cider with freshly caught mackerel by the coast is another phenomenal example.

Stretching beyond the apple, what about a spicy curry countered by a dollop of sweet chutney? Full-bodied sweet cider does the same job of neutralizing some of the heat (though beware tannins that can clash and create a nasty metallic taste).

In cooking, we substitute alcohol for water to add flavour rather than leaching it out when we boil, braise, poach, simmer or steam. We also substitute it for vinegar or juice in marinades or dressings. Cider works beautifully as the basis for anything from a meat casserole to a light salad dressing.

In matching food and drink, follow the same principles as anything else: think about body, weight and texture and begin by trying to harmonize light, medium and heavy. Then consider the basic components – sweetness, acidity and tannins – and where they might work with the flavours in the food. For example, the delicate, floral character of a sparkling perry complements and lifts white fish or turkey, whereas sweet, sparkling *cidre doux* from Normandy cuts through and refreshes soft, creamy cheeses such as Livarot. And at either end of the meal, a bottle-fermented cider or perry cannot be beaten as an aperitif, while a Pommeau or brandy is a perfect *digestif*.

Cider is hugely flexible, comparable to tannic red wine or crisp white wine, refreshing lager or mellow, full-bodied ale. And the lack of recorded 'rules' around cider, either as an ingredient or an accompaniment, means you have total freedom to experiment. And, if the worst happens and the match goes disastrously wrong, good cider is much cheaper than good wine!

The dinner table just became a whole new playground.

LEFT: The Hix Fix: a blend of brandy-marinated cherries and dry perry.

# CIDER AND FOOD MATCHING

### Light Commercial Style Cider

The refreshing fizz of a typical commercial cider makes it a good accompaniment to fried food. The sweetness of many mainstream brands also lends itself to hot food such as curries, where it can counter the spice as well as simply cooling the mouth.

### 'Apple Wine' Style Cider

Pairs with anything a fresh white wine such as Riesling would. Great with poultry and especially pork, the combination of low tannin and high acidity also makes it a great match for spicy dishes such as Thai or Malaysian cuisine.

### Farmhouse 'Scrumpy'

There's a *terroir* truth here that Somerset farmhouse cider is made to go with the local mature Cheddar. The minerally, tannic dryness makes it a great match for salty seafood, and there's enough going on for it to play a similar role to red wine or ale with a variety of dishes from lamb, pork and sausages through to duck and poultry.

### Spanish *Sidra*

The high acidity gives it the power to cut through fatty dishes, and in northern Spain it's often served with ham, chorizo and rib-eye steaks. But the funk also makes it a natural partner for pungent washed-rind cheeses.

### French-style Keeved Cider

Try with buckwheat *galettes* or crêpes, a natural pairing in Brittany, and they know their matches. The combination of natural carbonation and light funk also stands up well to mature soft cheeses such as Camembert or Vignotte.

### Ice Cider

The intensity of the balanced sweetness and acidity makes ice cider a perfect foil for even the strongest cheeses, and it's beautiful with blue cheeses such as Stilton. Also amazing with rich fois gras or pâté.

### Perry

The delicacy of perry means it can be easily overwhelmed, but thoughtful pairing with white meats, fish and seafood brings out all its tantalizing beauty. Also perfect with goats cheese.

### Pommeau

A great aperitif. Depth and richness make it a top match for blue cheese or foie gras. But the breadth of flavour from apple to oaky vanilla means it pairs with both light, fresh melon and dark-chocolate desserts. Also complements caramelization and savoury flavours in meat and pies.

### Calvados

The perfect partner for dessert. It might seem obvious, but pairing with apple pie or tarte Tatin is sublime. The deep, matured fruit flavours also work well with orange and marmalade, plus it's perfect with dark chocolate.

# THE SOMMELIER'S VIEW

French cider maker Eric Bordelet is clearly passionate about his wonderful ciders. The first time we taste his perry, it begs for a wonderful food match and I ask Eric – a former Michelin-star sommelier himself – what food he would pair it with. 'I cannot tell you that!' he barks. 'The art of a sommelier takes years to perfect! Oh, you have a lot of work to do.'

ABOVE: Stylish cider from a former sommelier.
OPPOSITE: Cider can do anything wine can – and more besides.

I know what he means, and while learning about food and cider matches first-hand is so pleasurable it can hardly be called work, it is a life's work without a few tips. Luckily Fiona Beckett, an English food and drink writer whose excellent website **www.matchingfoodandwine.com** covers all manner of drinks, is considerably more forthcoming. And Mathieu Chevrier, sommelier at Château Les Bruyères, Cambremer, Normandy, also gives us a few suggestions.

There are two overriding principles which, while not universal, do seem to be foolproof in creating the perfect match. The first is context, which we might extend to *terroir*: if you're in a region where things grow together, they go together. 'If you're in an area that produces wine, beer or cider you're more likely to enjoy the drink that is made locally,' says Fiona.

'Like wine, the characteristics of a good cider depend on its soil. That is why there is a wide variety of products across regions,' says Mathieu. To illustrate this point, both Mathieu and Fiona, independently of each other, enthuse about the perfect pairing of Camembert cheese and the AOC cider from Normandy's Pays d'Auge.

The second principle is ingredients. 'If a dish is cooked with apples, or has cider in it, then cider as your choice of drink is a no-brainer,' says Fiona. 'If you're eating a chicken pie made with cider, it's as obvious to drink cider with it as it would be to drink red wine with *coq au vin*.'

Cider has advantages in that it is lower in alcohol and often sparkling, which can help refresh the palate. Most ciders also have a residual sweetness that white wines often don't possess (which can make them pleasing with a wide variety of dishes), and an acidity that beer lacks. 'I think cider excels with white meats such as chicken and pork, especially with a light or creamy sauce, with fish and shellfish and with cheese. It's surprisingly good with mild curries and Indian street food,' says Fiona.

But however many rules and principles you follow, cider always has the capacity to surprise. 'I normally look to a pale ale or sparkling wine with fish and chips,' says Fiona, 'but last year I found that a light, medium-dry cider is an absolutely delicious accompaniment.'

So why on earth is cider not a default choice with food? 'It lost its cachet,' says Fiona. 'How many restaurants have a cider list? Virtually none. But that will change.' In Frankfurt, Andreas Schneider has already worked extensively with Michelin-starred chefs and has his products stocked in their restaurants. In Somerset and Normandy you'll find cider menus. There is a long way to go, but cider is inexpensive so it's easy to experiment with at home. Sitting around a dinner table with friends, opening a few bottles of cider and seeing how they go with different dishes is one of life's greatest pleasures.

'IT ALWAYS PAYS
TO DRINK LOCAL.'

## CIDER CURED SARDINES
Serves 4

*For the marinade*
300ml cider vinegar
300ml warm water
80g sugar
2 tsp sea salt
25–30 fresh green
  peppercorns
1 tsp fennel seeds
4 juniper berries
2 bay leaves

6 shallots, peeled
  and cut into rings
3 medium carrots,
  peeled and thinly sliced
16 sardine fillets,
  scaled and trimmed
40–50g sea vegetables
  (sea purslane, samphire,
  etc), trimmed of any
  woody stalks

1   Bring all of the ingredients
    for the marinade to the boil
    then leave to cool. Add the
    shallots and carrots. Mix with
    the sardine fillets, then lay
    the fillets in a non-reactive
    container (plastic, glass or
    stainless-steel) and pour
    over the marinade. Cover
    and leave to marinade in the
    fridge for at least 4–5 days
    before serving.

2   To serve, blanch the sea
    vegetables in boiling water
    for 10 seconds, then drain.
    Remove the sardines fillets
    from the marinade and dry
    on kitchen paper. Either fold
    them in half with the skin
    on the outside or lay them
    flat, skin-side up, on a
    serving plate with a few of
    the shallots, carrots and
    green peppercorns on top.
    Drizzle over a little rape-seed
    oil if preferred.

----------------------------------

## 'CIDER MAKES A MUCH
## BETTER SAUCE THAN WINE'

----------------------------------

MAIN: Fresh sardines
are enlivened by
a cider-vinegar
marinade.

# THE CHEF'S VIEW

Mark Hix is a British chef and restaurateur noted for a signature style focused around the use of seasonal British ingredients. Cider and its derivatives have always been an important part of this for him, and we were lucky enough to visit him to learn how he uses cider in everything from starters to dessert. We enjoyed this so much we asked if he would share his thoughts on cider and food for this book. This is what he had to say.

'I remember years ago lots of establishments selling local farmhouse cider under the counter to rosé-nosed fans of the apple drink. Now of course cider is becoming more popular, and often pubs will have as many draft ciders as real ales, not to mention bottled ciders. In Bridport, Dorset, there's even a bar at the Bull Hotel called The Stable that is totally devoted to cider. That's encouraging for both cider makers and cider lovers.

'What a lot of drinkers and foodies don't realize, though, is that cider is a perfect match for food, both in terms of cooking and supping with it. There are many dishes for which cider is actually a more appropriate accompaniment than wine. I'm not talking just meat here, either; fish and cider are also great partners. Sometimes the subtlety of some of the more refined, cleaner ciders creates a marriage made in heaven.

'I've found over the years that when slow-cooking meats like rabbit, chicken and veal, cider makes a much better sauce than wine – and what's more it comes in more convenient-sized bottles. Adding a final splash of cider at the end of cooking really brings the dish to life.

'For years now I've been making creamy onion and cider soup, which on a cold winter's day could not be more inviting and satisfying to warm up the cockles of your heart. And on that note, try steaming cockles and mussels in dry cider – the result puts any *moules marinières* to shame.

'I'm sometimes criticized for slightly overdoing the cider and cider brandy on my menus, but when you have a good friend like Julian Temperley at Burrow Hill Farm making the most of his Somerset apples, why wouldn't you use them in and around the menu?

'From the Hix Fix cocktail on arrival, featuring my neighbour's Morello cherries steeped in apple *eau de vie*, to a skate wing poached in Burrow Hill Cider then a Kingston Black and bramble jelly to finish off the meal, it's easy to fly the flag for our great British cider makers.'

RIGHT: Culinary wizard Mark Hix has every right to look pleased. He's just prepared an entire menu with cider in every dish.

## PORK TENDERLOIN WITH APPLES AND BRANDY
Serves 4

Pork and apples are a perfect classic marriage and always have been.
Add a little cider brandy to the pan and you are in for a real treat.

550–600g pork tenderloin,
  cut into 8 even-sized steaks and
  flattened a little
Salt and freshly ground black pepper
1 tbsp vegetable or corn oil,
  for frying
60g butter
2 dessert apples, cut into 8 wedges
  and the core removed
100ml double cream
4 tbsp cider brandy

1 Season the pork fillets, heat a heavy frying pan with the vegetable oil. Cook the pork fillets for about 3–4 minutes on each side over a medium heat, keeping them a little pink. While the pork is cooking, heat another frying pan with half of the butter in and cook the apples on a medium heat for 4–5 minutes, turning as they are cooking so they colour evenly.

2 To serve, remove the pork from the pan, add the cream to the pan and simmer until its reduced by half and thickened, then stir in the rest of the butter and season. Add the pork to the apples, pour in the cider brandy, and carefully ignite with a match, or you can tilt the pan over a gas flame if using a gas stove.

3 Arrange the pork on warmed serving dishes with the apples and spoon the cream on top.

# VENEZUELAN BLACK AND CIDER BRANDY TRUFFLES
Makes approximately 20

How nice it is to be able to feature a British cacao producer, and from the West Country! Willie Harcourt-Cooze's Venezuelan Black is not the type of chocolate you can munch on while watching a film: it's 100 per cent cacao, which means it needs to be cooked with rather than eaten. He makes it from carefully selected Venezuelan cacao pods and processes it in Uffculme in Devon using antique equipment – rather like Julian Temperley's old copper pot-still in which he makes his cider brandy. We thought we'd put these two West Country artisan eccentrics into a chocolate truffle.

400ml double cream
80g Venezuelan Black
  dark chocolate, grated
700g good-quality dark chocolate,
  finely chopped (reserve 300g
  for coating)
200g unsalted, softened butter
100ml Somerset cider brandy
60g good-quality cocoa powder

1 Bring the cream to the boil, remove from the heat and gradually stir in the Venezuelan Black and 400g of the dark chocolate with a whisk until it has melted and the mixture is smooth. Then stir in the butter and cider brandy. Transfer the mixture into a bowl and leave to cool in the fridge (about 1–1½ hours) until firm enough to spoon into rough shapes.

2 Line a baking tray with cling film and spoon the mixture out on it into roughly shaped blobs. Leave to set in the fridge until firm and solid. Then melt the remaining dark chocolate in a bowl over a pan of simmering water, stirring every so often. Remove from the heat and leave to cool.

3 Sift the cocoa powder onto a tray and have a third clean tray ready for the finished truffle. Using a thin skewer or cocktail stick, dip the truffle blobs quickly into the melted chocolate, ensuring as much excess as possible drains off, then dip them into the cocoa powder, shaking the tray so they become coated. When you have around 20 coated, shake off the excess cocoa with your hands and transfer them to the clean tray.

4 Store in the fridge in a container lined with kitchen paper until required, and bring them out of the fridge half an hour or so before serving. Don't keep them for more than a month. As if...

## CIDER BLOGS

**Pete Brown's Blog**
http://petebrown.blogspot.com
The co-author's blog focuses on beer, but since this book he has expanded to offer views and commentary on the global cider scene.

**IAMCIDER**
www.iamcider.blogspot.com
This book's other co-author lives and breathes his subject. Exploring the fringes of the cider world through a lens, photographer Bill Bradshaw searches for beauty among the detritus.

### GERMANY

**Cider-Blog.de**
http://apfelwein-blog.de
Frankfurt-based author Konstantin Kalveram's English-language blog tells the rest of the world everything there is to know about good German cider.

**Frankfurt. Apfelwein. Kultur.**
http://what-is-apfelwein.tumblr.com
A blog about Frankfurt's unique *Apfelwein* culture, plus cider reviews from around the world.

### SPAIN

**Cider Guerilla**
www.sidraglocal.blogspot.com
Spanish cider expert Eduardo Coto compares and contrasts cider styles around the world. This site is written in Spanish.

### UK

**Cider Pages**
www.ciderpages.blogspot.com
A pilgrim on a journey to try as many different ciders as possible, enjoy them and write about them.

**The Cider Blog**
http://theciderblog.wordpress.com
Cider, pubs, festivals reviews.

### UNITED STATES

**Old Time Cider**
www.oldtimecider.com
Dave White's blog about traditional North American craft cider and cider makers is wide-ranging, authoritative and simply essential. Also includes a world map of cider producers.

**United States of Cider**
www.unitedstatesofcider.com
Chronicle of two ciderphiles' explorations into the world of (hard) cider, with a focus on the American craft-cider revival.

### CANADA

**Cider Monger**
http://cidermonger.com
Reviews and news from a guy called Alex who lives, breathes and eats cider as well as drinking it. A lot of it.

**The West Cider**
http://thewestcider.com
A love letter to cider from British Columbia and beyond.

### AUSTRALIA

**All About Cider**
www.allaboutcider.com
One hundred per cent pure cider reviews, aged in intrigue with no added bigotry, celebrating all things cider.

## CIDER WEBSITES

### UK

**Cider Workshop**
www.ciderworkshop.com
Forum discussing all aspects of growing, making and consuming cider (and perry), from orchard to glass.

**Old Scrump's Cider House**
http://www.somersetmade.co.uk
Loads of resources for the cider and perry enthusiast.

**Real Cider**
www.real-cider.co.uk
Learn what makes real cider so special, how it's produced, how to enjoy it and where to buy it.

**UK Cider**
www.ukcider.co.uk
Cider website and directory with loads of detail which anyone can add to.

**Vigo**
http://www.vigopresses.co.uk
Everything you need to make your own cider.

**The Wittenham Hill Cider Portal**
www.cider.org.uk
Cider professor and Long Ashton research station veteran scientist Andrew Lea shares his knowledge with the world.

### UNITED STATES

**The Cider Digest**
www.talisman.com/cider
www.cider.org.uk/info.htm
Email discussion group with about 750 subscribers, moderated by Dick Dunn, an amateur mead and cider maker living in Hygiene, Colorado.

**The Cyder Market**
www.cydermarket.com
If there's something you want to know about cider that isn't on this website, there's a link to it somewhere else.

## CIDER BY MAIL ORDER

### UK

**Beers of Europe**
www.Beersofeurope.co.uk
Doesn't just sell beers and doesn't just source them from Europe. A good range of UK and French ciders.

**Bristol Cider Shop**
www.bristolcidershop.co.uk
Huge range all sourced within 80 km of a shop that sits handily between the UK's three main cider-making regions.

**Lilley's**
www.lilleys.biz
Good range of UK ciders.

### UNITED STATES

Due to Federal Government restrictions on custom orders between states, there are limited mail-order facilities for cider in the United States. Availability depends upon what individual states allow.

### AUSTRALIA

**Cider Insider**
www.ciderinsider.com.au
An independent Australian online liquor retailer for buying and blogging on all things cider.

**Dan Murphy's**
www.danmurphys.com.au
Some craft gems hidden among a huge range of commercial ciders.

## SPAIN

### Sidra de Asturias

www.sidradeasturias.es

The Designation of Origin Regulatory Board is the official body established to certify that a cider qualifies as designation of origin (DO) 'Cider of Asturias'. Monitors 25 cider houses, 267 growers and 587 hectares with plantations of Asturian apple varieties belonging to the 22 varieties listed in the DO regulations.

## FRANCE

### UNICID (Union Nationale Interprofessionnelle Cidricole)

www.info-cidre.com

Trade association for professional cider and perry makers in France.

## GERMANY

### Apfelwein im Römer

www.apfelwein-im-roemer.de

Consortium that organizes an annual world cider trade fair, which takes place in Frankfurt in March.

## AUSTRIA

### Most Sommelier

www.mostsommelier.at

Resource for *Most* producers in Austria.

## UK

### Campaign for Real Ale (CAMRA)

www.camra.org.uk

UK consumer organization supporting traditional British beer and pubs. Also supports 'real' cider with festivals and events.

### National Association of Cider Makers

www.cideruk.com

National trade body representing all UK cider makers.

### South West of England Cidermakers Association

www.sweca.org.uk

Supporting apple growers and cider makers in the region.

### Three Counties Cider & Perry Association

www.thethreecountiesciderandperry association.co.uk

The Three Counties Cider & Perry Association represents, supports and promotes the interests of craft cider and perry producers, primarily based in the Three Counties region of the UK (Herefordshire, Gloucestershire and Worcestershire).

### Welsh Perry & Cider Society

http://www.welshcider.co.uk

Full of information from the body that promotes Welsh cider and perry.

## IRELAND

### Cider Ireland

www.ciderireland.com

A group of like-minded craft-cider producers from the island of Ireland and the best source for real cider in Ireland.

## UNITED STATES

### United States Association of Cider Makers

www.unitedstatesofcider.com

Formed in 2013 to bring together and represent cider makers from all across the United States.

### Great Lakes Cider and Perry Association

www.greatlakescider.com

Body that promotes fermented apple and pear beverages and helps educate consumers and producers about them.

### Northwest Cider Association (NWCA)

www.nwcider.com

Promotes awareness of Northwest artisan-produced ciders among the general public and fosters cooperation within the industry.

### Rocky Mountain Cider Association

www.rmcider.org

Promotes the understanding and appreciation of quality cider in the region, and helps producers and suppliers work together.

### Vermont Ice Cider Association

www.vermonticecider.com

A group of dedicated artisanal producers committed to making ice cider in the tradition established in Quebec.

## CANADA

### Association of Independent Cider Producers of Québec (CAQ)

www.cidreduquebec.com

Trade body representing almost 50 Québécois cider makers.

### Ontario Craft Cider Association

www.ontariocraftcider.com

Formed in 2012 to help build Ontario's burgeoning cider scene.

## AUSTRALIA AND NEW ZEALAND

### Cider Australia

www.cideraustralia.org.au

National association for cider and perry growers and producers.

### Fruit Wine and Cider Makers of New Zealand

www.nzfruitwines.org.nz

Cider sits within this broader trade organization championing fruit wines, cider, mead and liqueurs.

Although the first of its kind, this book builds on and summarizes an array of publications that address specific aspects of cider. These include the following titles:

## CIDER BASICS

**Alwood, William Bradford.** *A Study of Cider Making in France, Germany and England, with Comparisons on American Work.* Washington: US Department of Agriculture. 1903.
**Bruning, Ted.** *Golden Fire: The Story of Cider.* Bright Pen. 2012.
**Pollan, Michael.** *The Botany of Desire: A Plant's-eye View of the World.* London: Bloomsbury. 2002.
**Stafford, Hugh.** *Treatise on Cyder-making.* London: Edward Cave. 1753. Ross-on-Wye: Fineleaf facsimile edition. 2009.

## GERMANY

**Kalveram, Konstantin, and Rühl, Michael.** *Hessens Apfelweine.* Frankfurt: B3 Verlag. 2008.
**Schick, Ingrid, and Zinzow, Angelika.** *Apfelwein 2.0.* **Neustadt an der Weinstraße:** Umschau Buchverlag. 2011.

## UK

**Bulmer, E. F.** *Early Days of Cider Making.* Hereford: Museum of Cider. 1980.
**CAMRA (ed).** *Cider.* St Albans: CAMRA Books. 2009.
**CAMRA (ed).** *Good Cider Guide.* St Albans: CAMRA Books. 2005.
**Clifford, Sue, and King, Angela.** *The Apple Source Book.* London: Hodder & Stoughton. 2007.
**Crowden, James.** *Ciderland.* Edinburgh: Birlinn. 2008.
**Foot, Mark.** *Cider's Story Rough and Smooth.* Mark Foot. 1999.
**French, R. K.** *The History and Virtues of Cyder.* London: Robert Hale Ltd. 1982.
**Legg, Philippa, and Binding, Hilary.** *Somerset Cider: the Complete Story.* Somerset Books. 1986.
**Mac, Fiona.** *Ciderlore: Cider in the Three Counties.* Little Logaston, Herefordshire: Logaston Press. 2003.
**Russell, James.** *The Naked Guide to Cider.* Bristol: Naked Guides. 2010.
**Wilkinson, L. P.** *Bulmers of Hereford.* Newton Abbott, Devon: David & Charles. 1987.

## USA

**Means, Howard.** *Johnny Appleseed: The Man, The Myth, The American Story.* New York: Simon & Schuster. 2011.
**Proulx, Annie, and Nichols, Lew.** *Cider: Making, Using & Enjoying Sweet & Hard Cider.* North Adams, MA: Storey Books. 1997.
**Watson, Ben.** *Cider, Hard and Sweet.* Woodstock, Vermont: Countryman Press. 2009.

## CANADA

**Leroux, Guillaume, and Perron, Alexis.** *Cidres du Québec.* Montréal: Modus Vivendi. 2009.

## AUTHOR'S ACKNOWLEDGEMENTS

The world of cider is contradictory and cantankerous. Here and there we met people who were almost hostile to the idea of this book, and others who were utterly indifferent. But for every one of those, we met 10 or a dozen people who went out of their way to help us, often to a degree way beyond what any reasonable person could even dream of, let alone ask. Thank you to everyone in the world of cider we spoke to for your time, help, knowledge, patience and product. Any errors are entirely our own.

Thank you to everyone who sent us samples of cider to taste and take pictures of. Hopefully any concerns that this might have been a scam to blag free cider have now proven unfounded.

Thank you to Louise Tucker, Robin Rout, Hilary Lumsden and Alexandra Labbe Thompson for helping bring this book home, and to Jo Copestick for believing in it.

Special thanks must also go to the following people in:

### SPAIN
Eduardo Coto gave us everything we needed to know on Spain, from history to tasting notes. Thanks also to Llucia Fernandez Marquez.

### FRANCE
Thank you to Guillaume Drouin, Christian Drouin, Jerome Dupont.

### GERMANY
This chapter would not exist without the tireless and tolerant help of Konstantin Kalveram. Huge thanks also to Andreas Schneider and Coady Buckley. And to Eduardo Coto again, whose passion and knowledge extend well beyond his native country and tradition.

### AUSTRIA
Thank you to Michael Oberaigner, without whom we would have missed something huge.

### UNITED KINGDOM
Thank you to Tom Oliver, Julian Temperley, Henry Chevallier Guild and Gabe Cook, for practical help as well as inspiration at every turn.

### IRELAND
Thank you top all at Cider Ireland, especially Mark Jenkinson.

### UNITED STATES
There would be no American section to this book without the passion and belief of Mike Beck, Steve Wood, Sharon Campbell, Dave White and Jennie Dorsey, who really did make the whole thing possible and enlisted the help of so many others on our behalf.

### CANADA
Thank you to Grant Howes, John Brett, Stephen Beaumont, Charles Crawford, Robert McKeown and especially Catherine St-Georges and Stéphane Rochefort, without whom this book would be missing one of its most wonderful discoveries.

### AUSTRALIA
Thanks to Max Allen, James Adams, Bryn Price and Coady Buckley again!

### ARGENTINA
Thank you, Juliana Mazzaro.

### REST OF WORLD
Thanks to Aiko Yazawa and Jacob Damgaard.

### CIDER WITH FOOD
Special thanks to Mark Hix, not only for being a tireless champion of cider in the kitchen and on the dinner table but also for taking time to show us how to cook with cider and kindly providing recipes. And to Fiona Beckett, food-and-drink matcher extraordinaire.

### IN ADDITION
Bill would like to thank Lisa (the 'cider widow') and the rest of his family for the time taken away from them so that he could pursue his cider-related adventures.

Pete would like to thank Liz Vater for her eternal patience and understanding.